D0898100

Let There Be Towns

Let There Be Towns

*Spanish Municipal Origins
in the American Southwest, 1610–1810*

Gilbert R. Cruz

Foreword by Donald C. Cutter

Texas A&M University Press

College Station

Contemporary maps researched and drawn by Chester B. Davis

Frontispiece:
"Market Plaza," San Antonio, by Thomas Allen, ca. 1878–79.
The marketplace was the life center of frontier towns.
Courtesy San Antonio Museum Association.

In 1985, the Board of Directors of the San Antonio Conservation Society
extended a generous grant, which facilitated the author's efforts to complete the
research and to organize the illustrations for the manuscript. The author and
the publisher wish to acknowledge the assistance afforded by the San Antonio
Conservation Society in the publication of this volume.

The paper used in this book meets the minimum requirements
of the American National Standard for Permanence
of Paper for Printed Library Materials, Z39.48-1984.
Binding materials have been chosen for durability.

Library of Congress Cataloging-in-Publication Data

Cruz, Gilbert R.
    Let there be towns : Spanish municipal origins in Texas and the
Southwest, 1610–1810 / Gilbert R. Cruz ; foreword by Donald C.
Cutter ; [contemporary maps researched and drawn by Chester B.
Davis]. – 1st ed.
    p. cm.
    Bibliography: p.
    Includes index.
    ISBN 0-89096-314-2 (alk. paper) :
    1. Municipal government–Southwest, New–History. 2. Cities and
towns–Southwest, New–History. 3. Southwest, New–History–To
1848. 4. Spaniards–Southwest, New–History. I. Title.
JS440.C78   1988
352'.0072'0979–dc19   87-33553
                                                                     CIP

For my sons,
ANDRÉS ANTONIO AND MIGUEL LUIS,
that someday they too may learn to appreciate
the marvelous pioneer heritage
of our
American Spanish Southwest

Contents

Illustrations

Maps

POPULATION GRAPHS

Foreword

By *Donald C. Cutter*

Let There Be Towns provides new insights into Borderlands history. The founding of a Spanish colonial frontier town was not an afterthought, as has seemed to be the case, but rather it was a logical sequential event. It was a last but far from least step in occupation of a new province.

Of the primary institutions of Spanish colonial control, the presidio, the mission, and the town—only the town was duplicative of the institution as it existed in the homeland. It was the most truly colonial in that it reproduced the Spanish town in the American environment. Neither the presidio nor the mission was intended as duplications of normal Spanish counterparts, but the town was a faithful copy of its Iberian antecedent. Both presidio and mission had Indian control as a primary and direct aim. The Hispanic town of the Borderlands may have obliquely contributed to control of native people, but when it did, it was done by indirect methods and such control was low on the scale of municipal priorities.

More than any other institution in the Spanish exercise of sovereignty, the town created a plan for permanent land tenure. The methods were long-standing and sanctified by association with the Reconquista of the Iberian peninsula. A Spaniard, if he had been miraculously transported from the countryside of Castile in Old Spain to the Internal Provinces of the north of New Spain, might not have recognized a presidio, he might have been estranged by a mission, but at one of the Borderlands towns he would have felt at home. He would have needed no introduction, no explanation, no orientation.

The Borderlands municipality can be traced to the Duero River Valley in the eighth century and to the reconquest of the Iberian peninsula from the Moors. The town was used to occupy physically those areas newly reconquered but lacking established government. Borderlands towns filled a similar role and were the farthermost outposts of a vast network of municipalities. When the new *vecinos,* the official residents, were given ceremonial possession of tracts of land, there was no doubt about the intent of the sovereign. There was nothing haphazard about the process; it was intended to be permanent. All was in strict conformity with the detailed codified laws regulating new towns, including the rights, privileges, and immunities thereunto pertaining. Such a systematic occupation procedure was at great variance with town founding in the Anglo-American West.

The infrequency of town founding in the Borderlands might strongly suggest that there would be limited local knowledge about the process, yet familiarity with the procedure to be followed was noteworthy. The men involved in laying out a new town went through the time-honored formalities and measurements without undue delay and with apparent assurance. The idea of what they were doing was so basic that specialists were not needed—only a bundle of stakes, a few cartloads of rock, a compass, a plow, and a standard measuring cord. But before these essential items could be brought into play, it was necessary to obtain a royal *ćedula* that decreed, "Let a town be founded." In the monolithic bureaucracy of the Spanish empire, such enabling documents were slow to run their lengthy course from the germ of the idea to final fulfillment. Nowhere is the old Spanish proverb of *del dicho al hecho, hay gran trecho* (roughly equivalent to "There's many a slip 'twixt the cup and the lip.") more appropriate. Once the many formalities and measurements had been completed with receipt of tracts of land in various categories, a new town was born.

The town was the least publicized but the most basic of the institutions of Hispanic control. National self-interest directed greatest publicity for the mission. That best-foot-forward stance gave conquest respectability even to the point of moral virtue. The presidio, the fortress that supported the religious aspect of frontier advance, is reasonably well known. The town, or pueblo, or municipality has up to now been the neglected area. Herbert E. Bolton, the great historian of the Borderlands, in a frequently reprinted brief essay, gave classic definition to the "Role of the Mission as a Frontier Institution." Since that time many historians have dealt with aspects of the mission but usually within the framework established by Bolton. One of Bolton's many students, Max

Moorhead, in his book *The Presidio: Bastion of the Spanish Borderlands* pushed the role of that military institution beyond anything that Bolton had done for the mission.

In *Let There Be Towns*, Gilbert Cruz has placed pueblo founding in the Borderlands in its historical perspective with his balanced treatment of Spanish town beginnings on the northern frontier of New Spain. The story is not without romance and heroic adventure, as exemplified by the long sea and land journey of the Canary Island pioneers of San Antonio and by the nearly two-thousand-mile march over desert trails from Sonora to California led by Juan Bautista de Anza. Underlying all was a penchant for legality. Town founding was the fulfillment of a desire to duplicate an institution greatly cherished in early Spanish history.

Let There Be Towns depicts the motivation, the preparation, and the implementation of the town-making process. It enriches the bibliography, not as the last word, but rather as a comprehensive overview of a basic step involving the least-studied of the major frontier institutions. It is a prelude for a full-scale treatment of the town as a long-term entity. After reading Cruz's study I have been forced to revise my earlier, frequently expressed, opinion that the mission, the presidio, and the pueblo were in that order of importance. This book will cause Borderlands students to alter such thinking, particularly in light of the fact that the municipality was the most durable of the three and the only one that from its inception duplicated Spanish culture and life as a mirror of the Old World.

This study, which had its origins in a doctoral dissertation, has been expanded and refined by Cruz's close association with the San Antonio area. His bicultural, bilingual background; his long association with one of the towns of which he writes; his familiarity with the appropriate documentation, all enhance this study. Cruz served as park historian at the San Antonio Missions National Historical Park, a position in which he viewed the historical interaction between missions, town, and presidio.

Let There Be Towns is more than the study of institution foundings, it is one that demonstrates a basic pattern of Spanish culture transfer from the Old World to the New.

Donald C. Cutter

Preface

This book serves as an introduction to the study of the municipal origins and early development of six of the first municipalities in the Southwest, which have endured through the centuries to the present. These town settlements and their *cabildo*s, or municipal governments, although proclaiming a history all their own, are representative of other Spanish municipalities in the northernmost provinces of New Spain. These distinct civil communities include San Antonio, Texas, and Laredo of the former colony of Nuevo Santander; and the New Mexican municipality of Santa Fe and El Paso, which in colonial times was reckoned a part of New Mexico. The origins of San José and Los Angeles, California, also an integral part of the narration, are depicted as two of the first northwesternmost town settlements of New Spain.

The hope of the Spanish imperial government was that these civil settlements, besides populating the Borderlands, would introduce industry, and as they prospered, they would contribute to the economy and defense of Hispanic Texas, New Mexico, and California. These plans were not entirely followed through, as this study indicates. However, these plans did reflect the crown's conviction that more than missions and presidios were needed to secure Spanish dominion over the northern Borderlands. This study also represents an effort to provide insights to actual events taking place at "city hall," namely, the town government in each of these civil communities. The *cabildo,* through its court system, served as a bastion for law and judicial procedure. The municipal government attempted to prevent the infraction of laws and to achieve a social structure in which the rights of life and property were guaranteed under the law.

In our own day, it is a regrettable fact that, in many cases, urbanists employed by state, county, and town authorities are trained mainly in disciplines geared to economic concerns, traffic congestion, and social conditions. Costly feasibility studies often reflect the planning of technicians skilled in accumulating massive data but who have little wisdom in their interpretation. Lamentably, public officials authorizing urban research are, at times, unaware until many years later that designs submitted to them are unhistorical and environmentally damaging. Planning historians, archeologists, urban sociologists, architects, and developers ideally should work together. When this collaboration is at least measurably accomplished, cities, which are organic in nature, take on a healthy, historically assuring, and often an aesthetic character. This volume, which attempts to create historical awareness of cities with colonial roots in the Southwest, hopes to contribute to bringing together citizens, urban specialists, and historians in harmony and successful planning.

The research for this manuscript was done in the Spanish archives deposited at the University of Texas at Austin, the University of New Mexico at Albuquerque, and the University of California at Berkeley. Donald C. Cutter, a recognized protégé of Herbert Eugene Bolton, has provided direction for this manuscript since 1975. Earlier, Félix D. Almaraz, Cutter's protégé, persuaded me to research the subject of municipalities in Spanish Texas. John Francis Bannon, S.J., the noted authority on the Borderlands who also once sat at Bolton's feet, directed me to enlarge the study to include Santa Fe and El Paso. Cutter suggested that Los Angeles and San José be included.

I am deeply grateful to these Borderlands scholars for their assistance over so many years. Special acknowledgment is due to Oakah L. Jones, whose prolific writings have always served as a source of inspiration. Others who have provided generous assistance include Charles Kielman, former director, Barker Texas History Center, University of Texas at Austin, and Vivian Fisher, director of the Microfilm Division, Bancroft Library, the University of California at Berkeley. Special thanks for their support are due to José Cisneros, first superintendent, San Antonio Missions National Historical Park, and to colleagues in the National Park Service with whom I engaged in cultural and natural research for both the development of an urban historical park and for the preservation, restoration, and interpretation of its resources.

This volume was made possible, in part, through a generous grant from the San Antonio Conservation Society. Mrs. Sherwood Inkley, the society's president in 1985, and her successor in 1986, Mrs. Sidney J. Francis II, graciously supported the grant award. In an age of tight budgets, Providence does, indeed, send angels to help those who keep the faith.

Let There Be Towns

I

The Iberian Municipal Tradition in New Spain

On March 9, 1731, the Alamo mission was following its daily pattern of training Christian Indians as it had for twelve years. From the mission the Franciscans and their neophytes were able to view the presidio across the west bank of the San Antonio River and in doing so witnessed extraordinary jubilation on that day. The unfurling of the banner of the Kingdoms of Castile and León in the lively breeze of the blue sky, the sound of the kettledrums, the ceremonial shot of musketry, and the hooves of the mounts of the escort marked the arrival of a caravan of fifty-six men, women, and children.

They were Spaniards from the Canary Islands. For six months they had endured a perilous ocean voyage to the port of Veracruz and a rigorous journey northward by horse and oxcart to the frontier province of Texas. The exhausted pioneers also rejoiced at their arrival. After a few days of rest in the best quarters of the soldiers stationed at the fort, their weariness faded. On March 12 the captain of the military outpost summoned all the heads of family to the spacious Plaza de Armas and proclaimed the orders of the king of Spain to build towns in the northern reaches of his New World empire. The time to lay the foundations for the city of San Antonio had come.

Whatever deficiencies the Spanish monarchs may have had, they were remarkable empire builders. One of the marvels of the history of the modern world was the manner in which the rulers of the small Iberian nation, during a time when wars in Europe were consuming many of its resources, took possession of the Caribbean archipelago and then went on, with few more than a handful of people, to implant Spanish culture, religion, laws, and patterns of life in much of the New World.[1]

3

By the late sixteenth century the political administration of the Spanish-American colonial empire had largely developed the structure it was to retain practically unchanged until the reform period under the Bourbons. Beginning in 1729 the Bourbon reforms brought about a number of changes in New Spain and the northern frontier provinces of Texas, New Mexico, and California. When the rule of the Hapsburgs ended in Spain, the Bourbon monarch who ascended the throne and his successors continued the traditional imperialistic and military patterns with an intensity equal to that of the Hapsburgs. But the Spanish Bourbons substituted the ideal of limitless progress through human exertion for the historical theory of divine guidance and revelation. They represented an enlightened monarchy endowed with vision, resolution, and energy.

Philip V, the first of the Bourbon monarchs (r. 1700–46), did not regard Spain as a satellite of its more powerful neighbor to the north, regardless of his French birth. He defended Spanish interests in the Mediterranean and found time to attend to the welfare of the Spanish-American colonies. He issued the decree under which present-day San Antonio was established. He was succeeded by Ferdinand VI, the peacemaker (r. 1746–59), who spent most of his time keeping Spain neutral in the Seven Years' War. His successor, Charles III (r. 1759–88), became the most acclaimed of the Spanish Bourbon monarchs. During his reign California's first two Spanish civil communities were established to protect the province from foreign penetration. The first, the "pueblo" San José, was founded in 1777 south of San Francisco Bay, along the banks of the River of Our Lady of Guadalupe west of the Coast Range. The second, Nuestra Señora la Reina de los Angeles, was established in 1781 near the banks of the Porciuncula River (now the Los Angeles River) west of the San Gabriel and San Bernardino mountains.

Endowed with determination and foresight, Charles III exerted pressure on his ministers to bring innovation to colonial administration. The monarch's discernment in selecting ministers of outstanding ability contributed enormously to the formation and expansion of the political machinery necessary for carrying out the Bourbon reforms. Charles III ordered José de Gálvez to conduct in New Spain a general visitation, an official inspection tour, which lasted several years and resulted in significant administrative changes.

The intendant system was an attempt to supplement the Laws of the Indies, the code under which Spain ruled her colonies around the globe. It simplified and made their provisions operative. The new system reached all parts of Spanish America and converted the colonies into uniformly governed intendancies, or administrative districts. The vehicle that carried the policies of Bourbon reform to the northern reaches of the Internal Provinces was a royal decree of August 27, 1776, under which Texas, New Mexico, California, and other northern provinces were placed under the control of a commandant general. The Bourbon reforms thus carried to the New World the traditional system of governance of the Castilian town and, at least in theory, a respect for its legal foundation.

About the time the Bourbon reforms were put in place, Indian uprisings threatened the northern frontier of New Spain, and there were fears of incursions by French, English, and Russian forces from the north. These pressures slowed the establishment of towns in the embattled northern provinces but never diminished the importance of municipal growth. When royal policy placed emphasis on military mobilization, all political and economic structures were redirected to support the military efforts.

The *cabildo secular,* or *ayuntamiento,* as it was also called, was the institution of local government in municipalities throughout Spanish America. This municipal form of local rule was an integral part of the political structure of Spanish America; the fact that more prestigious government agencies in the imperial bureaucracy have received the major attention of historians does not lessen their importance.

The traditions of the *cabildo* are part of the history of Spain from its beginnings in ancient times to the last years of Bourbon rule in colonial America. From the days when Phoenicia and Carthage promoted commercial enterprises in Spain and the Greeks introduced their laws and customs into littoral colonies on the peninsula, Spain continuously received settlers from many lands of the Mediterranean world.[2] Assimilating the best, and at times the worst, of the cultures of these ancient peoples, the earlier settlers adopted their customs and institutions. The Romans, coming somewhat later, made the most important contributions to Spanish urban traditions. In fact, Roman political institutions became so widespread and well grounded in Spain that the Germanic invaders of the fifth century A.D. did little more than modify them.[3] The Visigoths, less barbaric than the earlier Vandals and Suevi, assimilated the Roman caesars' code of laws and plan for civil order so thoroughly that the Roman Law of the Visigoths (A.D. 506) on government, family, and property became an early milestone of urban development.[4] Muslims from North Africa overcame the Visigoths, and during their rule, from the eighth to the fourteenth centuries, they implanted in Spain the best cultural traditions of the Moslem world.[5] The existing urban traditions were retained, however, and through wise policies of trade and commerce, the Moors helped Iberian cities grow and prosper.[6]

No other series of events contributed more significantly to the evolution of Castilian towns during the medieval period than the events of the Christian Reconquest of Spain. Encouraged by their kings, Spanish Christians of Castile and Aragon began settling in regained territories to protect them from Moslem enemies.[7] By establishing towns and cultivating the surrounding land, Spanish settlers secured the territory for their monarchs, who, in turn, not only promised them royal protection but also encouraged their continued cooperation by conferring on them *fueros,* or special privileges, which became a set of rights to self-rule. With the administrative structure of the *cabildo* established, there evolved the chief municipal officers, the *alcaldes ordinarios,* the *regidores,* the *alguaciles,* and the *escribanos.*[8]

Peace and economic stability fostered prosperity in Castilian towns once the Reconquest reached the final stages and Spain became united. Property owners, lawyers and members of other professions, and affluent artisans, traders, and merchants gradually formed significant elements in the towns in the kingdom. Moreover, in nearly every Castilian town was a proud upper class of knights, or *caballeros,* who had distinguished themselves in battle.

In the sixteenth century Spain emerged as the paramount colonizing power of Christendom. With the conquest of the Canary Islands in 1483, the crown acquired skill in establishing settlements and particularly in dealing with problems relating to regional and local administration. The reconquest of Granada in 1492 brought further experience in municipal organization.[9]

Now experienced in colonial rule, the crown confidently proceeded to nurture the growth of the empire on American soil. In effect, the intrepid conquistadors emulated the feats of the aristocratic *caballeros* in securing new lands. Following in the footsteps of conquerors, the artisans, merchants, and free commoners arrived to populate Spanish communities in the New World.

Understandably, America presented unique colonizing challenges to which Spanish resourcefulness adapted. The crown, in promoting the Spanish-American empire, implemented traditional patterns of town settlements and *cabildo* institutions reminiscent of the Reconquest of Spain.

Skilled administrators such as viceroys, tribunal officials, royal treasury agents, and governors formed the bureaucracy that ruled New Spain in the name of the king, but municipalities, proud of their Iberian heritage, constituted the firm base of royal power in Spanish America. Spanish communities, especially those with large populations, wealth, economic specialization, and industry, made the lands of the king secure. Regulating town affairs through their *cabildos,* the king's subjects promoted the common wealth and integrated the civil populace and its resources into the fiber of the empire.[10] Briefly, as the towns prospered, the king ruled mightily. Mexico City and Cuzco, in Peru, contributed extraordinary services to the crown with large donations of money and outstanding acts of loyalty, and were rewarded by being elevated to the rank of *ciudad* (city), which entitled each town to its own coat of arms.[11]

Spain's legacy to America began with the deeds of the conquistadors. Hernán Cortés, captain general and then governor of Mexico from 1522–1527, brought an image of Spain as a nation rich in ideas, with strong convictions and a proud awareness of its place in the world. The Spaniards had come to settle the land and to establish an empire in America.[12]

Cortés, skillful in the use of the sword, proved equally adept in the development of towns.[13] The reconstruction of the Aztec capital, Tenochtitlán, as Mexico City, in effect, symbolized the might of imperial Spain and the patterns of municipal growth that civil communities in New Spain were to emulate in centuries to come.

Mexico City and Municipal Style in New Spain

In the middle of August, 1522, after three months of incessant struggle, Tenochtitlán capitulated before the army of Hernán Cortés and his Indian allies. The conquistador's military achievements are famous. Less well known, though important to the social and economic organization of New Spain, were Cortés' efforts to rebuild Mexico City.[14] With peace restored to the former Aztec capital, Cortés began to repair the damage to the city by implementing traditional Hispanic policies in urban development:[15]

He named *alcaldes, regidores,* clerks of the market, an attorney, notaries, constables, and the other officers that a city council needed. He drew up a plan of the city, distributed lots to the conquerors, and sites for churches, squares, arsenals, and other public and community buildings.[16]

Implementing the *cabildo* structure, these appointed aldermen brought law and order to the conquered city and its environs until the crown could provide more elaborate civilian officers and organization from Spain.[17] As Cortés' epic conquest of Mexico was the necessary first pacification and consolidation of New Spain, the capture of Tenochtitlán was the preliminary step in the growth of Mexico City and the development of a colonial society throughout the new empire. Once he realized the implications of Cortés' dramatic military success, Charles V took steps to establish royal control over New Spain. He replaced the civil magistrates appointed by Cortés with crown officials.[18] In 1528 an *audiencia,* the civil government of the province, comprising a president and council members, was established in Mexico and its officers endowed with substantial governing powers. Nuño de Guzmán, the controversial first president of the *audiencia,* assumed his duties in the following year.[19] The overwhelming demands of government and the spread of the conquest soon made centralization necessary, and New Spain was proclaimed a viceroyalty, with Mexico City its capital. The first viceroy was Antonio de Mendoza, a nobleman of outstanding character and ability.[20]

The municipal officers of the viceregal city held meetings to prepare for the arrival of Don Antonio from Spain. On August 20, 1535, the *cabildo* appointed Gonzalo Ruyz and Francisco Manrique, both *regidores,* or city councilmen, to lead a reception committee to Veracruz and present the viceroy with official greetings from the capital. At a meeting on August 25 two additional *regidores,* Bernardino Vásquez de Tapia and Juan Mansilla, were named to represent Mexico City in further ceremonies for the viceroy. Enthusiasm ran high among the city fathers. When news of the viceroy's arrival at San Juan de Ulúa Island off Veracruz reached the *cabildo* members in Mexico City on October 2, they appointed an additional committee, furnished with credentials, to go forth and offer respects by kissing the hand of his majesty's representative.[21]

The fiesta planned by the *cabildo* in honor of the viceroy's arrival in Mexico City was scheduled for Sunday, November 14. Caught up in the festive mood of the occasion, city dignitaries, loyal knights, zealous clergymen, free commoners, and Indian vassals went forth to meet Don Antonio. Trumpeters in gay-colored attire and the roll of kettledrums greeted the entry of the viceroy and his royal entourage into the city. In the tradition of Iberian towns, a public crier proclaimed the royal commission of Mendoza in the presence of *audiencia* members, the town council, and citizens of the community. A city-sponsored celebration

Mexico City, in the age of the Spanish viceroys, claimed a majestic cathedral facing the great central plaza, the Zocalo, which was also bordered by the viceregal (now national) palace and the cabildo quarters. Illustration taken from Michaud y Thomas's *Album Pintoresco de la Republica Mexicana* (1848), courtesy U.T. Institute of Texan Cultures at San Antonio.

was climaxed by games in the plaza and a festive repast honoring the viceroy, his followers, and the sport contestants.[22]

The week after the ceremonies the viceroy conferred not only with the *audiencia* regarding the affairs of the state but also with the *cabildo* concerning affairs of the city. In view of Mexico City's role as seat of the viceroyalty, the king's representative, understandably enough, concerned himself with the welfare of the city. Nothing was to be proclaimed by the town crier without the viceroy's consent, nor could any act of the *cabildo* in the capital have legal character without his confirmation. The viceroy was to issue ordinances of his own but also was to share his authority with the *cabildo* in the promotion of municipal projects and to confirm laws passed by the *cabildo* before they were promulgated in the city.[23]

The viceroy's power over municipal affairs was accepted by the citizens of the capital. If the commands of the king's alter ego overshadowed decisions of all other officers and agencies in New Spain, whether civil, ecclesiastical, or military, municipal authorities were certainly aware of the viceroy's power to influence policies with the capital city. The viceroy, however, respected the traditional powers of the *cabildo*. The town council had jurisdiction in the city and fifteen leagues beyond it. Moreover, the *cabildo* exercised exclusive authority in granting town lots and in admitting new settlers into the town.[24]

Mexico City, as seat of the imperial goverment in New Spain, also served as the seat for the *audiencia,* the tribunal and court of the capital region.[25] The proposed plan of the crown in regard to the capital was designed so that members of the *audiencia* and the *cabildo* were to collaborate in the promotion of local improvements. Often enough, in efforts to serve jointly, the *audiencia* through its representative on the *cabildo* attempted to dominate municipal affairs and to interfere in the rights of the *cabildo*.[26] Such pressure, which became common, was resented by the town council. As *cabildos* proliferated throughout New Spain, external interference in municipal affairs continued. In the Borderland regions, whereas individual soldiers and missionaries generally welcomed and assisted civil communities, official agents of military and ecclesiastical institutions exerted their own authority and often raised obstacles to the free functioning of municipalities.

During the colonial period Mexico City was a large community with a growing population concentrated in an area on the ruins of Tenochtitlán. The new Main Plaza, now the Zócalo (or La Plaza de la Constitución), was carefully designed to serve as the center of events in the city. Important political and ecclesiastical officials lived around the plaza. The different social and economic levels of the citizenry often were defined by avenues, boulevards, streets, and lanes, the residents in the periphery reflecting more a rural than an urban mode of life.[27] Mexico City thronged with Indians, Spaniards, some mulattoes, and a growing number of mestizos going about their daily business. Cobblers, silversmiths, candlemakers, tailors, and merchants of medicinal drugs and wines imported from Spain sold their wares in shops and stores, while modest stalls in the public market displayed food, drink, and native wear.[28]

The *cabildo* was quick to realize that governing a municipality such as Mexico City with its continuum of economic and social development was expensive. Of great importance to the capital was a means of controlling serious flood conditions. From the earliest times of the new empire, the problem of disposing of vast amounts of surplus water accu-

Don Antonio de Mendoza served from 1535 to 1550 as the first viceroy of New Spain. Courtesy Nettie Lee Benson Latin American Collection, University of Texas, Austin.

mulated during the rainy season remained difficult to solve. Even with large amounts of money appropriated from taxes on the orders of the viceroy, flood control remained an engineering challenge.[29] As late as the eighteenth century, when the drainage canal of Huehuetoca was the principal means of removing water from the city, periodic inundation and contagion spread by floodwaters continued to plague the city.[30] Public health remained an important item on the agenda of the municipal government. The arresting of epidemics that ravaged the town population and rural inhabitants required joint planning on the part of the viceroy, *oidores* of the *audiencia,* and the *cabildo.*[31]

The city government also had to provide effective protection for life and property. It furnished revenue for the paving of streets and the installation and maintenance of illumination. Fire and property protection was implemented with the use of bells and pumps and the organization of voluntary companies to control fires and dragoon regiments to protect property and prevent looting.[32] The *cabildo* provided for fair practices in the marketplace by passing various ordinances controlling business transactions within city limits and by appointing supervisory personnel to make daily rounds of the markets and impose fines for violations of price regulations.[33] The need for an adequate supply of pure water in the city gave rise in 1535 to plans to build an aqueduct from Chapultepec to Mexico City.[34] During the colonial period the town council attempted to regulate the water supply by controlling its use, overseeing repairs of conduits, and maintaining patrols to watch for leaks and breakage in the aqueduct.[35]

Municipal governments constituted essential ruling institutions with viable political powers by means of which citizens were assured their daily needs. Transplanted into New Spain, the town council was a respected form of local government and was the center of the only significant growth in self-government in the Spanish colonies.[36] By the second half of the sixteenth century municipal governments began to dot the provinces of New Spain. In the newly explored lands of the vast northern frontier the *cabildos* reflected the peculiar aspirations, industry, and character of the town settlements they governed. In the Borderlands, history of the founding of Santa Fe and El Paso and their municipal governments reflects a descriptive account of the people of New Mexico, and the *cabildos* and civil communities of Texas and California reflected the pioneer life of the intrepid Spanish settlers in those regions.

Looming over all these frontier towns was Mexico City, the seat of the Spanish imperial government in New Spain. The viceroy, the king's personal representative, made his residence there. The emerging multiethnic character of New Spain was reflected in the inhabitants of the metropolitan city. Iberian municipal traditions of town planning and local government were best exemplified there. Understandably enough, the government and social structure of the frontier towns were far less complex. Even so, the inhabitants of civil communities across New Spain took pride in imitating the capital. A traveler just returned to the provinces from a trip to Mexico City was eagerly consulted on the latest municipal trends.

ZACATECAS AND DURANGO: SPRINGBOARDS FOR TOWN FOUNDINGS IN THE BORDERLANDS

In New Spain the *real de minas* was an organized mining community that was significantly important in the development of the north-central plateau regions. The *real de minas* was the first permanent settlement in a mining district, generally having been preceded by a more transitory camp of prospectors and miners called a *rancho*.[37] These adventuresome prospectors mined precious metal in stream placers or in mineral deposits formed by water currents descending over deeply weathered soils. In places where underground veins of high-grade ore necessitated the establishment of a large mining complex, the *rancho* was replaced by the more permanent Spanish mining community, the *real de minas*.

These town settlements encompassed the settlers and mines within a radius of five to fifteen miles. The *real de minas* became an administrative entity and, once its metallurgical industry was stabilized, came to be known as a *lugar, villa, ciudad,* or *alcaldía mayor,* depending on its size and significance.[38] The municipal features of a *real de minas* began to take shape in response to the capital investment and long-range planning demanded by the peculiar characteristics of underground vein mining. Engineering skills were required for sinking deep shafts, timbering, and constructing stamp mills in which ore was crushed to powder. Extensive mining of large veins led to the implementation of various engineering methods for extracting ore. Miners needed adequately constructed shafts for entry and exit and drifts and winches for downward passage to the ore bodies. To extract the ore from lodes, the laborers wielded heavy picks, crowbars, wedges, and sledgehammers. By the eighteenth century miners were using gunpowder cartridges to break up the ore. The cost of equipment continued to demand significant investments of capital.[39]

These mining activities and others elsewhere in New Spain were of great economic importance to the viceroyalty. By 1690 the value of the silver mined throughout New Spain, estimated from the quantity of mercury imported to refine the silver, amounted to more than four million pesos.[40] The internal economy of New Spain was greatly enriched by the rise of silver mining. The first large discovery of this metal, far inland north of Michoacán and Jalisco, intensified Spanish interest in the semi-arid hill country of Zacatecas and Aguascalientes, a land sparsely inhabited by the fierce nomadic Zacatecos and, on the east, other warlike Indian nations unaccustomed to bowing to imperial masters. For all the hazards and hardships that these northern nations, called Chichimecos by the Spaniards, promised the king's soldiers, their ancient hunting grounds were destined to become the northern El Dorado[41] and the site of the first civilian communities in northern New Spain.

The *real de minas* of Nuestra Señora de las Zacatecas was the first large mining settlement in New Spain. Founded principally by four Spanish explorers after the decisive confrontations of the Mixtón War of 1541–42, Zacatecas proved to be the first major success in the Spanish search for riches that started immediately after the conquest of Tenochtitlán.[42] A booming town settlement, preceded by the establishment of Guadalajara in 1531, Zacatecas was founded as a result of mining discoveries in the western province Nueva Galicia. By the end of the sixteenth century impressive houses and monasteries of five religious orders were among the prominent buildings and landmarks of the town, the most notable being the Convento Franciscano de Guadalupe, the Convento y Hospital de San Juan de Dios, the Convento de Santo Domingo, and the Colegio de la Sociedad de Jesús.[43] These religious institutions provided church services for the growing town populace, maintained care centers for the sick and the indigent, and served as inns for weary travelers. Equally important, these religious houses became significant centers for expanding missionary work among the Indians in Nueva Vizcaya and, in later years, for evangelization efforts in New Mexico, Texas, and California.

The growth of Nuestra Señora de las Zacatecas was phenomenal, and news of rich silver discoveries brought a flood of prospectors and mine workers, depopulating large sections of Nueva Galicia. On October 8, 1585, Zacatecas was granted the title *ciudad*. Moreover, in recognition of services to the crown in wars against the Chichimecos and for riches fed into the royal treasury, the municipality was granted a distinctive coat of arms with portraits of its four founders and the motto *muy noble y leal*.[44]

The rapid growth of Zacatecas, while making the town secure against Indian raids, presented the imperial government with serious challenges in consolidation and expansion. The most heavily traveled routes in the early stages of the Zacatecas mine rush were those from Guadalajara through Izatlán, Juchipila, and Nochixtlán. These roads must be kept in order and guarded, for along them were carried food and supplies vital to mine operations in the Zacatecas district and the silver output to the *caja real* in Guadalajara.[45]

The role of Zacatecas in the northward expansion of Spanish colonization has led historians to call the flourishing colonial community *madre y civilizadora* of northern Mexico. It is recorded that in 1554 Francisco de Ibarra, the youthful nephew of one of the founders, Don Diego de Ibarra, led expeditions from Zacatecas northward to the future sites of Mazapil and Avino, and the Guadiana Valley and back by way of Sombrerete.[46] Further explorations into these areas were triggered by the revival of a plan conceived by Don Luis de Velasco, the second viceroy of New Spain, to conquer New Mexico, or Copala, as it was called. Don Luis' interest in the extensive regions of Copala was reawakened by extravagant reports of mineral wealth brought back to the capital city and by qualified royal approval to make new efforts at northward expansion.[47] In 1562 an exploratory enterprise, again spearheaded by Don Francisco de Ibarra, although claiming more proximate goals than the future province of New Mexico, provided the groundwork for future steps toward the north.

Francisco de Ibarra's expedition—truly Zacatecan in the sense that it was financed by don Diego de Ibarra and its members were recruited in the city—passed through San Martín and other areas explored earlier. In October and November, 1563, the town settlements El Nombre de Dios and Durango were founded. Established on a site between the Río Santiago and the Río Grande where the two rivers empty into the Guadiana, the *villa* El Nombre de Dios was the first town that Ibarra established north of Zacatecas.[48] A few friars, civilians, and Indians had already settled in the area, but Ibarra officially registered the civil settlement, outlined the limits of the town, and appointed municipal officials. The fertile valley surrounding Nombre de Dios valley was well

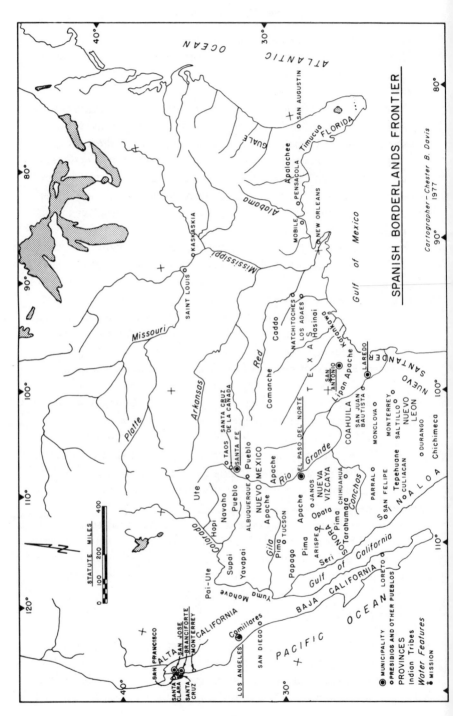

SPANISH BORDERLANDS FRONTIER

Cartographer—Chester B. Davis
1977

● MUNICIPALITY
○ PRESIBIOS AND OTHER PUEBLOS
PROVINCES
Indian Tribes
Water Features
† MISSION

16

suited to the cultivation of wheat and maize and soon served as a granary for the distant settlements of Sombrerete, Fresnillo, and Zacatecas.[49]

Next Ibarra ordered a contingent of his soldiers to select a location in the Guadiana Valley and make preparations for the establishment of a city. After mapping the city limits, Ibarra organized a municipal government, appointing *alcaldes, regidores,* and other town officials and proclaimed himself governor. At first the new town was called Guadiana, but later the name was changed to Durango, in honor of a town so named in the Basque province of Vizcaya, in Spain. Durango, admirably situated in a healthful climate, was also surrounded by fertile lands that supported agricultural crops and livestock. Ibarra spent considerable sums of money from his mines nearby for the construction of buildings and homes in Durango.[50] By the time of Ibarra's death in 1575, Durango had grown into a community of five hundred settlers, not counting the ranchers and miners who lived on the outskirts of town. In 1621, Durango was elevated to *ciudad* by the crown and came to be the capital of the newly formed Province of Nueva Vizcaya, a *reino* that included the present states of Durango, Chihuahua, Sinaloa, and Sonora and southern Coahuila.[51]

The *entrada* of Francisco de Ibarra had pushed the frontier beyond Fresnillo and Sombrerete to El Nombre de Dios, about 130 miles northwest of Zacatecas, and to Durango, whose site, the young governor claimed, was the best of any city in New Spain. In ill health at Chiametla, Ibarra, who had pushed himself beyond his physical limits, nonetheless closely followed the precarious growth of Mazapil and Cedros in the eastern sector of the province and noted with intense interest the steady advance of Spanish settlers across the lands of the hostile Tepehuanes to a site about 125 miles northwest of Durango, where they founded a *real de minas* called Inde. In 1567, after the subjugation of the Indians around Inde, the leader of the expedition, Rodrigo del Río de Loza, was ordered farther northwest by Ibarra to form the town settlement of Santa Bárbara in the San Bartolomé Valley. This *real de minas* proved to be rich in silver, but its production was limited by a shortage of mine workers. In 1579, to augment the labor supply, cabildo officials at Durango successfully petitioned the royal authorities in Mexico City for permission to encourage one thousand Indians loyal to the crown, mostly Tlascaltecans, to settle in the region.[52]

In the meantime, Santa Bárbara, with a population of thirty Spanish families and a small number of natives, established rich farms of wheat and corn and helped secure the northernmost area of New Spain. Santa Bárbara became the focus of sixteenth-century adventurers in northern Mexico. It was the "end of the line" for civilians, soldiers, and priests and a base at which new prospecting ventures were outfitted. There other expeditions, hopeful of finding "another Mexico" were conceived and launched. Probably no other center on Mexico's northern frontier so often nourished little groups setting out for the unknown interior.[53]

Such was the extent of the settlement of the Province of Nueva Vizcaya, especially Durango and southern Chihuahua. All of this exploratory and settlement enterprise was essential to the coming occupation of New Mexico and the American Southwest. In Nueva Vizcaya a group of frontier town communities, frequent subjects of political controversy between Ibarra and the Audiencia of Guadalajara, actually facilitated the growth of the Province of Nueva Galicia. Ibarra's colonization endeavors subdued the Indians threatening the Zacatecan miners and developed agriculture, especially in the fertile lands near Durango and El Nombre de Dios. Besides providing Zacatecas with added security and food, Ibarra advanced the frontier from Zacatecas to the *real* de Santa Bárbara, a distance of four hundred miles. All of Nueva Vizcaya and parts of Nueva Galicia in the area of Zacatecas bustled with evangelical movement, the sons of Saint Francis erecting nearly twenty-five monasteries in the newly created Franciscan province of Zacatecas, and the Jesuits building missions on both sides of the Sierra Madre Occidental around Sinaloa and Sonora.[54] Of course, not all of Chihuahua or Sonora was settled, but the prosperous city of Zacatecas and the growing municipalities in Nueva Vizcaya were able to support a major expedition into the mysterious kingdom of New Mexico, the land of Cíbola.

2

Santa Fe

THE FIRST CAPITAL
IN THE CONTINENTAL UNITED STATES

The Villa de Santa Fe, Nuevo México, the first capital city in the continental United States, was founded in 1610 and claims many American colonial landmarks.[1] In 1565, don Pedro Menéndez de Avilés built San Agustín on the eastern Florida coast. It served as a key post to guard Spanish territories around the Caribbean archipelago. This was the first town settlement on what would be U.S. soil. However, when silver mining shifted the crown's interest toward settlements in northern New Spain, this first European town community declined in importance, and Santa Fe became the key Spanish town within present U.S. boundaries. In 1607, Englishmen founded Jamestown on the shores of Virginia. Following similar feats by Spanish settlers in central Mexico more than three-quarters of a century earlier, this epochal event initiated English colonial history east of the Appalachian Highland. Unsuccessful in their search for gold, English colonists nonetheless converted the fertile soil of Virginia to good use. Through the cultivation of tobacco, English Amerians prospered in Virginia and, with profits from this new agricultural industry, were able to establish an aristocracy similar in elegance to that already in existence in central New Spain. Plymouth Rock was *terra incognita* when the municipal government of Santa Fe was being formed under instructions from Spanish sovereigns.

GOVERNOR JUAN DE OÑATE OF NEW MEXICO

Juan de Oñate accomplished the preliminaries to the founding of the Villa de Santa Fe. His father, Don Cristóbal, a noted trailblazer into the northeastern sector of Nueva Galicia during the 1540s, had founded the city of Zacatecas and become a wealthy and prominent figure in New Spain.[2] Don Juan also had served the crown on what was then the northern frontier of New Spain. His distinguished career, extending over two decades, had made a significant contribution in pacifying the unruly chichimecos and in establishing town settlements.

On August 27, 1592, the viceroy, Luis de Velasco, appointed Don Juan *alcalde mayor* of the mining district of San Luis Potosí. Soon after this assignment, the new *alcalde mayor* moved to San Luis Potosí for one year, during which he laid out the physical plan for the new municipality, distributed town lots to its citizens, and formed a well-organized *cabildo* to manage the affairs of the new civil community.[3] Don Juan's skills in civil administration made a favorable impression on the viceroy and probably contributed to his recommendation that Oñate lead the expedition for the colonization of New Mexico.[4]

The terms of the contract whereby the crown approved the Oñate expedition into New Mexico, after months of delay, made Don Juan directly answerable to the Council of the Indies, relieving, at least in theory, the need to deal with the king through the office of the viceroy.[5] Already in the final decade of the sixteenth century the later administrative position of *comandante general* in the future Provincias Internas seems to have been anticipated in Oñate's contract, an arrangement that was to affect the general government of the Borderlands, especially during the later Bourbon reform era.

On January 26, 1598, the expedition left Santa Bárbara to begin a journey across a roadless wilderness extending from the northernmost settlement of Nueva Vizcaya to the famous land of Cíbola. It was almost a year before all of the wagons in the caravan reached their destination.[6]

Oñate moved toward New Mexico at the head of a caravan four miles long. There were 129 soldiers in his company, some with families.[7] When he reached the Conchos River, there were eighty-three wagons and seven thousand farm animals in the party. The baggage carts carried wheat seed, farm tools, wine, oil, sugar, medicines, paper, flour and maize, arms, mining equipment, and church bells, all purchased by Oñate.[8] Several months later, a group of hardy Franciscan missionaries joined forces with Oñate.[9]

By virtue of his contract Oñate was empowered to form the political organization of the province, to make land grants with water rights, and to build new towns.

Don Luis de Velasco, viceroy of New Spain from 1592 to 1595 and from 1607 to 1611, was responsible for the policy that led to the founding of Santa Fe in 1610. Courtesy Nettie Lee Benson Latin American Collection, University of Texas, Austin.

When the land, province, and place [have] been chosen . . . let it be declared whether the pueblo that is to be settled is to be a city, town, or village [*"ciudad, villa o lugar"*] . . . so that, if it be a metropolitan city, it shall have a judge with the title of *adelantado,* or a governor, or *alcalde mayor,* or *corregidor,* or *alcalde ordinario,* who shall have universal jurisdiction and together with the *regimiento* shall have the administration of the commonwealth. . . . For the towns and village [*"villas y lugares"*] there shall be an *alcalde ordinario,* four *regidores,* one *alguacil,* one clerk of the council and public clerk and one *mayordomo.*[10]

It seems likely that Oñate followed the regulations of the ordinances of 1573, concerning the laying out of towns, at least as far as conditions in the province allowed. In keeping with the larger purpose of colonizing New Mexico, he expected the initial civil communities to take root, even though the main function of these town garrisons was to serve as the captain general's headquarters.

On July 15, 1598, Oñate approved a site, then a friendly Indian pueblo on the east bank of the Río Grande known as Caypa, to form the first Spanish settlement. He christened the town San Juan de los Caballeros.[11] Within three years, after leading a number of exploratory expeditions, Oñate decided to settle the Spanish colony of San Gabriel across the river near San Juan, a location that was to serve as the governor's headquarters until his resignation in 1608. San Gabriel continued to function as a stable pioneer community in the new province, at least until the founding of Santa Fe. By the end of the sixteenth century, Hispanic settlers at San Gabriel had already initiated the construction of a new church, had started work on an irrigation canal to bring water from the river to the town site, and had served as a militia for many exploratory enterprises across the vast province of New Mexico.[12] Moreover, the little town maintained a *cabildo,* which actively voiced the feelings of the settlers, who elected an *ad interim* successor to Oñate, his son, Don Cristóbal.[13]

With the Acoma uprising of December, 1598, quelled before the Pueblo nations were able to grasp the full extent of Spanish vulnerability,[14] the nascent town of San Gabriel had survived its first crisis. In the spring of the following year, Don Juan sent an enthusiastic account of the colony's prospects to the viceroy, claiming that " a great abundance and variety of ores [which] are very rich" were to be found in the province.[15]

New Mexico was not destined to produce booming mining towns, but Oñate was correct in declaring that the colony had taken root. Cattle, sheep, horses, and goats grazed on the banks of the Chama and the Río Grande. Corn, oats, barley, and vineyards began to sprout on the land grants of the new settlers. Creole and mestizo children were born. The *encomienda* system was implemented in keeping with the terms of Oñate's contract, forming new relationships between Hispanic and Indian populations.[16] Some of the Indians built houses, churches, and irrigation systems while others learned Spanish farming and livestock-raising techniques. The *encomienda* system, whereby tribute was obtained from an independent Indian populace by Spanish landholders, was a primitive economic form, yet lacking the mineral wealth of Nueva Vizcaya, anything more sophisticated could hardly be expected in the seventeenth century.

For more than a decade, Oñate maintained military surveillance over the vast province and promoted explorations for ores extending as far west as the mouth of the Colorado River and eastward to the buffalo plains of the Texas and Oklahoma panhandles and Kansas.[17] Only four supply caravans were dispatched to Oñate's colony, meager reinforcements indeed, and the continual colonization of the province could not be indefinitely financed by the governor's personal wealth.

After the near-bankrupt Oñate resigned,[18] the crown chose to retain New Mexico but discarded the *adelantado* and private-enterprise approach for a policy of gradual development of the land at royal expense.[19] This new policy entailed paternalistic supervision of the Indian vassals by Franciscan missionaries in New Mexico. The course taken in the development of Nueva Galicia and Nueva Vizcaya was not applicable to this particular province; the early traditions of town building prompted by the prosperity of the mining industry did not fit New Mexico. The crown had decided that it really had two choices: to implement the proposed policy of evangelizing the indigenous people of New Mexico, or to abandon the province and lose whatever there was to gain from Oñate's penetration into the northernmost reaches of New Spain. Fray Juan de Torquemada, the Franciscan chronicler, well might have rejoiced to know that the Franciscans' evangelical work, initiated as early as Coronado's entry into New Mexico, was now to be permanently supported by the strong arm of the king.[20] However much the new move might have elated Franciscans or promoted Catholic doctrine among Pueblo Indians—who in most instances had been quite content with their own form of religious cult—this royal decision to finance a project converting native inhabitants into wards of the state was second choice at best.

There were other unfavorable consequences following from the crown's new policy toward the province. The soldier-settler who had actually hoped to form prosperous town settlements, especially *reales de minas,* modeled after those in Nueva Vizcaya, now had to make the most of an *encomendero* form of life, the possibility of developing trade, commerce, and local industry having diminished to a large extent. With the Hispanic settlers frozen into an *encomendero* status that was on the wane in central Mexico and with the friars functioning as the crown's official custodians of a naturally free people, the cultural conflict that sparked Shaman Popé's revolt in 1680 was inevitable.

LA VILLA DE SANTA FE

Acting under orders from the viceroy to found a capital city for the province, Don Pedro de Peralta, the newly appointed governor of New Mexico, moved much of the Spanish colony of New Mexico to the site of present-day Santa Fe, the pueblo ruins of prehistoric Kuapoge.[21]

On April 30, 1609, Peralta was ordered to select an appropriate location to build a new capital city. The site was to provide quarters for Spanish settlers to live in proximity to each other and was to serve as a royal symbol of Spanish imperial power in New Mexico.

> When he [Peralta] shall have arrived at said province he shall inform himself of the conditions of said settlements endeavoring before anything else [to lay] the foundation and settlement of the Villa . . . so people may begin to live there with some cleanliness and stability, in which he shall allow the citizens to elect four councilmen, and two ordinary [regular] *alcaldes* each year who shall try civil and criminal cases which may occur in said Villa and within five leagues around it. . . . The said ordinary *alcaldes* and councilmen of said Villa may mark out for each resident two lots for house and garden and two *suertes* for vegetable gardens and two more for vineyards and for an olive grove and for a *cavaleria* [*sic*] of land. . . . They shall mark out as belonging to said Villa six *vecindades* and one square of the streets for the purpose of erecting Royal Buildings and other public buildings.[22]

The viceregal instruction to Peralta reflected the terms for creating towns in conformity with the current legislation, the Laws of the Indies and sections of the Ordinances of 1573. Briefly, the viceroy's instruction included the following points on municipal government: a form of rough democracy whereby town citizens were to elect mayors and councilmen, a *cabildo* with power to legislate city ordinances, a municipal court for *alcaldes ordinarios* to administer justice in town matters, and finally a town council with power to elect a constable of law and a clerk, both offices being subject to the governor's approval.[23]

Since the Coronado expedition in 1540, Spaniards had found the Upper Río Grande and its tributaries a promising environment with settlements to the west at Acoma, Zuñi, and Hopi, and to the east at Pecos Pueblo and the villages beyond the Manzano Mountains. The Río Grande drainage generally proved to be fertile land, as it supported large concentrations of river pueblos. In this area, specifically on the banks of the Santa Fe near the springs of Río Chiquito, Peralta thought to comply with the Ordinances of 1573 concerning the selection of a healthful location for the town site.[24] Apparently the place where the *villa* was established proved to be favorable, for amost a century later Fray Miguel de Menchero described the site of the capital as

> situated on a slope of highland, from which rises a crystalline river full of trout, which . . . are very savory and as good as those of our Spain. This river has its origins in a lake that lies on a summit, or crown, of this land, and its course runs through said villa, which is located in 37 degrees. It has the same climate as our Spain (that is, in New Castile) and rains at the same time; the spring is mild, and the summer extremely hot, so much so that cotton is sown and gathered the same as in tropical lands; it produces in abundance savory melons, watermelons, cucumbers, and all the fruit of the trees of Spain; the autumn is cold and the winter severe with cold, droughts, and snow.[25]

Throughout the two centuries of Spanish rule that followed its founding in 1610, the walled city of Santa Fe served as the seat for the political administration of the province and an important outpost for spreading the Christian gospel among the River pueblos.

Before the New Mexican province was destroyed in the Pueblo Rebellion of 1680, a relatively simple system of government prevailed. The governor personally ruled the northern sector of the colony, the Río Arriba, while a lieutenant governor administered the area of Río Abajo. New Mexico was further partitioned into six or eight subordinate districts, or *jurisdicciones,* which were administered by *alcaldes mayores* appointed by the governor. Although the office of *alcalde mayor* included no salary, it carried prestige and authority.[26] The *alcalde mayor* combined within his office practically all functions relating to government within his jurisdiction.[27]

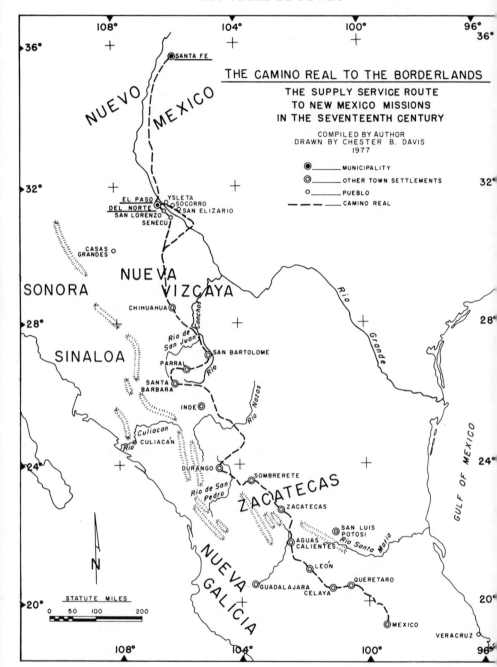

THE CAMINO REAL TO THE BORDERLANDS

THE SUPPLY SERVICE ROUTE
TO NEW MEXICO MISSIONS
IN THE SEVENTEENTH CENTURY

COMPILED BY AUTHOR
DRAWN BY CHESTER B. DAVIS
1977

⊚ ———— MUNICIPALITY
⊙ ———— OTHER TOWN SETTLEMENTS
○ ———— PUEBLO
– – – – CAMINO REAL

MAP 2

26

Only the Villa de Santa Fe and its municipal lands were outside the jurisdiction of an *alcalde mayor.*[28] This respect for municipal government suggests that law regarding the political autonomy of *cabildos* in managing the internal affairs of their towns was being widely implemented in New Mexico. Since the founding of Santa Fe, the *cabildo* had administered the affairs of the *villa.* Interestingly enough, the *cabildo* also served as an advisory board to the governor and as spokesman for all the settlers of the province before the crown.[29] By reflecting the functions of both the *audiencia* and the *cabildo* of Mexico City, the Santa Fe town council played a vital role in the political life of colonial New Mexico.

Originally rectangular and extending as far east as the site of the present cathedral, the Plaza Mayor of the Villa de Santa Fe has been the heart of the capital since 1610.[30] It was in this plaza, moreover, that embattled Spaniards remained barricaded within the governor's palace during the Pueblo Revolt of 1680, until they were able to slip away to El Paso del Río del Norte.[31] In 1692, the main plaza became the scene of Spanish triumph when General Diego de Vargas made the first successful *entrada* into the rebellious province to negotiate peace with the Indians, a diplomatic mission offering royal pardon but backed by the persuasiveness of two artillary pieces.[32] Peace was achieved between the rival parties and, while the banner of Castile and León was unfurled under New Mexican skies, Vargas took possession of the province in the name of Charles II, King of Spain.

> Thenceforward the gate of the Villa was thrown open without mistrust and in the *plaza principal* they constructed a shelter, made of the branches of pine trees, where the services and ceremony of absolution from their apostasy were performed, as also celebrating mass and baptism of their children; and after listening to a splendid sermon from the Father Custodio, they were absolved and with manifest joy their children were baptized; and on the following day, the 17th [of September, 1692] when another mass was said.[33]

Vargas completed the reconquest of New Mexico on his second journey, when he returned to the Villa de Santa Fe with settlers and provisions for the permanent possession of the province. He noted details of this triumphal *entrada*:

> On the sixteenth day of the month of December . . . I . . . made my *entrada* into the Villa de Santa Fe and, once within view of the walled village where the Tewas and the Tanos dwell, with soldiery on the march

Portrait of General Diego de Vargas, who twice—in 1692 and in 1693—led Spanish soldiers in retaking Santa Fe from rebel natives. Courtesy Museum of New Mexico, Santa Fe.

and in company with the very illustrious Cabildo of this Villa and the Kingdom, its *alguacil-mayor* and the *alférez* bearing our standard . . . we arrived at the Plaza where we found the natives assembled, the women standing apart from the men, without weapons and refraining from any warlike acts.[34]

An explicit mandate in the viceroy's instructions to General Vargas called for the immediate construction of royal buildings, the *casas reales,* as they were called. These buildings generally were to house everything that the governor needed to maintain control of the province in the name of the Spanish sovereigns. The original grounds of the royal buildings, also called the Governor's Palace, extended as far as the location of the present federal building. The grounds of the royal buildings provided space for the governor's dwelling, the official reception rooms, the military *quarteles,* an arsenal, the servants' quarters, and even vegetable gardens and orchards. Moreover, the *casas reales* had two *torreones,* or defense towers, on the east and west corners, the western one serving as a prison and gunpowder storage area.[35]

A modestly constructed chapel built for the original settlers was replaced in the 1620s by a parish church and convent under the direction of Fray Alonso Benavides, the *custos* of the Franciscan missions in New Mexico and commissary of the Holy Office for the same jurisdiction. An adobe *parroquia* built between 1714 and 1721, provided the Spanish settlers after the Reconquest with a parish church, the Chapel of Our Lady of the Rosary forming the northern portion of the building. Our Lady of Conquest, or La Conquistadora, a statue of the Virgin that accompanied Vargas back to Santa Fe in the Reconquest of 1693, was enshrined in the chapel.[36]

SANTA FE AFTER 1680

With the advent of the eighteenth century, significant changes appear to have taken place in the colonial plan of the Villa de Santa Fe, according to the municipal map of the capital furnished in the late 1760s by Joseph de Urrutia, a lieutenant to the noted Captain Nicolás de la Fora.[37] Situated on the Plaza Mayor opposite the governor's palace, the Chapel of Our Lady of Light, at times named the Capilla de los Soldados, was constructed at the expense of Don Francisco Antonio Marín del Valle, the governor of New Mexico from 1754 to 1760. This attrac-

A contemporary view of the *casas reales,* or administrative buildings, now called the Palace of Governors, located on the main plaza in downtown Santa Fe. Courtesy Museum of New Mexico, Santa Fe.

tive chapel, named the castrense because it was the military chapel, marked the northernmost extension of Mexican baroque style. Don Francisco even sponsored a religious confraternity devoted to the Virgin of Light, an association that was to receive deep praise from Pedro Tamarón y Romeral, bishop of the Diocese of Durango, when he visited Santa Fe in 1760.[38]

In 1776, the Church and Convent of Saint Francis were vividly described by Fray Francisco Atanasio Domínguez, a canonical visitor to the Franciscan mission area in New Mexico, officially known as the Custody of the Conversion of Saint Paul. Situated almost in the center of the villa, according to Fray Domínguez, Saint Francis Church constructed with nave, transept, and sanctuary, also had a choir loft. Its floor was of bare earth packed down to form a hard surface. The church had been

A nineteenth-century view (ca. 1867) of the parish church of Saint Francis of Assisi in Santa Fe. Photograph by Nicholas Brown and Son, courtesy Museum of New Mexico, Santa Fe.

furnished with three altars, one dedicated to Our Lady of Guadalupe, the second to Saint Francis of Assisi, and the third to Saint Anthony of Padua. On the gospel side, where the altar of Our Lady of Guadalupe was located, there was also a small chapel in which a three-foot statue of Our Lady of the Rosary, the Conquistadora, was enshrined.[39]

The fading prospects for a *real de minas* at Santa Fe meant that the economic development and growth of the town would lack the spectacular characteristics of the mining boom towns of Nueva Vizcaya. In effect, the economy of the province was to depend on the coffers of the government of New Spain and on an *encomendero* form of life. The bountiful treasury of the Spanish imperial government was to assume full responsibility for the support of the missions in New Mexico in 1609.[40] To furnish provisions for missionary activity, supply trains were sent about every three years. The gradual increase in the number of friars serving in New Mexico and the increase in the cost of transporting supplies from Central Mexico to Santa Fe made supplying the missions quite expensive. The costs prior to 1620 were about 28,000 pesos and, with an expanding missionary enterprise operated by forty-six friars, the expenses in 1629 were more than 81,000 pesos.[41]

Whereas the imperial treasury provided for the missionaries, the Spanish settlers sought economic security by exploiting the Indian population and by putting to use their land grants. The territory around Santa Fe became especially important. Even though much of the land in the vicinity belonged to the Tewa people, after the Reconquest, Diego de Vargas distributed land grants in the area to Spaniards,[42] probably in hopes of keeping the settlers grouped near the capital.

With the economy of early New Mexico dependent largely on missionary enterprises and the subsidies provided for these activities by the Spanish imperial government, local circumstances were hardly conducive to the expansion of civil communities. Moreover, an outmoded, in many ways feudal, *encomienda* system, tied the settlers to a primitive agrarian economy and hardly promoted the local industry required for town growth. Fray Benavides, the Franciscan superior of the province, claimed that by the second quarter of the seventeenth century in "the villa de Santa Fe, capital of the Kingdom, where the governor and the Spaniards reside . . . [there] . . . must be as many as two hundred and fifty . . . [and] . . . between Spaniards, mestizos and Indians, there must be a thousand souls."[43]

There was no spectacular population increase in the capital with the political reorganization of the province after the Reconquest. Bishop Tamarón during his visitation of New Mexico in the 1760s remarked that "this Villa de Santa Fe has 379 families of citizens of Spanish and mixed blood, with 1,285 persons. Since I have confirmed 1,532 persons in the said villa, I am convinced that the census count they gave me is very much on the low side. [There] . . . must be at least twice that given in the census."[44]

Without adequate resources to stimulate the municipal economy, trading at the marketplaces of Santa Fe remained limited, although levels were consistent, since Spaniards from outlying districts and Indians from nearby pueblos came to Santa Fe to shop and sell. There were, moreover, three water-operated grist mills at Santa Fe to grind grain harvested from fields in the vicinity.[45]

Some early Franciscan writers seem to have distorted the economic picture of the *villa*. In a letter to the crown on September 16, 1638,

POPULATION OF THE SANTA FE MUNICIPALITY
AND VICINITY DURING THE COLONIAL PERIOD

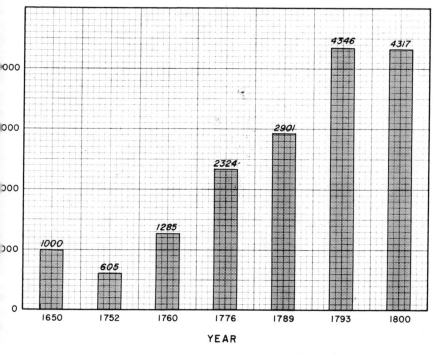

YEAR

FIGURE I

Fray Juan de Prado claimed that the commerce in Santa Fe had reached its nadir, since the people who traded in the *villa* were able "to neither buy nor sell," nor was there "any kind of money in circulation."[46] In March, 1776, Fray Domínguez had nothing more positive to say about the economy of the town, describing the *villa* as mournful in appearance.[47]

Actually, there had been active trade among the Pueblo Indians long before the first Spanish *entrada*. The crown, besides providing supply trains for Franciscan missionaries, imported specie to pay troops and to supply them.[48] This revenue filtered down to the people of the province, especially to those who provided livestock and agricultural produce for presidial garrisons. However, military expenditures in New Mexico could not stimulate the municipal economy without concomitant development of local industry.[49]

MUNICIPAL STABILITY AND THE PASTORAL INDUSTRY

In the years following the reconquest of New Mexico, the crown made significant changes in its view of municipalities in New Mexico. The establishment of new towns, which facilitated mobility, received special attention. Isolationism was no longer an attitude, only a geographical element to be overcome by emphasizing the importance of towns within the province.

Around the lands of the Pojoaque Pueblo, General Vargas settled the Villa de Santa Cruz de la Cañada in 1695. By the middle of the eighteenth century, this new settlement of Spanish and mestizo pioneers had grown to more than half the size of Santa Fe, with 556 settlers, of whom 99 were heads of family and 267, children. The town was defended by 135 arms-bearing men equipped with muskets, lances, and pistols, and there were 168 horses.[50] Moreover, Gov. Francisco Cuervo y Valdez approved on April 24, 1706, the founding of Albuquerque, "in the great grove of Doña Luisa located on the banks of the Río del Norte some twenty-two leagues" downriver below Bernalillo and Alameda. Situated on the vital route between Santa Fe and El Paso, this new *villa* provided additional protection for traders and a haven for wayfarers. By 1752, when Governor Tomás Vélez Cachupín visited Albuquerque, he could report that its total population consisted of 476 inhabitants, 297 of whom were children. There were 107 heads of family and 110 arms-bearing men equipped with swords, muskets, pistols, and lances. Moreover, the town had a herd of 389 horses, more than any other town in the province.[51]

The pastoral industry began to expand as sheep raisers made large quantities of wool available. Besides spinning cotton textiles in the prehispanic manner, Indians now began to produce woolen *mantas,* stockings, and coarse blankets. However, for reasons peculiar to the province, early weaving was not commercially promoted before Shaman Popé's revolt, at least not in the same measure as after the Reconquest. In 1664 the governor forbade "the masters of doctrine to employ Indian women in spinning, weaving mantas, stockings or any other thing without . . . express license" from his office.[52]

With the advent of the eighteenth century, colonial life in New Mexico reflected a new interest in sheep raising. The great number of sheep, along with other livestock, and the large quantity of raw wool exported southward with the regular caravans in November and December of each year, ultimately compelled the governor to establish trade regulations to retain enough of these resources for local needs.[53] In the later years of the colonial period, reports from the Villa de Santa Fe to the crown on agriculture, trade, and industry in New Mexico indicated that sheep raising abounded, with an export of about twenty-five thousand sheep to the Province of Vizcaya and some of its presidios. Economic necessity and the natural ability of the people had combined to develop the woolen textile industry, shoemaking, carpentry, tailoring, masonry, and blacksmith products. Some of the woven articles included blankets, coats, sackcloth, and carpets. These woolen products were often colored with indigo, local herbs, and Brazil nuts, which were imported from abroad. From cotton the settlers wove linen for tablecloths and stockings, as well as domestic shirting of twisted thread woven closer and stronger than that of Puebla.[54]

Manufactured woolen goods represented New Mexico's major export, many of these woven products reaching the Provinces of Chihuahua and Nueva Vizcaya.[55] The civil community of Parral and the town of Chihuahua were both active *reales de minas* with markets stocked with wares from Castile and from all parts of New Spain.[56] New Mexico merchants and settlers often returned from these commercial centers with purchased items or with silver pesos gained in exchange for their own products. As early as the 1620s, the governors of the province had been using the return trips of the New Mexico supply trains to get their salt, hides, and cotton cloth to the mines of New Spain,[57] with the intention of trading with Chihuahua and other towns in Nueva Vizcaya, and even with commercial centers in Central Mexico. It was not until sheep raising provided New Mexico with a viable industry that trade with neighboring provinces began to take hold, with recognizable economic results from this limited prosperity in the civil communities of New Mexico. By the last quarter of the eighteenth century, the Spanish government in the province began to encourage the woolen industry, "promoting the commerce in New Mexico and the establishment of factories of course weaves."[58]

3

El Paso

A STRATEGIC TOWN IN NEW MEXICO

NATIVES OF THE EL PASO AREA

Once the land of the Mogollon culture (A.D. 700–1400), the El Paso area extended northward into New Mexico, southwest as far as Casas Grandes (Chihuahua), eastward toward the Pecos River, and southward to the Big Bend country of Texas. When the Spaniards arrived in this part of their expanding empire, the Southern Athapaskans dwelt where Ciudad Juárez and El Paso now stand.

Alvar Núñez Cabeza de Vaca, in his odyssey from East Texas southwestward to Culiacán, a town on New Spain's west coast, was the first European to set foot in the general El Paso area.[1] When he arrived on the scene in 1536, there were two distinct El Pasoan nations at hand, the Sumas, or Jumas, and the Jumanos. Downriver from the El Paso crossing the Sumas dwelt on territory bordering the western fringes of the Jumano lands. The Sumas were a meandering tribe with a simple economic structure and probably related to the sedentary Jumanos, a nation living in the villages of the Río Grande Valley in West Texas around the Big Bend country.[2]

North of El Paso, within a hundred-square-mile area, lived a fiercer tribe called the Mansos, a group linguistically and racially similar to the Sumas and Jumanos.[3] In the land of the Mansos, at a point where the mountains came down to the river and formed a ford in the stream, a pass had creased the foothills; this geographic sector was destined to become the municipal districts of the twentieth-century twin cities of Juárez and El Paso.

On May 4, 1598, Juan de Oñate reached the pass of the river and was met by a welcoming committee of forty Manso tribesmen:

They had turkish brows, long hair cut to resemble little Milan caps, head gear made to hold down the hair and colored with blood or paint. Their first words were *manxo,* manxo, *micos,* micos, by which they meant "peaceful ones" and "friends." They make the sign of the cross by raising their thumbs. They told us very clearly by signs that the settlements were six days along the road. They mark the day by the course of the sun; in these things they are like ourselves.[4]

For all the solemnity in Oñate's taking possession of New Mexico at El Paso on April 30, 1598,[5] the hardy pioneers in Oñate's caravan were rank newcomers to this river crossing, a natural stopping place for travelers moving in all directions. The migration of some of the North American Indian tribes moving southward into Mexico and South America might have taken them through the pass. Even the expedition of Fray Agustín Rodríguez and Captain Francisco Sánchez Chamuscado in 1581 might have crossed there, and other Spaniards in search of souls or wealth in New Mexico during the same decade crossed routinely.[6] However, by carrying Spain's influence into New Mexico in 1598, Juan de Oñate, the veteran town founder from Zacatecas, turned El Paso from a natural water crossing into a vital way station between his province and the rest of New Spain. If town settlements in New Mexico were to secure the land and if the flag of Spain was to wave over the province, the district of El Paso del Río del Norte had to be recognized as an important logistical link by the Spanish imperial government in Central Mexico. The need for a civil community and presidio at the pass was to become even more vital in the eighteenth century with the gradual development of commercial ties between Chihuahua and New Mexico.

The historical antecedents to Spanish town settlements at El Paso are represented by the Franciscans' significant evangelical work among the Mansos, an endeavor under way several decades before Spanish municipal organization became evident. There was interest in the indigenous inhabitants around El Paso from the time the first religious entered New Mexico by the vital water crossing. Fray Alonso de Benavides, the *custos* of the Franciscan province in New Mexico from 1623 to 1629, had recommended that a mission settlement consisting of four religious and fifteen or twenty soldiers be established at El Paso.[7] Although offering pious descriptions of the Mansos' disposition toward Christian instruction and baptism, the articulate missionary hastened, with equal vigor, to provide King Philip IV with more mundane reasons for civil settlements at El Paso:

With this protection many very rich mining camps which are found all along this road could be settled, as well as magnificent farm sites with water and very fine land. Then one could travel that road every year, or as often as he wished; and it would not happen that for want of this protection, five or six years would pass without our knowing anything of the Spanish nation here in New Mexico.[8]

By the middle of the seventeenth century, zealous Franciscans from the Province of the Conversion of Saint Paul had succeeded in establishing several mission settlements in the El Paso district, the Indian pueblo of Senecú, upriver and in the Río Grande Valley near the future site of San Marcial, having been catechized by Fran Antonio de Arteaga by 1620.[9] The reported real founder of El Paso, Fray García de San Francisco y Zúñiga, with alms collected from citizens in New Mexico, established the pueblo of Nuestra Señora del Socorro and built in the Indian settlement a mission and convent, furnishing the newly built church and sacristy "with rich ornaments, organ and music."[10] Fray García directed his two companions, Fray Francisco Pérez and Fray Juan Cabal, to instruct the Mansos in Christian doctrine. Moreover, he grew lush gardens and rich vineyards around the mission center from which he supplied wine for weary travelers and for neighboring missionaries.[11] Meanwhile, Fray Pérez and Fray Cabal congregated some of the Mansos at the mission settlement, the latter extending his evangelical work among the nearby Sumas.[12] However, evangelical work was considerably curtailed when the supply caravan of 1658 failed to provide the additional religious assigned to New Mexico's mission centers in the El Paso district.[13] Moreover, a number of Mansos, nonagricultural by tradition, began to have second thoughts about the sedentary life at the mission centers and eventually rebelled, causing much disillusionment among Fray García's companions. "Never mind. Don't wear yourselves out, for the time has not yet come," advised Fray García, encouraging his comrades Fray Pérez and Fray Cabal not to be dismayed by setbacks in their missionary work among the Mansos and the Sumas.[14]

The Mission Center of Nuestra Señora de Guadalupe

In 1659 Fray García, who in his middle years had become vice-custodian of the New Mexico missions, had already embarked on more ambitious plans. Principal credit is due him for the establishment of the church

The famous church and convent of Nuestra Señora de Guadalupe, mother church of the twin cities of Ciudad Juarez, Chihuahua, and El Paso, Texas. Painting by Augustus de Vaudricourt from William H. Emory's *Report of the U.S. and Mexican Boundary Survey,* courtesy U.T. Institute of Texan Cultures at San Antonio.

and convent of Nuestra Señora de Guadalupe in present-day Ciudad Juárez.[15] With approval from the governor of New Mexico, Don Juan Manso, and with instructions from Fray Juan Gonzales, his religious superior, Fray García laid the foundation for the church of Nuestra Señora de Guadalupe, which became the cornerstone of the establishment of El Paso.[16]

Fray García recorded the founding of the church in the form of an *auto de fundación,* a document entered in the first administration books of the mission:

> Having received the patents from my superior, in which he orders me to descend for the instruction and conversion of this heathendom, and license from the said Señor Don Juan Manso governor; and having descended, with no little labor to El Passo del Río del Norte, on the border and province of New Mexico; and having congregated most

. . . of the Manso . . . and having offered them the evangelical word, and they having accepted it for their catechism, and permitted me to build a little church of branches and mud and a monastery thatched with straw."[17]

In 1661, with the arrival of the new *custos,* or religious superior, for the Franciscan missions in New Mexico, Fray García was relieved of his duties as vice-custodian, enabling him and his coworker Fray Benito de la Natividad to spend more time in the construction of a new church and convent. The humble mission of branches and thatched straw was to be replaced by a permanent church building and adequate living quarters for the missionaries, and the cornerstone for the new mission complex was laid on April 2, 1662.[18]

The whole establishment, located on the present site of the old cathedral of Ciudad Juárez, was completed and dedicated in honor of Our Lady of Guadalupe on January 15, 1668. Fray Salvador de Guerra, secretary of the Custodia of New Mexico during the dedication, vividly described the ceremonies.[19] Four hundred "natives of the nation of the Mansos" attended the ceremonies. During the day three missionaries were kept busy baptizing one hundred Indian converts, the men entering through one door of the church and the women by another. The baptized Mansos then proceeded to the middle of the church, where their marriages were blessed by missionaries.[20]

The indoor services were complemented by considerable festivity on the mission grounds. The church was decorated with a rich display of green silklike cloth, and the "Christian Manso Indians . . . celebrated the dedication of their church with a dance and signs of great joy."[21] There was a great display of fireworks and rockets constructed to resemble a beautiful "castillo [y] dos hombres armados" on the day of the mass and on the previous night.[22]

Described by Fray de Guerra as a church with two large bells and "with strong and unusual woodwork," Nuestra Señora de Guadalupe possessed a "beautiful arch" and a nave ninety-five feet long and thirty-five feet wide. On the main altar, approached by "altar steps [that] are very beautiful," there was placed an attractive painting of the Virgin of Guadalupe surrounded by a statue of Our Lady, one of the Divine Infant, and "a very handsome statue of our Seraphic Father St. Francis." One side altar of the church had a statue of the Immaculate Conception, and on the second side altar there was "a beautiful canvas of our

Father St. Anthony finished neatly and decently." The church also possessed a large choir loft "so spacious that the services of fifty clerics and of the Mansito choir boys could easily be celebrated there."[23] The baptistry was constructed under the choir loft and the sacristy, equipped with many sacred vessels and vestments, was furnished with carpets and candlesticks. In front of the church, gardens and fruit orchards were cultivated, producing abundant "grapes, apples, quinces, plums, peaches, and figs."[24]

To acquaint the Mansos with European agricultural techniques, their fertile lands near the mission were provided with an *acequia* and then plowed and sowed. Understandably elated by their success in converting the Indians of the Manso nation to neophyte Christians, Fray de Guerra recorded their docility toward doctrine, their joy at prayer, and their ability to be "good husbands and wives." The conversion of some of the Mansos meant much more, however. The Franciscan missionary, as an agent of the Spanish imperial government, had an obligation to convert the Mansos into worthy vassals of the Catholic kings of Castile and León, a duty almost synonymous with loyalty to religion and to his patron, Saint Francis. Elemental patterns of European life-style were introduced into the lives of the baptized Indians. Formerly nomadic, the Mansos at the mission now tilled their lands and tended cows and sheep. Moreover, the Mansos lived in little houses near the mission, wore proper attire, and used "pot and spoon."[25]

The Church and Convent of Nuestra Señora de Guadalupe became the focal point for town settlements at the ford of El Paso. It was the mother church for the missions of San Francisco de los Sumas.[26] La Soledad de los Janos, located about seventy leagues southwest in the direction of Casas Grandes, was generally referred to as belonging to the jurisdiction of New Mexico and was the main church of the Janos in the El Paso district.[27]

The magnitude of Fray García's achievements was seen in the thriving community of El Paso during the 1660s. The total number of parishioners reached one thousand, mostly permanent settlers who planted crops, orchards, and vineyards and had accumulated about nine thousand head of cattle plus thirteen thousand sheep and goats.[28] While most of the settlers were converted Indians, there was a growing number of Spanish families in the area. El Paso had become a refreshing way station for travelers reaching the ford from both directions.

SPANISH CIVIL COMMUNITIES AT EL PASO

The decade of the 1670s, a generally unsettled period in the Río Arriba and Abajo regions of New Mexico, witnessed the violence of church-state conflict and a drought and famine that affected both Spaniard and Indian.[29] This period was made more trying by the intensification of Apache raids on newly established missions in most areas, but particularly in the vicinity of the so-called saline pueblos. In that area between 1672 and 1677 the missions of Abó, Los Humanos, Senecú, Quarai, and Chililí were closed down.[30]

With the arrival of supply caravans, efforts to reestablish some of the mission centers were made in the late 1670s, but the attempt proved futile, as Apache attacks compelled some of the mission Indians to scatter and to find refuge farther south at Nuestra Señora de Guadalupe in El Paso. The number of Indian refugees that drifted into the mission center is uncertain; however, it appears that Nuestra Señora de Guadalupe was able to assimilate them, for names of Piros, Abós, Jumanos, Sumas, Tanos, and Apaches are in church records dating to the 1670s.[31]

Although the mission of the Mansos had ample food and stock for its original converts, the arrival of Indians fleeing Apache raids and of Spanish refugees from New Mexico taxed resources and tried patience.[32] Ultimately, the demands placed on the Indian settlements became so oppressive that the Mansos, Janos, and Sumas revolted in 1684, bringing additional hardships to the embattled New Mexican settlers.

The Manso mission attracted a small number of Spanish settlers from the start, the custom being often to send a Spanish family to care for the missionaries.[33] Hispanic town settlements were not possible because of the lack of settlers in the late 1660s. Even so, there were enough Spaniards in the vicinity to form an organized civil administration for the El Paso area. Captain Andrés López de García was appointed its first *alcalde mayor* by the governor of New Mexico, Bernardo López de Mendizábal. By 1680, Diego de Trujillo had succeeded López de García in office when the governor of Nueva Vizcaya appointed him *alcalde mayor* of Casas Grandes with jurisdiction over the El Paso district.[34] The appointment of *alcaldes mayores* by governors from two different provinces suggests that civil jurisdiction in the El Paso area was of little interest to either the crown or regional officials before the Pueblo Rebellion of 1680.

In tracing the existence of a Hispanic settlement in El Paso, the baptism, marriage, and burial records at Nuestra Señora de Guadalupe indicate that at least thirty-one Spaniards attended the mission for religious services.[35] There is other evidence pointing to the presence of a Spanish civil community at El Paso prior to Shaman Popé's rebellion. In the summer of 1680, Maestre de Campo Pedro de Levía and twenty-seven other settlers from New Mexico were in El Paso waiting to escort the triennial missionary supply caravan on to Santa Fe. On hearing of the Pueblo Rebellion, Pedro de Levía and his men hastened back up the river to assist the fleeing New Mexicans. In addition to Levía's men, the New Mexicans were assisted by fifty-one other armed men.[36] This increase in manpower suggests that some were drawn from the Spanish population already established at El Paso.

The retreat of refugees from New Mexico to El Paso in late 1680 introduced an unforeseen crisis. For twenty years, the relatively well established mission center at Nuestra Señora de Guadalupe had provided adequately for friars and Indian converts. Moreover, its two smaller missions, San Francisco de los Sumas, twelve leagues below El Paso, and La Soledad, located among the Janos southwest of Guadalupe Church, were at peace and actively engaged in converting neophyte Christians into productive vassals of the Spanish empire.

When Governor Antonio de Otermín's twenty-five hundred New Mexican refugees reached La Salineta just north of El Paso and on the right bank of the river, they required immediate help from Nuestra Señora de Guadalupe.[37] The semiarid lands around La Salineta, or "la Toma del Río del Norte," did not provide adequate resources for the destitute travelers from New Mexico. Immediate return to New Mexico was impossible, and the crossing of the river into El Paso would mean encroachment on Manso settlements. Yet to remain at La Salineta would only contribute to loss of morale and illegal departures into Nueva Vizcaya and Sonora.[38] On October 5, 1680, Don Antonio made arrangements for three temporary civil camps two leagues apart below the Guadalupe church and convent: San Lorenzo, where he and the Santa Fe *cabildo* resided; the Real de San Pedro de Alcántara; and the Real del Santíssimo Sacramento.[39] Fray Francisco de Ayeta, drawing mainly from food stored at the Manso mission, made generous provisions for the Spanish refugees and for the Piros and other allied tribesmen who followed the Spaniards from New Mexico.[40] The civil communities of the New Mexicans were not to be permanent but to serve as a base of operations for expeditions back into their province. In 1681, when Otermín's attempted reconquest of the Pueblo lands was thwarted, the governor and his advisers began making arrangements for an indefinite stay at El Paso. The viceroy and *junta general* in Central Mexico granted approval for stable Spanish settlements by the New Mexicans. Before locating the permanent organizations, the governor and several members of the *cabildo* examined both banks of the Río del Norte from Estero Largo to La Toma near the mission of the Sumas. The scouting party found no place that appeared more suitable for settlement than San Lorenzo, where the New Mexicans had already set up camp. They chose to maintain it until further orders from the viceroy.[41]

The Guadalupe church community had existed at El Paso without benefit of a neighboring presidio. However, because of the establishment of civilian communities, there was now a large population concentration at El Paso, and, with Shaman Popé's warriors in control of New Mexico, the need for a presidio had become more urgent. Luis Granillo, a *regidor* and the *procurador general* on the Santa Fe town council, informed Governor Otermín that a second *entrada* should be conditioned on the establishment of a fifty-man presidio in El Paso for the protection of the wives and children whom the expedition must leave behind.[42] Although Otermín enrolled the fifty men for the presidio, the plan was only provisional, since the enlistment of men and the actual construction of the fort were not made in accordance with Spanish imperial government orders until Don Domingo Jironza Petriz de Cruzate, Otermín's successor, became the governor of the New Mexico colony.[43] Before leaving Mexico City, Governor Petriz de Cruzate secured adequate equipment for the presidio and twenty men from Zacatecas for the fort, the balance of soldiers being recruited from among the El Paso settlers.[44] On his arrival in August, 1683, he located the new presidio seven leagues from El Paso, halfway between Nuestra Señora de Guadalupe Church and the civilian community of San Lorenzo. At the same time, Petriz de Cruzate, assisted by Fray Nicolás López, the ubiquitous vice-custodian of the New Mexico missions, reorganized the Spanish and Indian settlements and planted one new mission at Santa Gertrudis, about eight or twelve leagues south of the Manso mission center.[45] Moreover, Fray López, with the governor's approval, established seven missions among the Jumanos at La Junta, about one hundred leagues southeast of Nuestra Señora de Guadalupe Church.[46]

In El Paso prior to the Indian revolts of 1684 the Spanish settlers were distributed into four civil communities—San Lorenzo, San Pedro de

Alcántara, Señor San José, and La Isleta. The Christian Indians were divided among the pueblos of Socorro, San Francisco, Sacramento, Senecú, and La Soledad.⁴⁷ When the Indian insurrection occurred in 1684, the Spanish and Christian natives were grouped nearer to Guadalupe Church, where the presidio had been relocated.⁴⁸ The establishment of a presidio and two new Spanish settlements–San José and La Isleta–and one new Indian settlement at Sacramento had now converted El Paso into a fairly large population center embodying the three major colonial institutions of the northern Borderlands–presidio, town, and mission. Representatives from these three institutions–the governor, the town council, and the clerical leaders, respectively–contributed to El Paso's emerging political importance and introduced the need to clarify jurisdiction over the region. When Governor Otermín encamped the Spanish settlers from New Mexico at San Lorenzo, San Pedro de Alcántara, and Sacramento for an indefinite stay beginning in 1681, the viceroy formally placed the El Paso area under New Mexico's control.⁴⁹ The viceroy reaffirmed the grant of jurisdiction by appointing Petriz de Cruzate governor in 1682. With this move, he upheld the Spanish imperial government's position that New Mexico had not been abandoned and that the political organizations of the territory were intact, their quarters at El Paso being provisional until the new *entrada*.

The El Paso area comprised the lands between El Río del Norte and El Río del Sacramento, a region exerting political influence over Casas Grandes and its immediate environs. Understandably enough, the governor and citizens of Nueva Vizcaya, who traditionally exercised control over Casas Grandes, protested loudly enough before the viceroy to have the El Paso area restored to them.⁵⁰ However, this restoration was only temporary. The governor and the Cabildo of Santa Fe at El Paso informed the central government that the origins of the community of El Paso were rooted in the history of New Mexico,⁵¹ and that the future of the province and the reconquest of the Pueblo lands were vitally linked with their right to control the disputed territory. On November 28, 1685, the Junta General, impressed by the petitions from Governor Petriz de Cruzate and the Santa Fe *cabildo* in exile, restored authority over the El Paso area to New Mexico, and the viceroy issued a *mandamiento* to that effect on the same day.⁵²

The final decision on the disposition of the New Mexican settlers rested with the imperial government in Mexico City. Having spent more than a million pesos in New Mexico from the time of Oñate's penetration of the province to the Pueblo Rebellion,[53] the central government was not to be easily persuaded into thinking that Shaman Popé's declaration of independence was a *fait accompli*. The imperial government was mainly concerned with determining the most propitious time to embark on a successful *entrada*. In the meantime, the great challenge facing the viceroy was keeping the New Mexican settlers grouped together so that they would continue to form the foundation for the political organization of the province and the power base for the reconquest of New Mexico, the goal toward which the central government subordinated all other concerns regarding El Paso. The Junta General consolidated the political position of the New Mexican governor and his settlers when it persuaded the viceroy to place El Paso under New Mexico's jurisdiction in 1685.[54] Moreover, the viceroy commanded that a permanent presidio of fifty cavalrymen be established at El Paso by Governor Petriz de Cruzate for the security of both Spanish and Indian vassals, and as a base for the projected *entrada* into New Mexico.

After becoming the *procurador general* of the Franciscans in New Mexico, Fray Francisco de Ayeta bought wagons, mules, and supplies for the colonists. In 1676, he successfully argued before the viceregal courts in Mexico City for an administration in New Mexico that would treat the Indians justly. On February 27, 1677, he left for the north with provisions for the missions and reinforcements, military supplies, and horses for the embattled soldiers of the province.[55] His labors could only delay the catastrophe of 1680, however. Undaunted, he rallied his Franciscan brethren and enjoined them not to lose sight of the need to reenter the province and to correct the apostasy that had encompassed their mission lands. They were deeply aware that Shaman Popé's successes had undone almost a century of missionary work in New Mexico. Their missionary zeal had not diminished, though; even while residing in their provisional quarters at El Paso, the missionaries had cared for both Spanish and Indian settlers and, moreover, had penetrated deeply into regions of the Big Bend and established seven missions among the inhabitants of the Jumano nation. Furthermore, although the Indian revolt in the summer of 1684 stirred new dissatisfaction among the Spanish settlers, the friars remained steadfast, even though Fray Manuel Beltrán, the resident missionary at La Soledad, was added to the growing number of Franciscans who had lost their lives in New Mexico.[56]

The missionaries knew that the evangelization of New Mexico could not continue without effective Spanish civil communities in the province; the friars, in effect, were committed to the principle that Spanish laymen were entitled to moderate exploitation of native labor. The positive benefits of Christianity more than compensated the Indians for the loss of independence and the infringement of their property rights.[57] This was to be part of the reasoning behind future reconquest efforts in New Mexico.[58]

A SPANISH *CABILDO* AT EL PASO

The Cabildo of the Villa of Santa Fe in exile was the only full local government capable of representing the Spanish civil community in El Paso. Dutifully vocal since the time it reached La Salineta, the *cabildo* participated actively in everything that touched the lives of the New Mexican refugees. In the fall of 1680, representatives of the *cabildo* joined friars and military officials in a meeting to help the governor decide to settle the New Mexicans in El Paso.[59] The following year several members of the town council accompanied the governor in examining both sides of the Río del Norte for possible new town sites.[60]

Representing a distinct political entity, the members of the municipal government did not hesitate to disagree with the governor when they felt his decisions did not reflect the best interests of the civil community. In February, 1682, the representatives of the *cabildo* not only brought Governor Otermín to account before the viceroy for what they considered to be maladministration of soldiers and resources but also officially assigned messengers to deliver the letter to Mexico City without license from the governor for the couriers to leave the province.[61] When Governor Petriz de Cruzate arrived at El Paso in August, 1683, he was joined by three members of the *cabildo* (an *alcalde*, a *regidor*, and the *procurador general*) in a search for a suitable site for a presidio.[62] When the newly appointed governor attempted to move the Spanish civilian communities nearer to El Paso for better protection of settler and livestock, the settlers from New Mexico, accustomed to living in spread-out communities, issued through the *cabildo* an appeal to the viceroy that the whole colony be permitted to leave El Paso. The letter from the *cabildo,* dated July 6, 1684, described harsh conditions and the difficulty of obtaining food, which made it imperative that the settlers be allowed to abandon El Paso.[63] In addition, a plea to leave El Paso and requests for a license to settle in the valley of San Martín or along the banks of the Sacramento River, both sites within the jurisdiction of New Mexico, were often directed by the *cabildo* to Governor Petriz de Cruzate in the fall of the same year.[64]

The settlers, demonstrating signs of a desire for free choice, did not fail to rally behind their governor when they considered doing so to be in the interest of their community. Eleven of New Mexico's oldest settlers, taking independent action, strongly supported the governor when the disputed territory of El Paso was to pass to the jurisdiction of Nueva Vizcaya. These senior members of the community protested to the viceroy that the El Paso area extending as far west as Casas Grandes had its origins—at least according to their version—in the history of New Mexico and in the expeditions of Juan de Oñate.[65] And when news of the appointment of a successor to Governor Petriz de Cruzate reached El Paso well in advance of the expiration of his three-year term, he solicited the support of the *cabildo* to present the best possible record. In compliance with the governor's request, the municipal government executed a document expressing gratitude for services and listing in detail examples of his generosity, vigilance, and care for settlers and friars.[66]

Despite these signs of loyalty to the incumbent governor, however, the *cabildo* did not hesitate to endorse its own choice for Petriz de Cruzate's successor. In 1685, the *cabildo* provided Juan Domínguez de Mendoza, the rugged frontier captain from New Mexico, with a formal certification of his long and loyal service to the province in order to enhance his chances of becoming the next governor of New Mexico.[67] Even though Captain Domínguez de Mendoza was not selected by the viceroy, the *cabildo*'s expressing a choice demonstrated that the town council remained a vital force in the arena of New Mexican politics.

The vocal and often independent positions taken by the Santa Fe *cabildo* at El Paso evidenced a practice deeply rooted in the municipal traditions of the province.[68] Beginning in the early 1620s the Santa Fe *cabildo* at times openly opposed and at other times strongly supported both governor and friars. This was the practice in El Paso while Otermín and Petriz de Cruzate were governors and continued through the rule of subsequent New Mexican governors, particularly Don Pedro Reñeros, during Petriz de Cruzate's second term, and even during that of the leader of the Reconquest, Don Diego de Vargas.

While the *cabildo* was functioning in El Paso, apparently very few government or municipal buildings were constructed. Understandably enough, the town council, besides representing an impoverished civil community, had enough on its hands in regulating the political climate for benefit of the settlers and in providing the necessities of life for the Hispanic community. Even so, on August 18, 1685, the *cabildo,* in support of Governor Petriz de Cruzate, who had been directed by the viceroy to construct *casas reales,* had written a fairly clear description of the amount of work done on these buildings:

> And his lordship bought of the Manso Indians the site in this pueblo on which now his lordship has built some *casas reales* for the dwelling place of the governors. These [buildings] have a reception room, an apartment which serves as a secretary's office, another capacious apartment in which he is lodged, a cellar underground for the munitions of powder and balls, another apartment for a sleeping room, and two kitchens with their yard, and a pantry—all the aforesaid was built of adobe. Likewise his lordship has bought of the Mansos Indians three other houses adjoining the said *casas reales.* The one in which he has the guard-room, and which also serves as a jail, has two rooms; the other two adjoining it have, the one, two rooms, and the other, three rooms. Another house, which he likewise bought of the said Mansos, and which is beside the *casas reales,* has three small rooms. The wars and numerous expeditions upon which the governor and captain-general have set out have not given him an opportunity to finish the building.[69]

Apart from the construction of the presidio near Nuestra Señora de Guadalupe Church, the *casas reales* seem to be the only significant buildings constructed by the Hispanic community, the Indian revolt of 1684 having fairly well exhausted whatever limited resources the Spanish settlers might have accumulated in El Paso.

It is hard to estimate the exact population of El Paso during the years that Spanish settlers and refugee Indians resided there. When Governor Otermín arrived at La Salineta he estimated that he had 2,500 New Mexicans, but on completing a muster on October 2, 1680, the results revealed only 1,946 settlers of Spanish, mestizo, and Indian origins.[70]

Governor Tomás Vélez Cachupín, whose concern for the welfare of the loyal Indians in the province is manifested in his inspection report, made an official visitation of the El Paso community in 1752, and commented on the importance of this way station between the towns of New Mexico and the settlements in Sonora, Sinaloa, and Texas:

> At present there is no other settlement in the intervening area except Nuestra Señora de Guadalupe del Paso de Norte where there are four Indian towns and a community of Spaniards, mulattos and mestizos, and with a presidial garrison of fifty soldiers including a captain, one

POPULATION OF THE EL PASO MUNICIPALITY
AND VICINITY DURING THE COLONIAL PERIOD

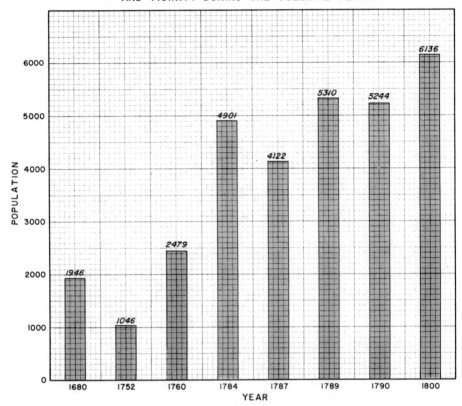

FIGURE 2

lieutenant, and an ensign who defend these four towns and check on those who enter and leave the province.[71]

According to his report the population at the El Paso community totaled 1,019: Guadalupe del Paso had 234 people, San Antonio Senucú, 297, San Antonio Isleta, 353, and Concepción de Socorro, 135. There were 305 heads of family and 462 children in the four pueblos. This vital outpost was well guarded by 361 men and more than 450 horses.[72]

The population at El Paso appears to have increased, for, about ten years later, Bishop Tamarón in a visitation indicated that the community had "354 families of Spanish and Europeanized citizens," totaling 2,479. The Indian population had diminished considerably since the in-

50

spection of 1752, there being only 72 Indian families comprising 249 persons.[73]

Even so, El Paso remained a vital link between the communities of the reconquered province of New Mexico and the town settlements of northern New Spain. While economic development continued at a relatively modest pace, mostly in view of its way-station status, essential agricultural production began to show signs of revitalization. Despite seasonal floods in late spring and early summer, Bishop Tamarón in 1760 pictured El Paso as a stop that exhausted travelers could anticipate with pleasure.[74]

By the close of the eighteenth century, the central government was providing New Mexico with tax breaks to encourage the production of woolen textiles and had established an annual fair in Chihuahua where the people of New Mexico might sell their goods quickly and profitably. Interested citizens in Santa Fe requested that the fair be located at El Paso, probably because, besides considering El Paso far closer than distant markets in Chihuahua, they viewed it as a community sufficiently attractive to draw prospective buyers from mining towns in northern New Spain for the purpose of doing business.[75] Governor Joaquín del Real Alencaster forwarded the petition to the viceroy by way of Nemesio Salcedo, then *comandante general* of the Provincias Internas. Unfortunately, there seems to be no record of a response from Mexico City regarding the request.

Whatever the economic potential of El Paso might have been during the late colonial period, the importance of the community in the early frontier history of New Spain can scarcely be overestimated. During the most critical period in their history, Spanish colonists in New Mexico made El Paso their bulwark against the threats of Shaman Popé's warriors. Moreover, the defensive measures implemented by the embattled Spanish communities in El Paso provided safeguards for the coveted *reales de minas* in Nueva Vizcaya. Under no circumstances would the Spanish government surrender the district of El Paso del Río del Norte. Eventually El Paso made it possible for Spain to repossess the Province of New Mexico.

Interestingly enough, early expeditions originating at El Paso strengthened Spanish claims to the "Kingdom of Texas."[76] These Spanish explorations, by mapping what is now the West Texas landscape and by planting missionary outposts across this vast land, played an important role in the northern frontier history of New Spain.

4

San Antonio

EARLY MUNICIPAL FOUNDINGS IN TEXAS

THE INTERNATIONAL SCENE

The War of the Spanish Succession (1710–1714) introduced powerful nationalistic forces into the Anglo-Franco-Hispano struggle for colonial supremacy in the New World.[1] With the advent of the eighteenth century, English naval strength had increased tremendously and posed a growing threat to Spanish claims in America.[2] As early as February, 1699, English designs against Spanish colonies in Georgia and Florida were suspected. The Spanish governor in Havana became deeply alarmed when he received intelligence reports revealing that the English were even contemplating the occupation of the Gulf Coast in an area between the Mississippi and the Bay of Espíritu Santo in Texas.[3] The Spaniards were able to restrict English plans directed against Spanish settlements along the Gulf Coast, particularly at Pensacola and at least during the War of the Spanish Succession.[4] However, as early as the spring of 1699, the Spanish governor in Florida began to report to viceregal officials that the French were beginning to encroach on Spanish possessions on the Gulf Coast.[5] France, the nominal ally of the Spanish crown, viewed the lower Mississippi Valley as part of New France. Moreover, French entrepreneurs regarded the Mississippi River as a vital trade route between Canada and emerging colonial trade centers in the Gulf of Mexico. France's attempts to strengthen its hold on the Louisiana drainage basin were supported by the establishment of strategically placed trade posts that challenged the Spanish imperial government. In less than twenty years, the French planted four settlements in the Lower Mississippi Valley: Biloxi in 1699, and Mobile in 1702, both along the Gulf Coast; Natchitoches on the Red River in 1713; and New Orleans above the mouth of the Mississippi in 1718.

Before the 1700s there were no battles between Spaniards and the French over Louisiana, even though French imperial designs along the Gulf Coast became openly manifest with Robert Cavelier, Sieur de la Salle's ambitious attempt to colonize East Texas in 1685.[6] However, conditions on the international scene changed in the eighteenth century. The fate of Louisiana was determined in Europe in France's favor due mainly to the diplomatic successes of the Duke of Harcourt, the French ambassador to Madrid, who prepared for his mission by carefully reading the lengthy dispatch drawn up on March 23, 1701, by Jerome Phelypeaux Pontchartrain, the minister of marine, who ardently promoted French establishments in Louisiana. In the royal court of Madrid, the Spanish monarch, Philip V, Bourbon in blood, sympathies, and education, readily acquiesced to his grandfather's plan that, to protect Spanish Gulf Coast possessions from the English, France must be allowed to settle Louisiana.[7] The Spanish War Council, or Junta de Guerra, reconsidered the plan to establish French outposts in Louisiana and, understandably enough, objected. Even so, Spain's questionable ally in North America quietly moved its settlement from Biloxi to Mobile Bay, a point closer to the Spanish Florida border. In 1702, when the members of the Junta de Guerra protested French encroachment, Philip V rebuked the council and the matter ended.[8] Thus, Spain, ruled by a Bourbon king and persuaded by French diplomatic maneuvers, allowed France to occupy Louisiana.

However, as the eighteenth century unfolded, the Spanish imperial government began to view more clearly the full picture of French colonial designs in the Mississippi Valley, both in the Illinois Country and in Louisiana. When Alonso de León, the governor of Coahuila, led a military expedition into East Texas in 1689, he was eyewitness to vestiges of La Salle's ill-fated attempt to claim Texas for France, the Indians having killed most of the Frenchmen and destroyed their outpost.[9] All the same, Gallic intentions to convert the lower Mississippi and the Louisiana drainage basin into exclusively French territory had not died; theirs was a dormant plan that was eventually to challenge Spanish claims to both Florida and Texas. France was not without able entrepreneurs to exploit the natives and resources of the Gulf Coast area, Antoine de la Mothe Cadillac, the Sieur de Bienville, and Louis Juchereau de Saint

Denis being familiar names to military officials in charge of New Spain's northern frontier defenses.[10]

In view of the French presence in the Lower Mississippi Valley, the Spanish imperial government felt obliged to protect the Gulf Coast of northern Mexico both in East Texas, and in the Seno Mexicano, particularly the area comprising the coast of Tamaulipas and sections of South Texas. In the 1690s, Texas had been declared a frontier province and Domingo Terán de los Ríos appointed first governor of the newly designated province. Moreover, the Neches missions had been established in East Texas, but a few years later were abandoned because of the expense involved in maintaining them.[11]

The inability of the royal treasury to support outposts in East Texas was overcome by necessity. With the advent of the eighteenth century, the Spanish imperial government was compelled to embark on an all-out effort to hold and colonize Texas; French encroachment in the province and the determination of Fray Francisco Hidalgo and other Franciscans to maintain missions among their Hasinai charges influenced the crown's officials in New Spain.[12] Spanish authorities in Mexico City commenced the long, tedious, and expensive preparations needed for the reoccupation of Texas, a move eventually leading to the establishment of the San Antonio civil community and *cabildo* in 1731.

Fray Juan Agustín Morfi, the noted chronicler of the Spanish Southwest in the eighteenth century, was familiar with the frontier and stressed the need to consider the international scene in recapitulating Texas history during the first years of the period: "So close are the events of the history of Louisiana connected with those of Texas that it is not possible to narrate with clearness what took place in the second without giving at least a brief summary of the first."[13]

ROYAL PLANS FOR TEXAS TOWNS

With ambitious French leadership firmly established in Louisiana and traders from the Lower Mississippi Valley spreading in all directions, the Spanish imperial government felt obliged to bolster New Spain's defensive posture throughout the Borderlands, a move that strengthened the new hold on Nuevo México and in particular fortified largely uninhabited Texas.[14] The proximity of Spanish Texas to Louisiana made the province especially susceptible to French influence. To defend the

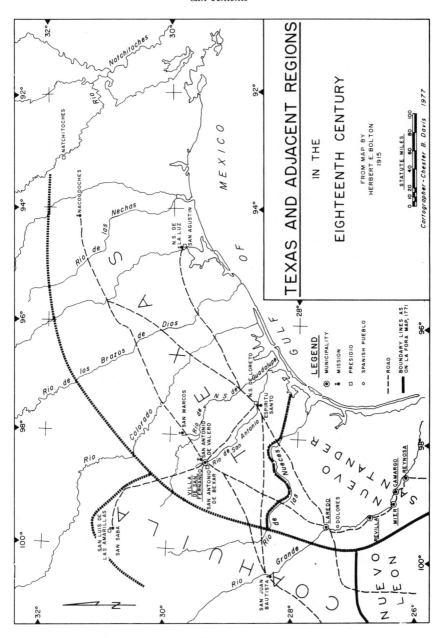

Map 3

northernmost Borderlands, the presidios were revitalized, missionary efforts were renewed, and ultimately chartered town settlements with *cabildos* were established. These three agencies played distinct roles in making New Spain secure from both internal rebellion and foreign encroachment. One frontier institution could not replace another, yet all three had the common goal of securing the land. By the second half of the eighteenth century, during the Bourbon reforms of the northern frontier, all three institutions played an important role in the formation of a line of defense extending from the shoreline of California to the Gulf Coast of Texas.[15]

The mission centers received more attention than the other two colonial institutions, at least in the early phases of the Spanish colonial period. The Christianized Indians assembled their families within the mission compound, where the friars instructed them in religion, in the art of tilling fields and caring for livestock, and in handicrafts.[16] The mission settlement, designed for the frontier, was to be turned over to the secular clergy, at least theoretically, within ten years, once the Indian became a worthy vassal of the king and was assimilated into the social structure of New Spain. This regulation was based on experience with the sedentary Indians of Central Mexico.[17] Indians in Texas were mainly nomadic, grew few crops, and, oftentimes, rejected organized mission life. Consequently, the crown began to place more responsibility on the presidial system. Spanish soldiers were to secure the land, pacify unruly natives, and defend the provinces from foreign intruders. Moreover, troops were to protect the missionaries and provide the physical strength needed to bring order to mission centers.[18]

The Spanish imperial government ultimately decided to lay out town settlements in Texas as part of its three-pronged attempt to secure the Texas Borderlands. In contrast to the presidio and the mission, the municipal settlement was populated mostly by *peninsulares* (Spaniards from the motherland), Creoles (American-born Hispanics), and mestizos (offspring of Indo-Hispano marriages). Many of these settlers were from families of soldiers assigned to outlying presidios; others were merchants, farmers, or ranchers with land grants in the vicinity.[19]

In Texas, the presence of these frontier agencies—mission, presidio, and municipality—was reflected as early as the Espinosa-Olivares-Aguirre expedition, which had as its objective to establish contact with the Tejas Indians and prevent them from trading with the French.[20] On April 4, 1709, Captain Pedro de Aguirre, commander of the presidio of the Río

Grande del Norte, escorted Fray Antonio de San Buenaventura Olivares and Fray Isidro Espinosa, both Franciscans from the Colegio de Santa Cruz in Querétaro, north to the San Marcos River, the object being a meeting with the Tejas Indians.[21] Maintaining a remarkably steady pace, the expedition reached the site of San Pedro Springs in present-day San Antonio on the thirteenth of the same month. The location was vividly described by Fray Isidro Espinosa:

> We named it San Pedro Springs and at a short distance we came to a luxuriant growth of trees, high walnuts, poplars, elms, and mulberries watered by a copious spring which rises near a populous *ranchería* of Indians . . . numbering . . . about 500. . . . The river, which is formed by this spring, could supply not only a village but a city, which could easily be founded here because of the good ground and many conveniences. This river not having been named by the Spaniards, we called it the river of San Antonio de Padua.[22]

The expedition failed to meet with the Indians of the Tejas nations, but succeeded in demonstrating the emerging phases of the three frontier agencies at a site destined to become San Antonio, Texas. The expedition reflected Spanish intentions to establish a mission for the Indians at San Pedro Springs and the San Antonio River; the presence of Captain Aguirre's soldiers symbolized the role of the presidio near the mission; and, last, the expedition defined the location where the first Texas municipality was to be established twenty-two years later.

The French penetration into Spanish Texas was the initial step toward more ambitious economic plans devised by French entrepreneurs; their main purpose was to establish trading alliances with northern town settlements in New Spain, particularly the wealthier *reales de minas* on the northern central mesa. French persistence to form commercial ties with New Spain was part of the economic policy of the proprietor of Louisiana, Antoine Crozat, a wealthy financier and merchant.[23] In 1714, Saint Denis, Cadillac's remarkable commander at Natchitoches, and a small band of Frenchmen traveled across Central Texas to the Presidio de San Juan Bautista del Río del Norte with the intention of facilitating trade relations with Spanish soldiers and settlers on the Río Grande and near French Louisiana.[24] The central government in Mexico City was shocked by the news of French traders deep in northern New Spain and sent orders initiating an expedition into eastern sectors of the province under Domingo Ramón, captain of the San Juan presidio, to investigate the extent of French incursions.[25] The Spanish imperial government was not interested in allowing silver pesos to be exchanged for European goods, which, in many cases, sold in Louisiana at far cheaper rates than those registered at the port of Veracruz.

From intelligence reports received from Captain Ramón's investigation, the central government concluded that the French were much too close for comfort. In the plans of the Spanish imperial government the source of the San Antonio River was now to be the site for the establishment of a mission and the construction of a presidio, both of which were to serve as a way station between remote outposts in East Texas and town settlements in northern New Spain. The Alarcón-Olivares expedition of 1718 led to the formation of the new way station.[26] Captain Martín de Alarcón and Fray Antonio de San Buenaventura Olivares, at times at odds with each other during the expedition,[27] contributed yeoman work in erecting a permanent settlement in San Antonio. On May 1, 1718, the cherished dream of Father Olivares became a reality with the establishment of the mission of San Antonio de Valero, later popularly called the Alamo. Five days later, Captain Alarcón founded the Villa de Béjar, actually a military outpost, "designated as a site where settlers and soldiers were to be established."[28] During the same year the French in Louisiana established the port town of New Orleans.[29]

In 1719, France and Spain clashed over European questions, and the War of the Quadruple Alliance had its impact on the Texas-Louisiana frontier. The viceroy promptly issued orders to equip an army for the defense of Texas and the expulsion of the French from Spanish soil. Joseph Azlor Vitro de Vera, Marqués de Aguayo, appointed commander of the expedition, mobilized eight companies of cavalry comprising five hundred men.[30] In November, 1720, Aguayo, who was also the wealthy governor of Coahuila, left Monclova in haste with his mounted infantry, wagonloads of military provisions, and five thousand fresh horses in reserve. In Texas, he reinforced the presidio at San Antonio and then headed for the eastern sector of the province, commissioning a detached garrison to guard the Matagorda Bay area.[31] Aguayo's swift occupation of strategic points on the Texas frontier led the French to conciliatory reaction. "Peace had now been declared and at the Neches River, Aguayo was met by Saint Denis, who swimming his horse across the stream for a parley," informed the Spanish commander that the European war was over and that French entry into Texas had been abandoned.[32]

Governor Aguayo wrote a report of his expedition in Texas, recommending to the central government that effective dominion over the province must rest on the settlement of families in Texas. He considered the settling of two hundred families from Galicia or the Canary Islands essential to the security of the new province and to the reduction of expenses in maintaining large concentrations of troops in Texas. He indicated that town settlements were needed at San Bernardo, the presidio of San Antonio de Béjar, and a point between the two. Aguayo's suggestion was not entirely new. However, French encroachment on Texas soil gave the recommendations for Spanish town settlements new importance, even though hard-pressed missionaries in Texas had been urging such action since the time of Ramón's expedition in 1716.[33] Moreover, the Council of the Indies had suggested to the Spanish monarch that a large number of families from the Canary Islands or Galicia be sent to Texas, long before Aguayo's expedition to counteract French encroachment on the province.[34]

Hispanic plans to establish town settlements in Texas varied but deserve attention so that the functions of the *cabildo* in the eighteenth century, can be appreciated. Initially, the crown rejected the recommendations to dispatch Spanish citizens from the Canary Islands to Texas.[35] The monarch wanted assurances that the frontier site could be supported militarily and financially, and he wanted strategic districts in Texas settled with families from New Spain, whose transportation would be less costly to the royal treasury.[36] However, after reading the long communication from the viceroy and the recommendations of Aguayo, the Spanish sovereign changed his position and decided to supply Texas with two hundred families from the Canary Islands, who would be located in the vicinity of the Bay of Espíritu Santo, one of the original sites indicated by Aguayo.[37]

Adopting measures in 1723 to occupy Texas permanently as an effective barrier against French encroachment, the Spanish crown issued two important *cédulas*. On March 18, 1723, the king's ministers sent orders to Juan Montero, intendant of the Canary Islands, to publish a proclamation throughout the islands calling for volunteers who wished to settle at San Bernardo Bay near the Texas Gulf Coast.[38] The second *cédula*, issued May 10, 1723, ordered the governor of Yucatán to supply all families sent by royal mandate from the Canary Islands with everything they needed and to provide food and shelter for them while at Campeche awaiting passage to Veracruz.[39] The Spanish sovereign's interest in the welfare of the settlers was further demonstrated in the instructions forwarded to the viceroy of New Spain notifying him that the crown was to be informed of the departure and arrival of the Texas colonizers and that arrangements were to be made for their reception at Veracruz.[40]

There were several reasons why the monarch selected Canary Islanders to settle Texas. In other colonizing endeavors throughout the empire they had proved to be good settlers. Moreover, the Canary Islanders, besides being closer to Spanish America, welcomed the opportunity to find new homes in more fertile lands. The "Isleños" disposition to form town settlements in Texas reflected the kind of enthusiasm that was to sustain them through a hazardous ocean voyage and the nine-month journey northward from the port of Veracruz to the frontier district of San Antonio. On September 19, 1723, a letter from the Canary Islands declared that in reply to the royal proclamation, two hundred families had already registered voluntarily for the proposed trip to Spanish Texas. Moreover, Juan Montero, a *cabildo* official who was answering the crown's proclamation, claimed that the Canary Islanders were willing to outfit two vessels at their own expense to assist the colonists to reach their destination and were prepared to pay all expenses until the settlers were under the care of the officials at Veracruz.[41]

The defense of Texas was only one of the many problems in Spanish America that concerned the Council of the Indies during the first quarter of the eighteenth century, however. The imperial government continued to discuss Aguayo's colonizing plans for seven years after the king had issued orders for the transportation of the two hundred families recommended by the viceroy of New Spain, Juan de Acuña, Marqués de Casafuerte. Because of the delay and the continuing reassessment of plans to colonize Texas, fewer than one hundred finally reached the frontier province. On July 3, 1727, Joseph Patiño, the private secretary of the monarch, transmitted an order instructing the Council to put into effect already approved plans for the relocation of the colonizing Isleños.[42]

In view of the fact that two more years passed before any action was taken, the monarch issued a long *cédula* on February 14, 1729, on the need for civil settlements in Spanish Texas. The royal document contained four significant points: (1) it summarized Aguayo's plan for civil settlement with families from Spain or the Canary Islands and Tlaxcala; (2) it ordered that four hundred families (a number recommended by the Council of the Indies) be sent from the Canary Islands for the purpose indicated and that in this number the original two hundred families be included; (3) it reflected the king's concern for the welfare of the settlers by stating that they were to be provided with everything needed

Don Juan de Acuña, Marqués de Casafuerte, whose orders to lay out the main plaza for the Villa de San Fernando gave rise to the Spanish community of San Antonio. Courtesy Nettie Lee Benson Latin American Collection, University of Texas, Austin.

for their journey to Texas and for the raising of first crops; and (4) it indicated that the families should be established in the places formerly designated, namely, the vicinity of La Bahía del Espíritu Santo, the Presidio de San Antonio de Béjar, and Los Adaes, and a settlement at a convenient location between the last two.[43]

By modern standards, the implementation of the king's orders should have been simple, but an opinion in 1729 from Casafuerte, the viceroy of New Spain, indicates that to him the matter was not that easy. He received the *cédula* on November 27, 1729, ordered a copy made, and entrusted it to Brigadier General Pedro de Rivera, "who was still in Mexico and was constantly consulted by the marqués . . . on all matters pertaining to the interior provinces."[44] Rivera's criticism of certain aspects of Aguayo's plan coupled with his strong influence on the viceroy thwarted extensive population in Texas in the form of Spanish civil communities. Rivera's report questioned the number of families needed in Texas and whether the money, always an important factor to the viceroy, expended on so many town settlements was warranted. Rivera also indicated that transportation from the Canary Islands to Veracruz, and thence to the Bay of Espíritu Santo, involved considerable expense and hardship and that the proposed plan for civilian settlements excluded the traditional patterns of communication with towns in north central New Spain, in the case of Texas, the need to link Texas settlements with vital supply towns in Coahuila such as Saltillo, Monclova, and Allende. Therefore, Rivera contended, it was inadvisable to attempt the foundation of a large number of new communities in Texas, particularly those proposed near the Gulf Coast. Rivera submitted his own ideas on where settlements should be located in Texas. His suggestions, though not entirely acceptable to the viceroy, led to substantial changes in the original plans.[45]

Upon receipt of Rivera's recommendations, the viceroy sought the counsel of Juan de Oliván Rebolledo, who, as *auditor de guerra* since 1715, was well acquainted with the conditions on New Spain's northern frontier. On July 17, 1730, Oliván Rebolledo strongly urged the establishment of a civil community near the Presidio de San Antonio. He also informed the viceroy that the settlers were entitled to organize their own municipal government and that for that purpose a group of ten families constituted the minimum number required by the Laws of the Indies.[46] Moreover, Oliván Rebolledo, aware that the viceroy was a strict interpreter of the law, recommended that the Isleños, Spaniards by birthright and founders of town settlements by royal mandate, be granted all the rights and privileges as well as titles of "Hijo Dalgo" prescribed by the Laws of the Indies.[47]

The fate of the first Texas municipality was determined, in large measure, by the decisions of Viceroy Casafuerte and his counselors, Aguayo, Rivera, and Oliván Rebolledo. Joseph de Azlor, the marqués de San Miguel de Aguayo and governor and captain general of the Province of Texas and Coahuila, had enlisted and equipped soldiers to save Texas from French encroachment. His ability to reinforce the presidio-mission defense structure on the Texas-Louisiana frontier received deserved recognition and his plans to introduce civil settlements secured royal attention. Brigadier General Pedro de Rivera, the former commander of the fortress of San Juan de Ulúa at the Port of Veracruz, had spent a three-year inspection tour on the northern frontier. Despite his policy of cautious reserve in the implementation of civil settlements in Texas, his unlimited devotion to the crown was well known and his position as consultant to the viceroy a highly respected one. Juan de Oliván Rebolledo, an alert administrator with more than fifteen years of experience as New Spain's *auditor de guerra*, demonstrated an ability to clear up practical legal questions associated with the status of the *cabildo* of the town settlement that the Isleños were to found on the Texas frontier. Despite the delays caused by the parleying from his council, the marqués de Casafuerte was a staunch supporter of the royal mandate to colonize Texas, his solicitude for the needs of the Isleños from Veracruz to San Antonio in Texas being openly manifest. Even so, the viceroy and his council, for all their individual concern in promoting Spanish colonization in Texas, have been held responsible for its limited implementation.

On March 9, 1731, the arrival of the little group of Canary Islanders in San Antonio was a relief to the new settlers and to royal officials of the central government. With the exception of a five-year-old child who died en route, the ten families and five unattached bachelors (fifty-nine persons) completed the nine-month journey northward across Mexico.[48] Francisco Duval, the official guide of the Texas-bound Canary Islanders, presented to Captain Juan Antonio de Almazán, commander of the San Antonio presidio, a list of the families and an inventory of all the supplies and equipment distributed to the Isleños at Cuautitlán, a village south of Mexico City. Moreover, there was submitted a list of additional provisions supplied to the settlers at Saltillo by order of the Spanish imperial government. After a few days' rest in the best houses of the soldiers stationed at the presidio, the new Texans from the Canary Islands regained strength. On March 12, 1731, Captain Almazán summoned all heads of families to appear for an important meeting.[49] The time had come to lay the foundation for the city of San Antonio.

LA VILLA DE SAN FERNANDO

In 1731, the Villa de San Fernando was skillfully laid out in accordance with the Royal Ordinances of 1573 on the establishment of towns in Spanish America. More than a century earlier, Pedro de Peralta had used this document in laying the foundations of the Villa de Santa Fe. Moreover, both municipalities were established by distinct viceregal decrees. Don Pedro received orders from Luis de Velasco, marqués de Salinas, to select a site for a new capital city for Nuevo México on April 30, 1609. He complied with the mandate by founding a town on the banks of the Santa Fe near the springs of Río Chiquito. On November 28, 1730, Captain Juan Antonio de Almazán was commanded by Juan de Acuña, marqués de Casafuerte, to lay out the town foundations of the Villa de San Fernando along the fertile banks of the San Antonio River, deep in Spanish Texas. Further, both viceregal documents provided specific orders for the establishment of municipal governments for the administration of the internal affairs of each town.

Municipal plans for the creation of both towns might have indicated further similarities. However, accounts of the design for Santa Fe are generally lacking. With the loss of the *Actas de Cabildo* of the Villa de Santa Fe in the Pueblo Rebellion of 1680, there remains little local documentary evidence on which to re-create descriptions of the initial events in the construction of the new capital of Nuevo México. The beginnings of the Villa de San Fernando in San Antonio, which became the capital of Spanish Texas thirty-one years after its founding, are clear in documents that have lasted through the centuries, particularly its *Actas de Cabildo* and the Bexar County Archives. Similarities in the construction of the Villa de Santa Fe and its sister community in Spanish Texas may be inferred from the vivid descriptions available on the establishment of the Villa de San Fernando.

Casafuerte's decree of November 28, 1730, for the construction of the Villa de San Fernando was in keeping with the Royal Ordinance of 1573 regarding the laying out of such a city. These regulations had been drafted "in a conference of officials at the Escorial, to which the King had invited architects, engineers, meteorologists, hydrographers, and other technicians of his realm in order to obtain the best advice and counsel possible for municipal planning."[50] Their skills combined to select sites and physical form and to direct future development of the cities and towns of New Spain.[51] Their comprehensive blueprint, forwarded by Philip V, indicated that the elements of geography, health, and security were to play an important part in the development of the first Texas municipality.

The Isleños spent their first few months in Texas cultivating the land and planting crops. By July 2, 1731, a harvest had been gathered and the settlers' attention now turned to the actual layout of their city. Casa-fuerte had directed Captain Juan Antonio de Almazán to select a site with certain specifications:

> The captain . . . is to . . . go in company with the most intelligent persons available at that point and examine the site, which is a gunshot's distance from the said presidio to the west, where there is a slightly elevated plateau suitable for the establishment of a fine settlement, on account of its location. It will have the purest air and the freshest waters, which flow from two springs or natural fountains situated on a small hill a short distance from the Presidio de Béxar.[52]

The geographical selection of a site was just the start. The viceroy continued his letter with a description of how the city was to be laid out:

> After having examined the elevation and plateau, the said governor shall measure the land, lay off the streets and blocks, the main plaza, the site or block for the church, the home for the priest, the municipal hall or *casa real,* and other buildings shown on the map that is appended, so that in accordance with measurements in feet or *varas* indicated in each direction he may mark, with a cord, each square, each street, site for the plaza and *casa real* and maybe a furrow with a plow. In order that each block may be separated from every other block, he shall place a wooden stake in the corner of each. He shall have a hole dug in the center of each square and a stone placed therein to mark the spot.[53]

Don Juan Antonio, aware of the historical significance associated with the viceroy's orders to build the first civil settlement in Texas, executed his duties well. He spent considerable time in laying out the city in compliance with the directions of the viceregal decree. The official establishment of the Villa de San Fernando was outlined in his letter to Casa-fuerte dated July 11, 1731.

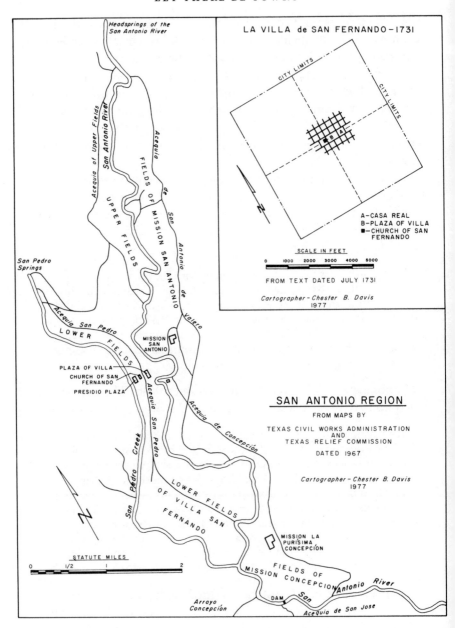

MAP 4

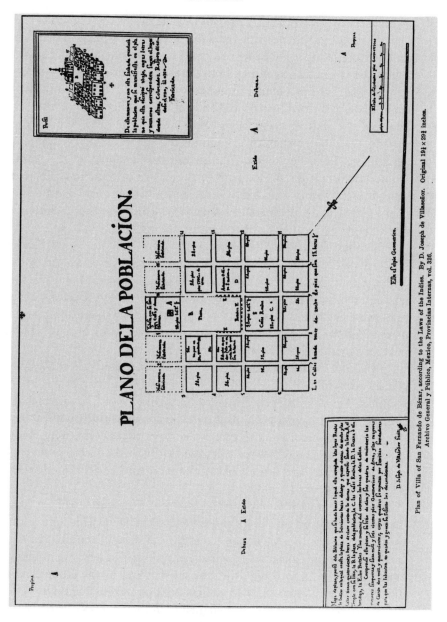

Plan of Villa of San Fernando de Béxar, according to the Laws of the Indies. By D. Joseph de Villaseñor. Original 19¼ × 29¼ inches. Archivo General y Público, Mexico, Provincias Internas, vol. 326.

MAP 5

Each family gathered two cartloads of large stones and ten stakes and brought them to the site designated by Casafuerte. A place was chosen for the church and a public square, "and with the aid of a sundial and a fifty-*vara* chain, a line running from southwest to northeast was determined. Using this as a base, the survey was begun."[54] Captain Almazán drew a line in a northeasterly direction for a distance of 200 varas, or 600 feet, the starting point being the center of the main door of the church. "Having finished this, I laid off the square facing the church, designating it for the *casa real*."[55] Almazán next marked out the plaza. A line was run at a right angle from the center of the church for 230 varas, therein "being included . . . the width of the street." By the end of the first day, the plaza and the square on which the church and *casa real* were to be located had been measured out.

The following day, July 3, Captain Almazán, "in company with the majority of the sixteen families of Islanders," continued the survey by marking out the lot of the *aduana,* or customhouse, and another for one of the most prominent families, both of which were located on the northwest side of the plaza. On the southeast side two similar lots were marked off, "each being 240 feet or 80 *varas* on each side," both of which were designed for the colonists.

July 4, 1731, was a special day for most of the settlers, since the specific location of each residential lot near the plaza of the *villa* was to be assigned. Almazán laid out thirteen additional lots for houses, "each of the said squares having been made 240 feet square with this difference: . . . the two squares lying to the two sides of the *casa real* were made 320 feet, equal to 106.7 varas."[56] In keeping with the viceroy's suggestions, the corners and centers of each lot were further delineated "with a furrow made with a plow."

By providing each family with a town lot, the viceroy had, in fact, carried out one of the king's most benevolent laws. This regulation was deeply rooted in Reconquest tradition as it had been used to encourage Hispanic Christians to settle communities in newly conquered lands. Later, in New Spain, the law, written out in the *Recopilación*, directed the viceroy to grant to settlers bent on developing towns residential lots on lands of exceptional quality in the name of His Majesty, provided that the grant did not impede the rights of any other subject of the king.[57]

Almazán presented the titles for the house lots to the new citizens of the *villa* in the following order:[58]

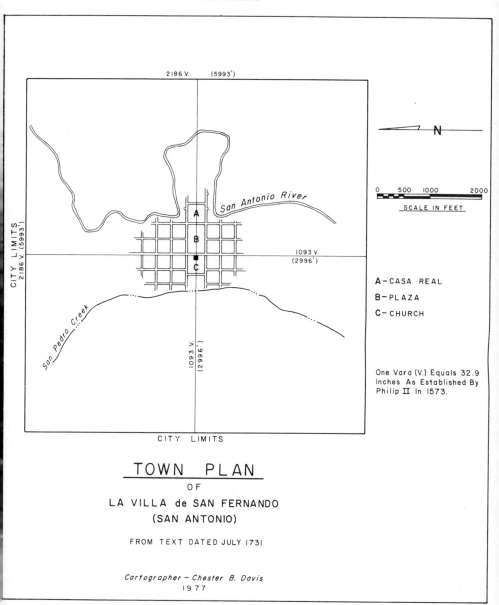

2186 V.   (5993')

CITY LIMITS
2186 V. (5993')

San Antonio River

1093 V.
(2996')

San Pedro Creek

A
B
C

1093 V.
(2996')

CITY LIMITS

N

0   500   1000   2000
SCALE IN FEET

A – CASA REAL
B – PLAZA
C – CHURCH

One Vara (V.) Equals 32.9
Inches As Established By
Philip II In 1573.

TOWN PLAN

OF

LA VILLA de SAN FERNANDO
(SAN ANTONIO)

FROM TEXT DATED JULY 1731

Cartographer – Chester B. Davis
1977

MAP 6

Lot Number	Name
1	José Cabrera on behalf of his widowed mother
2	José Leal, newly married son of Juan Leal Góraz
3	Salvador Rodríguez
4	Juan Leal Alvarez
5	Antonio Rodríguez, *mayordomo de los propios*
6	Francisco de Arocha, council secretary
7	Vicente Alvarez Travieso, *alguacil mayor*
8	Francisco Delgado
9	Manuel de Nis
10	José Padrón
11	María Rodríguez, widow
12	Juan Delgado, on behalf of his mother, Mariana
13	Antonio Santos
14	Juan Curbelo
15½	Martín de Armas for himself and three other single men
16	Juan Leal Góraz, first *alcalde ordinario*

He reminded them of the viceroy's instructions regarding the need to follow established methods of urban development: "The houses shall be adopted for defense, for cleanliness, and the healthfulness of the inhabitants. They shall be so built, that as indicated in the map, the four winds, north, south, east, and west, may enter the four angles or the corners of the settlement and each of the houses, making them more healthful."[59]

On July 5, 1731, Captain Almazán staked out the city limits of the new *villa*. His method was fairly simple: "Having reached the spot, from the place designated for the church across the four squares (that is, the center of the main entrance of the church), I ordered a measurement made in direction of the northeast of 1,093 common varas." The terminal point was then indicated by a hole and large stone and used as a marker and boundary for the quadrilateral. Returning to the main entrance of the church, another line was run to the southwest, for 1,093 varas, and another marker placed as before. "From this point I returned to the church door and, to the northwest, I ordered 1,093 varas laid out," the terminus being marked by a large stone as before. Once more, from the center of the main church entrance another line was run for 1,093 varas to the southeast, the end of the measurement being marked as the other two. To square his plan, Almazán "ordered measurements with the same cord from the four extremes to the amount of 1,093 varas, for each side of the area or the plan, this quadrilateral being a perfect square of 2,186 varas on each of the four sides." The intended quadrilateral was thus formed, since "the measurements were taken from the extremes of the first measurements of the cross, 1,093 varas, and then the same amount in the opposite direction."[60]

On the same day, Captain Almazán also surveyed a large section of the *bienes comunales,* or the town common. He refers to the sector as the *ejidos* in his letter to the viceroy. In the sixteenth century, the term *"ejidos"* originally designated collective lands in the hands of Indians subject to the crown, whose religious and economic well-being was under the supervision of a religious order.[61] As time went on, *"ejidos"* began to take on a larger meaning. More than a century later, the term was being used to designate lands relating to the *bienes comunales,* namely, the common lands of civil communities.[62] Almazán seemed interested solely with surveying the *villa's bienes comunales.* From the northeast corner of the city limits, he extended a line of 1,934 varas long and marked off the initial boundary of the town common. From the northwest corner of the city limits, he measured 1,039.5 varas in that direction, the terminus marked with a deep hole and a large rock. It was not possible to lay out the lands for *bienes comunales* to the east because, with the first measurement of the town, the banks of the San Antonio River were reached.[63] Since the river served as a boundary between the civil settlement of the Canary Islanders and the Indian lands of the missions, especially the mission of San Antonio de Valero, Captain Almazán respected the eastern river boundary and extended the first three measurements used to determine the town common.

Spaniards realized the importance of agriculture, especially in frontier towns. They were concerned with locating irrigable farmlands and using selected pasturelands for horses, beef cattle, oxen, and other livestock. On July 6, Captain Almazán, in company with a majority of the settlers, continued to survey the pasturelands suggested by the instructions of the viceroy. Since there was no room to the southeast, it became necessary to seek pasturelands on the three remaining sides. Beginning at the northeast corner, from which point the commons had last been marked, Almazán measured another 3,825.5 varas, the terminus point again marked with a large rock, "to serve as a perpetual boundary." The complete boundaries of the *bienes comunales* may be summarized in the following manner: on the northeast, they extended from the head of the principal springs of the San Antonio River along a straight line to the site of the Arroyo de Novillo; thence west, "along the quadrilateral line" to the Real de Nicolás Hernández, which is slightly to the northwest; thence south beyond a point called Llano de León, on to a spot called Real Lagunilla, "which is to the right of a place called Los Jacalitos; thence turning to the northeast straight to the Paso de los Nogalitos," where the final angle of the quadrilateral is closed. "To the east of the *bienes comunales* are the *labores* [probably the already-developed farmlands of the missionaries] . . . and the San Antonio River, which runs north to south."[64]

The indefatigable Captain Almazán added to this day's work a survey enabling him to set aside one-fifth of the measured *bienes comunales* for exclusive use by the *cabildo*. The proposed city council was to exploit and to use this municipal property "to produce revenues through rents, and funds . . . [which were to be] . . . used for the ends and purpose that His Majesty has ordered."[65] The *bienes comunales* exemplified the principle of collective ownership characterizing the contemporary Castilian municipality.[66] Almazán, by assigning a fifth of the *bienes comunales* to the municipal government, had, in effect, defined the *Villa's propios,* that is, the special property rights of the town council "as a corporate personality for maintenance and function." *Propios* were designed to enable the *cabildo* to obtain the financial resources needed to meet future city expenditures. The *propios,* for all their importance, in the long run provided only limited financial resources, however, since with the growth of a town, operational costs increased. Experience from long-established *cabildos* indicated that provisions had to be made for religious and civil fiestas, the prosecution of lawsuits, and contributions occasionally required by the crown.[67] Captain Almazán did not enumerate all these costs in his letter, but by writing that funds from the *propios* "may be used for the ends and purposes that His Majesty has ordered," he might have had them in mind.

Captain Almazán declared the boundaries of the *propios* of the *villa* thus: on the south side they began at the point where the *bienes comunales* ended and extended as far as the Paso de los Nogalitos, thence to the southwest to La Lagunilla and "La Escaramuza" to the Real de Nicolás Hernández, where another corner was located, and then to the east to the end of the survey. The fifth part of the farm and irrigable lands would later be set aside in a similar manner and for the same purpose.[68]

Almazán completed his civil engineering duties on July 7, 1731. To provide the viceroy with an overall view of the new municipality, he summarized its geographical boundaries in the following manner.

This quadrilateral, though an imperfect one, was laid off with all possible care, the land measured off for the town proper, those for the
commons, as well as that for pasturelands and those, for final measurement, [i.e., finally] arable lands lay within the following boundaries: to
the east, the San Antonio River; to the west, Arroyo de León; to the
south, the lands of San José Mission, through Paso de Nogalitos; and
to the north, Arroyo del Salado.[69]

First Municipal Government in Texas

Captain Almazán, having put into effect the viceroy's blueprint for the
establishment of the Villa de San Fernando, now proceeded to create the
political life of the new town, again according to the instructions of the
viceroy. On July 20, 1731, Juan Leal Góraz, the oldest of the settlers and
their leader, was appointed first *regidor,* or councilman. Almazán declared
that this office had been conferred on Leal Góraz because the senior
settler was fully qualified and had the required knowledge and experience
and thus all settlers were to respect and honor his office. Captain Almazán
further appointed, in descending order of official importance, Juan Curbelo, Antonio Santos, Salvador Rodríguez, Manuel de Nis, and Juan
Leal Alvarez, son of Juan Leal Góraz, associate *regidores* of the *cabildo.*[70]

The *regidores* were primarily administrative officers, although at times
they did exercise judicial power. Among the six *regidores* the *alcalde* could
designate "various administrative duties not performed by himself, by
the *alguacil mayor,* or the *procurador* or *mayordomo.*"[71] In the initial stages,
the *alcalde* with the *regidores* looked to the presidial officers for guidance and even orders. In later years, there were times when the offices
of the presidio and the *cabildo* meshed. However, by the end of the
century, the duties of the *regidores* were fairly clear. In 1797, late in the
period of Bourbon reforms, a royal decree dated May 3 ordered that
salaries be fixed for the *regidores* in the *ayuntamientos* of the Indies (which
included Texas) and that reports be forthcoming from all *cabildos* indicating the duties discharged by various officers. In compliance with the
regulation, the San Antonio *cabildo* included in its report the designated
duties of the *regidores*:

> The *regidor decano,* at times, served as alcalde, and saw that superior or-
> ders were carried out; the second *regidor* acted as *alcalde provincial,* and
> saw to the security of the prisons; the third *regidor* acted as *fiel ejecutor*
> and had charge of weights and measures; the fourth *regidor* was *depositario*

de los embargos [depository for illegal merchandise]; the fifth *regidor* had charge of unclaimed property falling to the King; the sixth *regidor* had only to vote in the cabildo.[72]

With the appointment of the first *regidores* completed, and their names forwarded to the viceroy for approval, Almazán proceeded, on the same day, July 20, to select Vicente Alvarez Travieso, who demonstrated signs of leadership, for the office of *alguacil mayor,* with the right of remuneration for the performance of duties as assigned by the *alcaldes.*[73] The *alguacil mayor* was a law-enforcement officer assigned to maintain order within the jurisdiction of the *cabildo.* In the Spanish-American empire there were usually two law enforcement officers, the second being called *alguacil mayor del campo,* who were to assist the *alcalde* in the administration of justice throughout rural areas of the municipal district.[74] However, in Texas, with a garrison of presidial troops nearby, there was little need for a second law-enforcement officer at the new *cabildo,* and the citizens of the *villa* decided that one municipal police officer was sufficient. Besides being charged with the duties of night watchman and of arresting culprits as ordered by his superiors,[75] the *alguacil mayor* voted in the *cabildo* and remained aware that he held office at its pleasure.[76]

Francisco de Arocha was appointed to the important office of *escribano de consejo y notario público,* or council secretary.[77] A person of some education, he was indispensable for the functioning of the town council. His principal duties were to keep the minutes of the sessions and to maintain an account book of the local treasury with a record of the receipts.[78] His other duties ranged from transcribing court proceedings to the preparation of inventories of the property of deceased.[79] Arocha remained in office until 1757, at which time he "presented a petition to the *cabildo* to be relieved of the duties of his office."[80]

The appointment of *mayordomo de los propios* fell to Antonio Rodríguez. His role was that of municipal treasurer and bursar and his main duty was to collect revenues due the city and to pay its debts and obligations. In some of the older *cabildos* of New Spain, the *mayordomo de los propies* also leased buildings, lots, and utilities owned by the *municipality* and collected rents from the leases.[81] Rodríguez was expected to indicate the amount received as rent on the sale of products raised in *propios* set aside to benefit the government of the Villa of San Fernando.[82] He had no authority to spend or distribute any of these public funds without the consent of the *cabildo.* He also had to make an annual report to the *cabildo.* Later he was called, without apparent preference, *mayor-*

domo or *procurador,* even *síndico procurador general,* since his duty remained "to manage city funds."[83]

The political climax of the establishment of the Cabildo de la Villa de San Fernando was the first municipal election in Texas.[84] The electoral system in the municipalities of New Spain, though rooted in a tradition beginning in 1519, when a *cabildo* elected Hernán Cortés "Governor and Commander of New Spain," underwent numerous changes during the two centuries of Hapsburg rule. These alterations were apparent in the first municipal elections in Texas years later. Politically, the municipality was characterized by two stages: an era in which colonists had considerable leeway in the selection of municipal officials, and a subsequent period extending into the time of the Bourbon dynasty (from 1703) in which this right was much restricted by crown policy. The first stage, "lasting well into the reign of Philip II (1556–1598)," was a time when the *cabildos* were to a large measure free to conduct their own elections. The founders, usually *adelantados,* appointed the first members of the council, after which "the principle of self-perpetuating corporation was adopted, the retiring officials meeting annually for the election of their successors."[85] However, the right to confirm all elections or to nullify them was retained by the crown. This limited degree of self-government was patent recognition of the importance of the *cabildos* in the colonization of the New World and of the strong influence of ancient Castilian customs.[86]

In the first Texas municipality, there was a combination of electoral freedom and royal restriction. On August 1, 1731, in compliance with the viceroy's orders, Almazán summoned the six *regidores,* the *alguacil mayor,* the *escribano de consejo,* and the *mayordomo de propios* to appear before him for the first city council meeting of the Villa de San Fernando.[87] It was customary that on January 1 of each year elections for council offices take place in the town hall if one existed, in the residence of the governor, the church, or the home of a prominent citizen.[88] Since the municipal government needed to be formed to regulate the internal affairs of the new town, the election date did not apply to the first Texas *cabildo.* There being no public buildings available, Captain Almazán invited the members of the *cabildo* to meet at his home for the purpose of electing the first two *alcaldes ordinarios.* Without prejudice to the right of the *adelantados,* the oldest *cabildo* tradition also called for a greater voice in elections by municipalities, especially on the frontier of the Spanish-American empire. The *Recopilación* directed that the *alcaldes ordinarios* and other officers be elected by the colonists.[89] The *alcaldes ordinarios* were not elected directly by all the citizens of the Villa de San Fernando, but since it took the majority of the town's adult males to fill the council, which elected the city leaders, in effect the *alcaldes ordinarios* did take office by a kind of popular vote. Thus these elections to public office in 1731 were of historical significance in that they were the first free elections in Texas.

To lend greater prestige and dignity to their offices, the council members took individual oaths and then elected the two *alcaldes ordinarios*.[90] Since the prospective candidates had to be members of the *cabildo,* the names of Juan Leal Góraz and Juan Curbelo were forwarded as nominees for the office of first *alcalde* and the names of Salvador Rodríguez and Manuel de Nis for the second mayoral office.[91] Juan Leal Góraz was elected first *alcalde ordinario* by a majority vote. Salvador Rodríguez was elected *second alcalde ordinario*.[92]

In many towns and cities throughout the Spanish-American empire, a kind of secret ballot was adopted to elect magistrates.[93] Although the manner of voting at the San Fernando *cabildo* is not described in the documents, the secret ballot was probably utilized. It was also customary after elections for the governor or his deputy to announce the names of the successful candidates and to present them with their symbol of authority, often called the *vara.* Thus, when the *alcalde* took an oath of faithful and impartial performance of duty, Almazán proclaimed him legally elected and delivered to him his insignia of civil authority. He then sent a copy of the minutes of the meeting, the official appointment of all members of the *cabildo,* and the returns of the elections of the two *alcaldes* to the viceroy for his final approval and confirmation.[94] On October 24, 1731, the viceroy approved the appointments and ordered ten patents for each of the new officers.[95]

The most important office was that of *alcalde,* or mayor. In keeping with the Spanish predilection for combining judicial and administrative functions in the same office, the *alcalde* was lawmaker, judge, and policeman. In the absence of the governor or his deputy, the first *alcalde* presided at the town council meetings.[96] He issued city ordinances for the preservation of order and the promotion of public health and cleanliness. Although in the mid-seventeenth century, Philip IV enormously reduced the position of the *cabildo* as a judicial body by decreeing that appeals from the *alcalde*'s decisions were to proceed to the governor, *corregidor,* or *audiencia,*[97] the *alcalde* continued to make arrests and to punish individuals for allegedly disobeying city ordinances.

Several examples illustrate the *alcalde*'s power to issue ordinances and in certain cases to enforce them through punitive measures. In 1735, Juan Leal Góraz issued a city regulation requiring "the heirs of fields . . . [where] . . . farmers of the Villa de San Fernando are at present planting crops . . . to repair the said fence" and ordering that "all residents and stock breeders who have horses and cattle . . . place them in charge of a herder who shall take care of them during the day and shut them up at night." To impress on the settlers that he did not intend to let unattended livestock damage crops, he instituted a penalty of "four pesos in silver."[98] If Alcalde Joseph Curbelo enacted the first Texas curfew law in 1744, prohibiting "citizens from going upon the streets after nine o'clock at nights,"[99] he also may have had it abrogated. In 1745 Alcalde Juan Montes de Oça, one of the few non-Isleños to hold office in the *cabildo* at San Fernando prior to 1750, issued a law ordering "all settlers . . . not go out or walk in the street after eight in the evening . . . since this is a region subject to [Indian] war." His decree also forbade the carrying of small arms in the city "under the penalty of forfeiting the weapon, a fine of twelve pesos and imprisonment for one week." A bit stern with single men, Alcalde Montes de Oça ended his decree with a law "commanding all bachelors, ruffians, and others . . . without any work . . . to look, within a period of one week for masters whom they may serve . . . or . . . depart from this *villa*."[100]

The citizens of the new municipality, elated with civic achievement, also studied the question of naming their town. Alcalde Leal Góraz suggested Nuevo Arrecife, after a town on the island of Lanzarote. Manuel de Nis, a council member who likewise was nostalgic for the Canary Islands, suggested the name Villa de Gran Canaria. Some of the settlers recalled the port of Santa Cruz in Tenerife, and the time they embarked from there on the *España* for their long journey to New Spain. In fact, Francisco de Arocha, the council secretary, presented the idea that the new settlement bear the name of the Holy Cross. The Marqués de Casafuerte had considered the question of naming the first Texas municipality late in 1730. His advisers urged that the new municipality should be named Villa de Casafuerte.[101] The viceroy, moved with loyalty to the monarch, in turn suggested that, since Philip V had sponsored the undertaking, it was only proper that the new settlement bear either his name or that of some other member of the royal family. Although final authority to select a name rested with the viceroy, he and his counselors reached a compromise by selecting Villa de San Fernando.[102] Thus officially named, it was only a question of time before the new municipality as-

The parish church of the Villa de San Fernando, viewed here across the military plaza, was completed in 1749. Drawing by Arthur Schott, from William H. Emory's *Report of the U.S. and Mexican Boundary Survey.*

sumed the name of the Presidio de San Antonio situated within its city limits. Interestingly enough, toward the end of the century, both settlers and government officials accepted the notion that the presidio-mission-*cabildo* communities and their environs constituted a trinity of three distinct institutions making up one citadel of civilization amid the wilderness of south-central Texas.[103]

With the years, the *cabildo* status of the Villa de San Fernando contributed additional importance to the San Antonio community. Although Casafuerte had designated the *villa* as the seat of the provincial government, the capital had remained at Los Adaes in East Texas since the Aguayo expedition there in 1722. However, with Louisiana passing to Spanish control in 1762, the viceregal government transferred the capital to San Antonio, in response to the recommendations of the Marqués

POPULATION OF THE SAN ANTONIO MUNICIPALITY
AND VICINITY DURING THE COLONIAL PERIOD

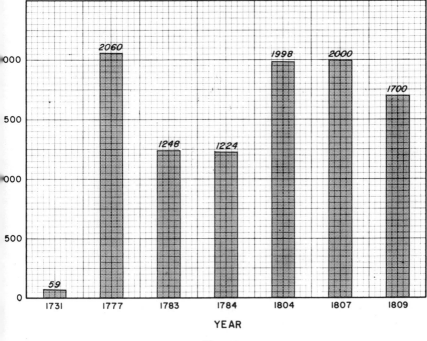

YEAR

FIGURE 3

de Rubí, deputy to royal Visitador José de Gálvez, during his inspection of the northern provinces.[104] Despite the added prestige that the rank of municipality gave to the San Antonio area, its growth was obviously slow by later standards, and observers, both transient and indigenous, did not hesitate to point out the *villa*'s dilatory progress.[105] Approximately fifty years after the municipality's establishment, one visitor, Fray Juan Agustín Morfi, staunch defender of the Texas mission institutions, caustically described the *villa*:

> On the west bank of the San Antonio river, about a league from its source, above the point where San Pedro creek joins the river, is situated the villa de San Fernando and the presidio of San Antonio de Bexar, with no other division between them than the parochial church. . . . The church building is spacious and has a vaulted roof, but the whole is so poorly constructed that it promises a short life. The town consists of fifty-nine houses of stone and mud and seventy-nine of wood, but all poorly built, without preconceived plan, so that the whole [town]

resembles more a poor village than a *villa,* capital of so pleasing a province.[106]

Obviously, not every individual appreciated the Isleños' tireless efforts on behalf of their municipality. Even so, this *villa,* modest by most standards, must have manifested itself as an oasis of civilization to most frontiersmen, missionaries, and soldiers, all recent arrivals from the vast, untamed land of the province.[107]

Who were the Isleños? Why did they come to America? They were "of the lower or farming class" and one would except "such to be chosen for the Texas wilderness." As did many other colonists, they came to the New World to seek social and economic opportunities. Moreover, in their petitions and correspondence they demonstrated, at least to twentieth-century minds, "an exaggerated idea of their own importance" and continually sought to impress "upon the governor, or viceroy, or presidial captain the great favor they rendered His Majesty in coming to this remote frontier settlement." Their humble origins contributed in large measure to an obsession for recognition, since, perhaps with the exception of Francisco de Arocha, few were able to read or write.[108] Although at times the viceroy considered some of their demands impertinent,[109] the Isleños "transported from an island home to the wildest of inland wilderness" might well have considered a bit of clamoring necessary for survival. For example, Alcalde Leal Góraz, aware of a responsibility to his constituents, returned to Mexico City only six months after his journey to Texas to ask the viceroy for horses. According to the viceregal decree of November 28, 1730, the settlers were to be provided with livestock, but no mention was made of horses. Even so, Leal Góraz, aware of the horse's importance on the frontier, thought differently. The viceroy approved the request for horses for the colonists of the *villa,* but at the same time wrote to Captain Almazán directing him to prohibit the Isleños' leaving Texas,[110] and forthwith issued an order that, thereafter, under no pretext were the Canary Islanders to leave the province.[111]

Whatever stipulations the viceroy may have laid down as policy for the future, the fact was that the Canary Islanders were now settled in Texas in sufficient numbers to establish the first chartered town settlement under the harsh conditions of the frontier province. Moreover, their municipal government at the Villa de San Fernando pioneered the way for law and order in civil communities and introduced local rule in the management of the affairs of town citizens in Texas.

5

Laredo
ORIGINS OF A SOUTH TEXAS MUNICIPALITY

The war of the Spanish Succession ended with the peace of Utrecht in 1713. England won limited trading rights in Spain's Caribbean possessions; however, these English prerogatives led to much friction over smuggling. In 1738, international tensions between the two empires came out into the open with Captain Jenkins's temporary incarceration by Spanish revenue authorities in Jamaica. An English task force retaliated by capturing Jamaica. On the mainland, the clash of arms was largely confined to the frontiers of Georgia and Spanish Florida. In 1745, the War of the Austrian Succession continued, enveloping the small-scale scuffle between English and Spanish forces in America into a global war that angered and frightened the central government in New Spain.

English pressures on Florida might now possibly extend westward along the Gulf Coast of Mexico beyond French settlements in the Lower Mississippi Valley. France was also at war with England, but limited concentrations of French forces in Louisiana could not be expected to challenge English sea power along the Louisiana Gulf Coast. Even so, for more than a century, the area around Matagorda Bay in Texas and as far south as present-day Tampico, Tamaulipas, had been the undisputed territory of New Spain. Now Spain's claim to this territory was challenged. Government officials in Mexico City were quick to realize that this enormous region bordering the Gulf of Mexico was largely unexplored and unattended, which would make possible the unopposed establishment of English posts in the area.

In 1746, the Junta de Guerra, the general council on war and finance in Mexico City, authorized an expedition to "conquer one hundred leagues or more from East to West on the coast of the Mexican Gulf occupied by many barbarous, gentile and apostate nations."[1] Named Nuevo Santander after a city in northern Spain, this newly designated province included in its original boundaries approximately sixty-eight hundred leagues. More precisely, Nuevo Santander was to claim as its natural boundaries the Pánuco River region on the south, the Gulf of Mexico on the east, La Bahía del Espíritu Santo in Texas on the north, and the Sierra Madre Oriental on the west.[2]

Don Juan Francisco de Güemes y Horcasitas, count of Revilla Gigedo, one of New Spain's most able administrators, became viceroy in 1746. Almost immediately he began studying reports on potential leaders to settle Nuevo Santander. On September 3, 1746, the viceroy appointed José de Escandón, the founder of Sierra Gorda, to conquer and colonize regions of the Seno Mexicano, namely, the largely unexplored areas of Nuevo Santander north of the Tampico Bar. In the service of the crown since the age of fifteen, when he enlisted as a cadet in the Spanish army in Yucatán, Escandón was well respected for his integrity and leadership ability.[3] While *corregidor* of Querétaro, he accepted a commission to lead a campaign against unruly Indians from La Sierra Gorda, a sizable area north of the towns of San Miguel el Grande and Querétaro. Escandón managed to pacify the Indians but did not tyrannize them nor did he permit other Spaniards to do so.[4] Under his leadership strategic *villas* and mission centers were founded among the native populace at Pacula, Fuenclara, Guadalupe, Jalapa, Landa, Tilaco, Tancoyal, Conca, La Divina Pastora, Palmilla, and Jaumave, the last two settlements located as far north as the Guayaleyo River.[5] During the 1740s, Escandón began to consolidate Spanish control over the area by founding towns at San José Vizzarón, Peña Millera, Herrera, and at Juamave,[6] a settlement refounded after having been destroyed by hostile natives. These new civil settlements, besides assuring the pacification of La Sierra Gorda, served to support subsequent movements northward into the Seno Mexicano.

For his achievements Escandón received the title of conde de la Sierra Gorda, although he was familiarly known as "El Conde." More important, he was appointed lieutenant governor and captain general of the unexplored region of the Seno Mexicano and commissioned to settle the area. Before the main body of his expedition moved northward, Escandón explicitly stated the goals of his colonizing endeavors:

Viceroy Juan Francisco de Güemes y Horcasitas, one of New Spain's most able administrators. Courtesy Nettie Lee Benson Latin American Collection, University of Texas, Austin.

Governor José de Escandón, "Colonizer of the Rio Grande." Drawing by J. Cisneros, *Riders across the Centuries* (1980), by permission of Texas Western Press of the University of Texas, El Paso.

It is our purpose to explore, pacify, and settle the unknown lands that now form a sort of bay lying between Tampico, Panuco, Villa de los Valles, Custodia del Río Verde, Nuevo Reyno de León, and the Bahía del Espíritu Santo, . . . The general reconnaissance of this area can only be practiced by a general *entrada*. . . . The central point of the lands to be explored lies more or less halfway between Tampico and Bahía del Espíritu Santo, in the vicinity of the mouth of the Río Grande del Norte.[7]

84

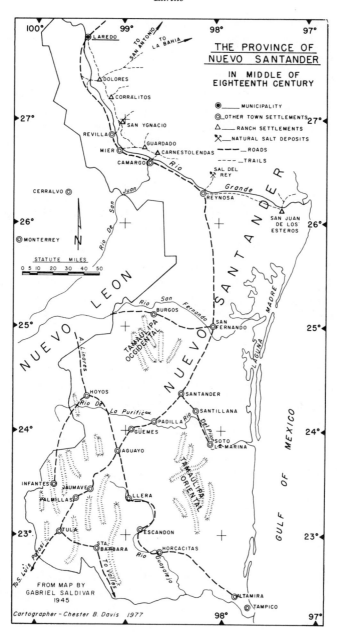

THE PROVINCE OF
NUEVO SANTANDER

IN MIDDLE OF
EIGHTEENTH CENTURY

◉____MUNICIPALITY
◎____OTHER TOWN SETTLEMENTS
△____RANCH SETTLEMENTS
✕____NATURAL SALT DEPOSITS
━ ━ ━____ROADS
- - - -____TRAILS

FROM MAP BY
GABRIEL SALDIVAR
1945

Cartographer - Chester B. Davis 1977

MAP 7

A thorough organizer, Escandón divided his strategy into two parts: first a reconnoitering expedition, and then a general colonization thrust northward into the province. The reconnoitering mission was launched in January, 1747, with seven military parties, comprising about 765 soldiers, penetrating the new province from distinct points of origin–three from Sierra Gorda in the south, three from Nuevo León and Coahuila in the western sector, and one from the northeastern province of Texas.[8] The use of regular troops and militiamen from the Borderlands provinces cut down expenses, the soldiers furnishing their own equipment and pack mules. Escandón, experienced in pacifying unsettled regions, proposed that the entry into the Seno Mexicano from diverse directions would discourage Indian resistance. Moreover, he instructed the officers of each military party to record and to observe accurately all natural features of the terrain, listing the rivers, mountains, and hills, and to maintain a journal on the types of Indians they encountered. At the mouth of the Río Grande del Norte, El Conde was to hold a general consultation with all his officers, a month after departure, to map the surveyed regions and to set up concrete plans for future settlements in the province.

Six of the scouting parties reached Escandón on time; the soldiers from Texas were compelled by pressing frontier duties to return to La Bahía del Espíritu Santo and Los Adaes. However, the Texas military contingent under Captain Joaquín Orobio Bázterra completed its mission on the northern sector of Nuevo Santander and submitted a report to Escandón's messengers at Cantaro Ford, a crossing where the Río Alamo joins the Río Grande. Orobio reported what he believed to be the best sites suited for town settlements north of the Río Grande, notably at the mouths of the Nueces and San Antonio rivers.[9] He was the first to indicate that the Nueces River emptied into the Gulf of Mexico, correcting the misconception that it flowed into the Río Grande. He mapped out large areas between the Nueces River and the Río Grande and recommended sections of the coastal prairies that could be cultivated or used for livestock grazing. Moreover, his report to Escandón indicated that the bay area at the mouth of the Nueces River was an ideal site for the establishment of a large municipality. More than a century later, the founding of the port city of Corpus Christi confirmed his choice.

By early 1749, José de Escandón was ready to embark on the second phase of his colonizing projects into Nuevo Santander. With more than twenty-five hundred colonists, consisting of numerous contingents of

Spanish and mestizo families, he moved out of Querétaro. He enlarged his caravan with additional settlers and zealous missionaries who joined his expedition at towns and *villas* through which he passed. While pushing northward toward the lower Río Grande Valley, Escandón established numerous towns in the central parts of Nuevo Santander.[10]

Some of the settlements, such as Güemes, Padilla, and La Villa Capital de Nuevo Santander, proved to be worthy way stations for future expeditions into northern sectors of the province. In March, 1749, the colonists, assigned to settle the Lower Río Grande Valley, reached the confluence of the San Juan River and the Río Grande. Within a short time, Escandón had executed one of the best-conceived and ultimately most-successful colonizing moves into the Borderlands. More than twenty towns were established by Spanish, mestizo, and converted Indian families. Most of these settlements were in the northern sector of the province south of the Río Grande.[11] Some of the most prosperous Spanish towns—Camargo, Reynosa, Mier, and Revilla—were on the southern bank of the Río Grande, civil settlements that have endured to the present. Dolores and Laredo were founded on the northern bank of the Río Grande, Laredo about ten leagues up the river from Dolores. Dolores was eventually abandoned, but Laredo took hold and at present is the only municipality in modern Texas whose origins can be traced to one of the most successful colonizers on the Borderlands frontier.

TOWN FOUNDINGS ON THE SOUTH BANK

Before Nuevo Santander was created by royal decree in 1746, interest in the northern province of Nuevo León had been centered in the gold and silver mines near Cerralvo, a *real de minas* forty miles northeast of Monterrey and about sixty miles from the Río Grande. Groups of Indian laborers from the Río Grande delta had gone to the mining district of Cerralvo to work, and the relationship between the Indian chieftains and Spanish settlers apparently paved the way for the successful subjugation and colonization of the Lower Río Grande Valley in 1747.[12]

José María de la Garza Falcón of Coahuila, one of Escandón's veteran collaborators, had received authority from Escandón to proceed with colonists to a site near the juncture of the San Juan River and the Río Grande. The Spanish pioneers from Coahuila, determined to build their settlement on firm foundations, brought their cattle, horses, goats, and sheep, and as many household goods as their wagons could carry. The women brought flower and fruit seeds, small pieces of needlecraft, dishes, and small silver and gold articles.[13] The civil community established by the settlers was christened La Villa de Santa Ana de Camargo by Escandón in ceremonies taking place on March 5, 1749.[14] Before the arrival of the governor, the colonists hastily made a clearing, constructed huts, dug preliminary irrigation canals, and even built a temporary structure to serve as a church, a mission named San Agustín de Laredo. Fray Simón de Yerro's interesting description of the ceremonies for the founding of the Villa de Camargo suggests the importance that the Spanish imperial government and the colonists gave to town settlements springing up along the southern banks of the lower Río Grande:

> At the sounding of the drums all of the soldiers and settlers gathered with their arms in the open plaza in front of the rude arbor erected to serve as a place of worship. Here, with the captain of the *villa* standing at the door, the church was blessed, and Colonel Escandón then addressed the captain, administering to him the oath to defend the *villa* and to comfort and encourage the settlers. He ended by saying that in all things ecclesiastical, the *villa* was to be in charge [of the Franciscan friars] of the College of Zacatecas."[15]

The occasion was aptly celebrated with a high mass and the singing of hymns. The soldiers, moreover, discharged their muskets during the ceremonies in honor of the event. Fray Simón Yerro, similarly interested in recording the social aspects of the festivities, indicated that a bottle of wine was brought out after the ceremonies by the officers, who drank to the health of José de Escandón from silver goblets and praised him for providing them with leadership.[16]

The second *villa* established on the south bank of the lower Río Grande was Nuestra Señora de Guadalupe de Reynosa. Situated on a bluff about twelve leagues downriver from the juncture of the San Juan and the Río Grande, this new civil community comprised forty settlers who, under the command of Captain Carlos Cantú, had migrated from the province of Nuevo León.[17] On March 14, 1749, José de Escandón christened the new town settlement presumably in the same type of civil ceremony that he used on other such occasions. A church very probably existed, since on the date of the town founding Fray Márquez was appointed pastor to the community.[18]

On October 10, 1750, Don Vicente Guerra, a prominent rancher from Coahuila, brought forty families from Nuevo León and established the

Villa de San Ignacio de Loyola de Revilla at a site called Los Moros, near the juncture of the Salado River and the Río Grande.[19] Guerra had petitioned only for the rights and title of colonizer and succeeded in establishing the town without cost to the royal treasury, an achievement that undoubtedly won Escandón's praise. About two years later, Lugar de Mier was established along the banks of the Alamo River and José Florencio Chapa was placed in charge.[20] Escandón founded this town with thirty-eight families who had come earlier from Cerralvo to join about nineteen families already living on ranches in the vicinity.[21]

The success of the town settlements in the Río Grande delta is due in large measure to the plans used to stimulate the interest of settlers from other provinces. Two of the most persuasive arguments promoting the Río Grande colonies concerned the chance to acquire free land and tax exemptions for settlers signing up for the first *entrada*. The fertility of the soil and the possibilities of river irrigation made the land grants even more appealing. The proximity of salt deposits just north of Reynosa also made the Río Grande settlements attractive, large quantities of salt nearly always being in demand in the mining towns.

Interestingly enough, people from all walks of life were drawn to the new territories of the valley. Wealthy ranchers from Coahuila and Nuevo León became interested because the move provided them with cheap land for their large herds. For the poor, besides being given an allowance of one hundred pesos for traveling expenses, the journey to valley settlements meant securing a homestead free from taxation. For enterprising traders, development in the valley meant new outlets and marketplaces for goods and services. For zealous missionaries, particularly Franciscans from the famed College of Zacatecas, the opportunity to civilize and Christianize the Indians east of the Sierra Madre was irresistible. Wealthy *caballeros*, proud members of noble families in New Spain, demonstrated increasing interest in colonizing the largely unexplored Río Grande delta, since the move provided opportunities to emulate the feats of Spanish conquistadors and to gain fame in the crown's service.

Preliminaries to the Settlement of Laredo

The central government in Mexico City had authorized Escandón to settle the entire Province of Nuevo Santander. He interpreted this mandate to mean that the northernmost reaches of his territory bordered the boundaries of Coahuila and the Province of Texas. Before making plans to settle Nuevo Santander, Escandón marked out on a map the settlements projected for the left banks of both the Nueces and the San Antonio rivers. The authorities on the Junta de Guerra in Mexico City who had sanctioned Escandón's expeditions approved his map, thus clearly indicating that Nuevo Santander was to be settled northward beyond the Río Grande.[22]

The northernmost sector of Nuevo Santander served as the eastern part of a larger strip of territory extending into West Texas and New Mexico on which powerful Apache tribes roamed almost unchallenged. The entire Apache territory had proved to be a haven for braves after successful raids on Spanish horse and cattle herds. The area south of the Nueces River, which Escandón hoped to settle, was actually one of many favorite hunting grounds for the Lipan Apache. Undaunted by Indian threats, Escandón began to push northward toward the Nueces River, a move that the embattled governments of Coahuila and Texas welcomed.[23]

In 1749, Escandón ordered the presidio and mission of La Bahía moved westward toward the San Antonio River to a site where Goliad, Texas, is now situated. This relocation was preliminary to coordinating a settlement complex that was to be enlarged by the founding of two civil communities, the Villa de Vedoya and the Villa de Balmaceda.[24]

Unfortunately, plans for the projected towns were unsuccessful. The Villa de Balmaceda was never subsidized by the royal treasury, thus making it virtually impossible to get the settlement under way. Captain Diego Gonzales, a wealthy rancher from Nuevo León, was able to lead a band of settlers northward and to establish the Villa de Vedoya east of the Nueces River, a site that in a short time proved to be unsuitable. Moreover, nomadic Indians suspicious of civil settlements in the midst of their lands had become deeply hostile. They compelled the Spanish pioneers to return to Nuevo León. Their leader, Captain Gonzales, died eight months later.[25]

Ranchers and wealthy *hacendados* whose lands were located in Nuevo León and Coahuila along the borders of Escandón's province remained undaunted by the hardships involved in pushing the frontiers northward. With permission from Escandón these Spanish ranchers had already succeeded in planting settlements on the south bank of the Río Grande. With their sights on lands across the river, some of them applied for concessions to organize settlements in the northern sectors of the Río

Grande delta. In 1753, Captain Blas María de la Garza Falcón and his father-in-law, Don Nicolás de los Santos Coy, petitioned Escandón for individual allocations of land on the north side of the Río Grande. Escandón reviewed the plans and granted them one hundred *sitios de ganado menor.*[26]

Captain de la Garza Falcón selected an elevated section of land overlooking the Río Grande for his ranch headquarters, his herds roaming in the delta north of the river and northward over the hills and plateau of his new land grant. Garza Falcón and Santos Coy agreed to bring fifteen new families from Camargo within six months to the *rancho,* which was called Carnestolendas. The ranch headquarters thus became more a small village. The settlement did not grow much larger during the Spanish period, however, for it remained a mission outpost, or a *visita* served by the priest from Camargo.[27] Even so, Carnestolendas, present-day Rio Grande City, served as a stepping stone to future settlements on the north banks of the Río Grande.[28] Santos Coy pushed westward about nine miles and established his ranch, Guardado, at the present site of Carceno, Texas. Although Guardado remained a *rancho,* because it employed more than one hundred workers, the settlement bustled.

Permanent ranch settlements on the north bank of the Río Grande were not a new venture for wealthy Spanish ranchers from the neighboring provinces of Coahuila and Nuevo León; they were continually attracted by the grazing lands in the northern sectors of Nuevo Santander. As early as August 3, 1750, Don José Vásquez Borrego from Coahuila had established the ranch settlement of Nuestra Señora de los Dolores on the north bank of the Río Grande at a point nearly ten leagues downstream from present-day Laredo, or approximately eighty miles upstream from present-day Rio Grande City. Experienced in cattle raising, Don José sent his son Juan José from his Hacienda de San Juan el Alamo, northeast of Monclova, to negotiate a land concession with his close friend José de Escandón. Escandón granted the Borrego family approximately 329,000 acres of land, comprising large sections of present-day Webb and Zapata counties. Exempt from taxation for ten years by Escandon's order but directed to develop the land, Vásquez Borrego expanded his control over the new land grant by establishing two other ranch headquarters along the north banks of the Río Grande downstream from the villa of Dolores, notably Corralitos and the Hacienda de San Ygnacio. Corralitos was assigned to José Fernando Vidaurri, Vásquez Borrego's grandson; San Ygnacio, a small community north of Zapata, Texas, was placed in the charge of José Fernando, the youngest of Vásquez Borrego's three sons.[29]

Although Vásquez Borrego had borne the expense of establishing the new communities and had encouraged families to move into his newly acquired land grants, he remained for the most part on his hacienda near Monclova. He placed his nephew Bartolomé Borrego in charge of the Villa de Dolores, the principal settlement on the north bank of the Río Grande. In 1755, José de Escandón visited the community, noting that its principal occupation was cattle raising.[30] The Vásquez Borregos had invested large sums of money to develop the livestock industry on the north bank of the Río Grande. There were few resources available to cultivate the agricultural potential of the land, but adequate provisions and ranch equipment arrived at Dolores from Don José's hacienda in Coahuila.[31]

Even though twenty-five families (nearly one hundred persons) lived in the settlement, they had been unable to attract a resident priest to minister to the Spanish settlers and the small number of Indians who dwelled with them. Two years later, when José Tienda de Cuervo made an inspection of the Villa de Dolores, the settlement had changed little: the population had remained stable; there was still no chapel; and Fray Miguel de Santa María, a Franciscan from the College of Zacatecas who lived in Revilla, attended to the spiritual needs of the settlers, which he had done since the earliest times of the *villa*.[32] The inhabitants spent most of the day caring for José Vásquez Borrego's many cattle, horses, mules, donkeys, and oxen.

Dolores, although reflecting the character of a small community, was involved in two significant developments in the growth of Spanish Texas. First, the settlement was located on the most direct route to San Antonio de Béjar and La Bahía, the former, according to Vásquez Borrego's report to Tienda de Cuervo, being about sixty leagues directly north, the latter northeast nearly seventy leagues.[33] Wagons bearing military supplies and mounted soldiers of the Spanish imperial government often used the ford near Dolores en route to the province of Texas. Moreover, Franciscans from Zacatecas frequently crossed the Río Grande near Dolores on their way to Texas missions under their care. This flow of visitors remained fairly steady until nearly all major traffic from New Spain into the province of Texas was absorbed by the Camino Real, which passed through Laredo. The Villa de Dolores also paved the way for the founding of the Laredo settlement. José Vásquez Borrego, captain of the *villa*, persuaded Escandón to extend necessary land concessions to Laredo's founder, Tomás Sánchez de la Barrera y Gallardo.

The establishment of a town in this remote corner of Nuevo Santander was a challenging undertaking for the first settlers, a band of four families.[34] They left from the Villa de Dolores on May 15, 1755, and directed their wagons and livestock westward under the leadership of Tomás Sánchez, the newly appointed captain of the Laredo site on the north side of the Río Grande, about ten leagues north of the Villa de Dolores.[35]

LA VILLA DE SAN AGUSTÍN DE LAREDO

As Vásquez Borrego had once searched for pasturelands in the vicinity of the Villa de Dolores, Captain Sánchez, a notable proprietor from Coahuila, had reached the Río Grande in quest of grazing lands for his growing herds of horses and cattle and large flocks of sheep and goats. Sánchez crossed his livestock to the north bank of the Río Grande at a ford within the limits of Nuevo Santander.[36] This strategic location had been discovered and used by soldiers stationed at the Presidio de San Juan Bautista, a military outpost situated where Eagle Pass, Texas, now is. Sánchez named the ford after Jacinto de León, a frontiersman who was probably a lineal descendant of Alonso de León, the leader of expeditions from Coahuila into Texas during the time of French threats from La Salle in the 1680s.[37]

Faced with an expanding number of livestock at his settlement on the north side of the Río Grande, Sánchez went to see Escandón, who was at Revilla in 1754. The enterprising cattle baron proposed to establish a town at his new ranch and to bear the expenses of bringing in the families needed to form the settlement. Escandón accepted the proposition but as he had not abandoned the idea of settling lands along the Nueces River, he requested that Sánchez examine the Nueces country and select a suitable location there for a village. Sánchez embarked on a reconnaissance of the Nueces River region but was hampered by bands of Apache braves. He submitted a report to Escandón indicating that projected settlements were impractical in the Nueces country until the native population was civilized by Spanish standards. Escandón, who had returned to his estate near present-day Tampico, Tamaulipas, left orders with his friend José Vásquez Borrego advising Captain Sánchez to proceed with his original plans of converting his ranch on the north bank of the Río Grande into a town settlement.[38]

Sánchez selected an ideal location for the new town, an area of elevated land overlooking the river. The center of the town was established near where the plaza and church of San Agustín are now situated. The town commons was sizable, comprising fifteen *sitios de ganado mayor.*[39] The emerging community was originally named the Pass of Jacinto de León, but Escandón renamed it San Agustín de Laredo in honor of a town on the Bay of Biscay in Santander, his native province in Spain.[40]

The terrain around Laredo was semiarid, furnishing little timber for building. However, other materials were plentiful. As the town began to take form, adobe houses, built from clay bricks dried in the sun, were constructed. The more fortunate families erected homes surrounded by stone walls; other settlers built small huts, or *jacales.*[41] Settlers continued to arrive in Laredo across the well-traveled pass of Jacinto de León a short distance to the north. A second ford a few leagues south called El Paso de Miguel de la Garza proved to be particularly suited for crossing livestock.[42] By 1757, Laredo's population numbered eighty-five persons composed of eleven families and a few single men,[43] two of whom lived with their widowed mothers. The settlers actually were *vaqueros,* skilled in the use of horses and arms, who maintained close watch over their well-stocked ranchlands. The grazing land around Laredo was ideally suited for breeding livestock. Within two years the herds had increased to more than eight hundred horses and mules and more than one hundred cattle. Moreover, the open range proved particularly suitable for flocks of sheep and goats, their number totaling nearly ten thousand in 1757.[44]

Interestingly, the El Paso settlement in Nuevo México resulted from government-funded missionary activity, whereas the founding of Santa Fe in the same province and of the Villa de San Fernando in Texas were largely supported by the royal treasury. Laredo, however, reflected the enterprising frontier spirit characteristic of the American West of a century later and developed independently of a mission or presidio.[45] Captain Sánchez, who bore the major expense for the founding of the town, was charged with the political and military administration of the community during its early years.

The livestock industry was the principal means of livelihood for the inhabitants of Laredo. Throughout the countryside, particularly at daybreak, a great number of horses and mares, along with wild herds of deer, were to be seen grazing on open pasturelands on the outskirts of the small community. Enormous flocks of sheep and goats provided the settlers with plentiful meat. Moreover, the raw wool produced by the large flocks of sheep provided the inhabitants with a marketable commodity. Cowhides, sheepskins, and tallow were sold at marketplaces in towns located in central Nuevo Santander.[46] Settlers from Laredo often returned to their small town by the Río Grande with purchases of clothing and food staples or even silver pesos received in exchange for their products.

Laredo was the sixth settlement established in Nuevo Santander along the Río Grande. As did sister communities downstream, Laredo depended on the long river. Nature had stocked it with numerous perch. Bass probably abounded in the streams, since they are still found, but catfish particularly flourished in the sediment and muddy color of the river. The inhabitants of Laredo were well acquainted with the "very large perch" of the Río Grande, the presence of which was recorded as early as 1757 by Tienda de Cuervo during his visit to the new settlement.[47] The Río Grande also provided water transportation for the people in Laredo who were anxious to visit friends and relatives at the Villa de Dolores and at larger settlements farther downstream on the south bank, notably Camargo (with 638 inhabitants) and Reynosa (with 470). Frequent trips were made in *chalanes,* or small flat-bottomed boats, which were often loaded with local produce to be traded for food at Carmargo and for salt at Reynosa.[48]

In view of the depth of the riverbed, it was not possible to engineer irrigation canals to the elevation where the town was located. However, attempts were made to plant crops on small, flat beds near the bank, a move often thwarted by floods. Actually there were "very good lands for cultivation" near Laredo, but drought and intense heat made farming impractical.[49]

All the same, the Río Grande continued to play an important role in the economy. A group of settlers under Tomás Sánchez agreed to construct a small ferry on the bank of the river in front of the town, a project continually delayed by the lack of suitable timber.[50] Even so, the plans were practical in view of the growing number of travelers crossing the Río Grande at Laredo on trips between Coahuila and Texas. Apparently, the Laredo ferry went into business, since fees were regulated in 1767. There was to be no charge for the settlers of Laredo; however, they were expected to maintain it. Travelers were charged two reales, or approximately twenty-five cents per head, and one real for each package. The accumulated funds were set aside for town improvements.[51]

A number of colonists became interested in Laredo and sought permission from Captain Sánchez to settle there. By 1767, the population had increased to about two hundred. The reports made by José de Escandón in 1755, and by the Cuervo Commission in 1757, indicated to the central government that, whereas settlements had not taken hold in the Nueces country, the towns planted on the banks of the Río Grande were steadily growing. New colonists continued to arrive at the *villas* and ranch settlements in the Río Grande delta. Camargo and Reynosa received the greatest number of new settlers.

It became necessary for a team of surveyors officially commissioned by the central government to go to the Río Grande settlements to confirm the land grants made to the first settlers and to partition new lands in the town areas for the latest colonists. Joaquín de Monserrat, the Marqués de Cruillas, who was appointed viceroy in 1760, organized a commission known as the General Visit of the Royal Commission to the Colonies of Nuevo Santander to visit the Río Grande settlements in 1767, an official visitation that Escandón, now sixty-seven years old, had been urging the central government to form for more than two years.[52] Juan Fernando de Palacio, the new governor of Nuevo Santander, was appointed to head the commission, joined by José de Ossorio de Llamas, secretary of the Royal Council, Palacio's special assistant, and several minor officials. The members of the commission began their journey to the northern sector of Nuevo Santander early in 1767, reaching the Río Grande settlements in May of that year.[53]

It was thirty-six years after the founding of the Villa de San Fernando that the royal commission arrived at Laredo and converted this Río Grande settlement into an officially chartered municipality. On June 9, 1767, Don Juan Fernando de Palacio and Don José Ossorio ordered a review of the land grants and a survey of the town and the extent of its jurisdiction. The municipal character of the settlement also was reflected in the legal arrangements required for new tracts of land for individual settlers and in the requirement that transactions be properly recorded to provide all citizens with clear titles to their lands.[54] Royal officials and Laredo citizens collaborated in the survey of the town, a procedure reflecting the same plan implemented by Captain Almazán in laying out the Villa de San Fernando at San Antonio de Béjar in 1731. Citizens proudly se-

lected their neighbors Miguel Díaz, Juan Bautista Villarreal, and Prudencio García, a pragmatic surveyor, to represent them on the royal commission.[55] The royal commission began determining the Laredo boundaries by surveying the town commons, an area of municipal lands that
Captain Almazán and the Isleños had laid out toward the end of their
survey of the Villa de San Fernando. Even so, the descriptions of the
surveys of the Laredo town commons, or *ejidos,* and the *propios* of the
Villa de San Fernando bear a remarkable resemblance. In a deposition
of the surveyors witnessed by Palacio on June 10, 1767, the boundaries
of the Laredo town commons were vividly depicted:

> We set apart for town commons grazing lands and pastures properly
> belonging to the town, one league around its center measured to the
> four cardinal points of the compass and declare for their limits—on the
> south the five thousand varas which were measured to the place called
> San Francisco de Paula; on the east, the Arroyo de Mal Paso; on the
> north the Laguna de Abajo, and on the west, on the side of the river,
> the place called San Gregorio, marked out as hereinafter reported by the
> surveyors, who for better evidence shall [measure] out this said district
> to the banks of the river on the other side, for the use and benefit of
> the community who may exact and such regularities as may be deemed
> conducive to the best interest of the public.[56]

The extension of the limits of the Laredo town commons onto the
south bank of the Río Grande appears to have been motivated by two
reasons. First, Laredo residents wanted secure title to the grazing lands
in the vicinity of their town. This official survey was to assist in curbing
encroachment by ranchers from towns on the south bank on grazing
lands near the Laredo municipality. Moreover, a small number of Laredo
inhabitants had settled on the south bank. To incorporate their dwellings into the newly founded municipality, Governor Palacio declared
on June 13 that the residences on the south bank were to be "annexed
to this town and to its secular and ecclesiastical jurisdiction."[57]

In a procedure recorded in terms strikingly similar to those used by
Captain Almazán at the Villa de San Fernando, the surveyors on the
royal commission went on to describe to Governor Palacio the task of
laying out the downtown area of the Laredo municipality:

> And forthwith we, conjointly with the aforesaid surveyors, those se-
> lected by the Laredo citizens, proceeded to select a suitable spot for the
> public square and building lots for the public buildings thereunto be-
> longing, and determined upon a level piece of ground situated in the

center of the present settlement, concluded to laying it off prolonged into a square, and, considering the number of inhabitants and their probable increase, we deemed sufficient a length of one hundred varas by a depth of eighty varas in which are included twenty varas at each corner occupied by the outlets and entrances of their respective streets, with a width of ten varas in order to pass in and out unmolested on horseback.[58]

With the main design of the town square surveyed and "marked out with visible and durable stakes," the north and south sides of the plaza were laid out with four lots of twenty varas wide facing the town center and forty varas in depth, these principal lots customarily being set aside for the leading families of the community. The large frontage area allowed for plenty of room to construct a home facing the main plaza, while a depth of forty varas provided ample space to build pens and shelters for riding horses and prized livestock.[59]

The west side of the town square was marked for a small cluster of buildings required for the administration of law and order, notably a municipal government building, a residence for the *alcalde*, at times called justice or captain, and a jail, symbolizing the town's determination to protect the security of its citizens.[60]

The east end of the town square was to serve as the location for a parish church and residence for the curate.[61] For the first several years, the settlers had depended on Fray Miguel de Santa María of Revilla, a town twenty-three leagues downstream on the opposite bank of the river. The missionary who ministered to the people at the Villa de Dolores visited Laredo once a year, for which the settlers provided him with a stipend of thirty pesos.[62] In 1757, the residents at Laredo had informed Tienda de Cuervo of their need for a minister and had asked that this pastoral ministry be made available to them at royal expense, such a petition being common among frontier settlements. Tienda de Cuervo concurred with the idea of a permanent priest on the north bank, but believed that the combined resources of Laredo and Dolores could support the curate.[63] His belief was not unreasonable, since both communities were already accustomed to providing stipends for the missionary from Revilla for baptisms, marriages, burials, and the celebration of mass. Few parish priests were available, however, and an emerging civil community on the untamed frontier was hardly a priority of central government officials in Mexico City.

The spiritual needs of Laredoans were vividly revealed by the Bishop

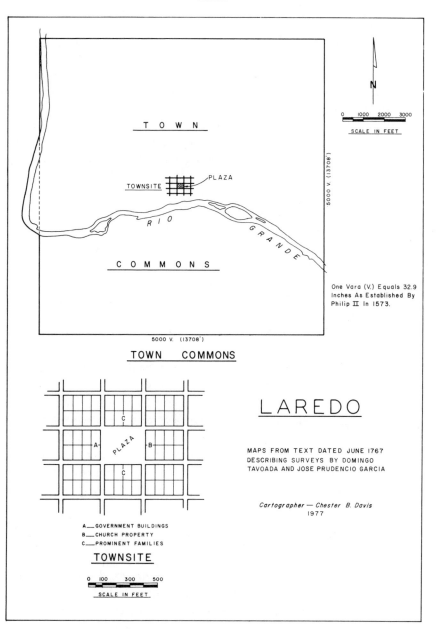

T O W N

TOWNSITE ⌐ PLAZA

5000 V. (13708')

R I O

G R A N D E

C O M M O N S

One Vara (V.) Equals 32.9 Inches As Established By Philip II In 1573.

5000 V. (13708')

N

0 1000 2000 3000

SCALE IN FEET

TOWN   COMMONS

C

A- PLAZA -B

C

LAREDO

MAPS FROM TEXT DATED JUNE 1767
DESCRIBING SURVEYS BY DOMINGO
TAVOADA AND JOSE PRUDENCIO GARCIA

Cartographer — Chester B. Davis
1977

A__GOVERNMENT BUILDINGS
B__CHURCH PROPERTY
C__PROMINENT FAMILIES

TOWNSITE

0 100 300 500

SCALE IN FEET

MAP 8

99

of Guadalajara, Martínez de Tejada, during his visitation in December, 1759. On his return from La Bahía in Texas he stopped in Laredo for three days, baptizing many children and confirming over one hundred settlers. On December 26, 1759, he noted in a letter to the viceroy that the spiritual conditions at Laredo were regrettable, the settlers "neither hearing Mass nor the Word of God."[64] In 1767, when the town was laid out, there was still no indication of a curate permanently living in Laredo. However, the residents were persistent in petitioning both crown and church for a parish priest. The request for a pastor apparently proved to be successful, for Fray Gaspar José de Solís, in his diary regarding visits to the missions in Texas in 1767–1768, noted that a curate, Joseph Gutiérrez, had come to Laredo.[65]

The arrival of a priest did not mean that royal funds were available for supporting a minister and constructing a church. On August 31, 1769, Governor Palacio wrote to the Laredo *alcalde,* Joseph Martínez de Soto, and asked him to urge residents to construct a church according to their own means to recall to them the spiritual benefits they would accrue from a religious temple.[66] It is not known how quickly the settlers followed the governor's advice. However, in a census report drawn up in Laredo by the lieutenant *alcalde,* Miguel Ponce Borrego, in 1789, it was noted that a stone church had been erected with a priest in charge of the spiritual needs of the people.[67]

In 1767, the royal commission proceeded to promote Laredo's municipal government by granting town lots to settlers who agreed to build homes within two years. The lots, equal in size to those facing the town square, were assigned to the settlers by lottery and were to be in the possession of their owners within two months. The sale of these properties, particularly to ecclesiastical orders, was prohibited by law. The intent of the royal commission had been to increase municipal interest by encouraging the settlers to augment the value of their properties through house building and thus to defend the town more vigorously from possible Indian attack or foreign invasion.[68]

To provide each settler with adequate grazing land and a continual source of water for livestock, the engineers on the royal commission decided to survey the lands bordering on the town commons into about eighty-nine *porciones.*[69] Each *porción* was a rectangular piece of land measuring nine-thirteenths of a mile of river frontage and eleven to fourteen miles long. The surveyors measured out more *porciones* than there were applicants for grazing land. This made it possible for the royal commission to assign the land grants with little difficulty and to set aside vacant *porciones* for new colonists wishing to settle at Laredo. Tomás Sánchez received two *porciones,* and nine other Sánchezes, mostly sons and relatives, each received an additional *porción.* After all the applicants had been assigned *porciones,* sixty-four of approximately eighty-nine tracts had been assigned to the settlers.[70]

A large land grant sixty leagues north of the *porciones* surveyed by the royal commission was given to Tomás Sánchez as part of the crown's attempt to carry out Escandón's original plan to settle northward into the Nueces country.[71] Although the plan had failed in 1755, it was never abandoned. Spanish officials hoped that the colonizing plans that originated with Escandón would begin to unfold once travel into the northern reaches of Nuevo Santander became secure. Laredo was to play an important role in pushing the frontier northward. The town comprised Spanish and mestizo families with strong feelings of loyalty to the crown, and because there were hardly any Indians among the settlers, the Spanish imperial government had never considered the establishment of a mission or a presidio to Christianize or to civilize the indigenous population. Sánchez had established his town without the help of Indian vassals. The nearest Indians were bands of Coahuiltecans about forty leagues away. These friendly Borrados, Carrizos, and Bocas Prietas were numerous but caused no trouble.

The relationship between the colonists and the Indians was one of neighborliness, there being plenty of space for all, at least during the first twenty years. More important, Sánchez had earned the respect of the unpredictable Lipan Apache who dwelt to the north of the Río Grande. These mounted braves often visited with the colonists in peace.[72]

Under Sánchez's leadership Laredo had become a strategic center in the crown's attempt to push the frontier onto the land of the Nueces River. To effect this plan the central government approved an order that all land between the northern limits of the Laredo municipality and the Nueces River were to be made subject to Laredo's jurisdiction.[73]

The citizens of Laredo, acting on the new municipal charter granted by the crown, held elections for offices on the town council in the fall of 1767. Don José Martínez de Sotomayor was elected *alcalde ordinario* of Laredo. The *regidores* of the newly organized municipal government were councilmen Salvador Gonzales Hidalgo and Nicolás de Campos Castellanos. The new municipal officers were confirmed by the governor of Nuevo Santander, Juan Fernando de Palacio, in a letter that his secretary, José Ossorio, sent to the members of the *cabildo* on April 8, 1768.[74]

Although the Laredo *cabildo* appeared considerably smaller than that formed at the Villa de San Fernando in 1731, it apparently performed its duties to the satisfaction of the citizens for several years. Under the *cabildo*'s direction, records were kept and archives began to accumulate. The second municipal elections within the present boundaries of Texas had taken place, and the town government of the little village went about the business of regulating Laredo's internal affairs.

An indication that the municipal government at Laredo was alive is seen in the political friction that attended Alcalde Martínez de Soto-mayor's attempt to exceed the powers of his office by directing a move to depopulate the main town site and to remove town records to that sector of town situated on the south bank of the river. Alcalde Martínez de Sotomayor maintained his ranches and home on the south bank and apparently wanted the river barrier against possible raids from unfriendly Indians north of the Río Grande.[75] Many citizens were deeply loyal to the crown and became incensed by the mayor's decree. They were aware that the founding of their town on the north bank had been encouraged by the imperial government in New Spain primarily to serve as a bulwark against raids on interior settlements by unruly Indians. These fearless citizens, spearheaded by Tomás Sánchez, made haste to inform Don Vicente Gonzales de Santianes, the new governor of Nuevo Santander. After some spirited correspondence, Governor Gonzales de Santianes assessed the situation and on July 5, 1770, sent a decree to Captain Sánchez removing Martínez de Sotomayor from office and naming Sánchez in his stead.[76]

The new *alcalde,* hoping to reaffirm the importance of the original town site, asked those settlers misled by Martínez de Sotomayor to return to their residences in Laredo. To encourage the move, he issued a city ordinance assessing a fine of twelve pesos, which was to be applied to the construction of the new church, and placing delinquents in stocks in the public square for a period of eight days.[77]

As time went on, Laredo recovered from the friction resulting from the attempt to change the town site. It began to assume the air of a bustling civil community as new settlers moved in, homes were constructed, and private property accumulated. To guard the peace and tranquillity of the citizens and to offer security to their goods, Sánchez proclaimed a municipal curfew law on May 29, 1779. He directed that one hour after eight o'clock in the evenings, at the sound of the kettle drum, all citizens were to retire to their homes. A sentinel assigned by the *alcalde* was to police the village on horseback, and all persons idling on the streets were to be brought before the justice. Citizens of high estate were to receive a maximum fine of twelve pesos and fifteen days in jail, ordinary citizens being liable to a fine of six pesos and one month in the city jail.[78]

Whereas curfew laws at Laredo seem stringent, at least by present standards, these ordinances designed to protect the civil community were acceptable legislation in Spanish frontier communities. Joseph Curbelo, the *alcalde* of the Villa de San Fernando, enacted the first curfew law in Texas in 1744. It prohibited citizens "from going upon the streets after nine o'clock at night."[79] Juan Montes de Oça, Joseph Curbelo's successor, issued a law in 1745 forbidding the use of small arms within the town limits and compelling citizens to retire an hour earlier by changing the start of the curfew to eight in the evening.[80] The *alcalde* in Laredo, by declaring a curfew law, was acting in what appeared to be the custom of *cabildo* officials in the Borderlands; namely, he was attempting to provide security for citizens and municipal property. Lawlessness was not to become commonplace.

By the last quarter of the eighteenth century the population in Laredo had grown considerably, and the town indicated notable signs of prosperity, at least by the standards of the harsh northern frontier of New Spain. In a census report on January 28, 1789, to the governor of Nuevo Santander, Alcalde Miguel Ponce Borrego indicated that the total population of Laredo was 700 inhabitants, comprising Spaniards, mestizos, mulattoes, and a new addition of 110 Carrizo Indians,[81] probably in Laredo to seek protection from Apache warriors who were becoming increasingly restive with the close of the century. Besides a rock church and a house for the local curate, the town boasted a total of eighty-five dwellings and barracks for the troop of soldiers recently stationed in the town to discourage Lipan Apache braves north of Laredo from menacing the civil community.[82]

Whatever demands the grim conditions of the frontier were to require of them with the advent of the nineteenth century, Don Tomás Sánchez, the first founding families, and the later arrivals were now settled in sufficient numbers to convert Laredo into the second permanent chartered town settlement in what is now Texas. As had the Canary Islanders who settled the Villa de San Fernando about thirty years ear-

POPULATION OF THE LAREDO MUNICIPALITY
AND VICINITY DURING THE COLONIAL PERIOD

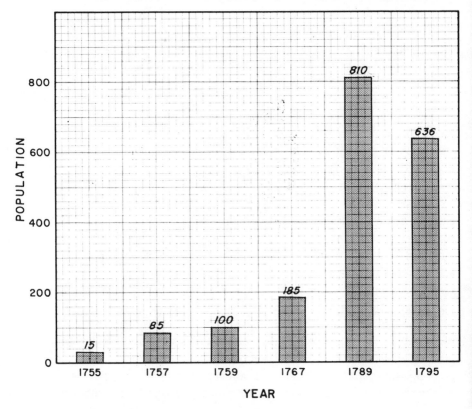

FIGURE 4

lier, the Laredo settlers promoted their distinct forms of municipal government and saw to it that as early as the mid-eighteenth century local rule in the management of town affairs became part of the scene of present-day South Texas.

6

San Jose and Los Angeles
TOWN SETTLEMENTS IN CALIFORNIA

ANTECEDENTS TO CIVIL COMMUNITIES

When Father Junípero Serra and his Franciscan brethren created the Mission Trail more than two hundred years ago, they laid the cornerstones for many of California's modern cities by selecting ideal town sites. Establishing San Diego de Alcalá in 1769 in the south and extending to Sonoma in the north, the Franciscans built twenty-one missions spaced a day's travel apart on horseback so that a traveler could rest and shelter at the end of each day's journey. They named the road linking the missions El Camino Real–The King's Highway. Although not more than a wagon lane in those years, the Camino Real constitutes today much of scenic U.S. Highway 101. The mission centers and the presidios were the first institutions implemented by the Spanish imperial government in its attempt to strengthen Hispanic control over the natives and land of Alta California. Since town settlements figured prominently in Spanish colonization plans in California, the pueblos were sure to follow.

Two hundred years before the introduction of missions and military forts, Spain had sent expeditions under Juan Rodríguez Cabrillo, Sebastián Rodríguez Cermenho, and Sebastián Vizcaíno to explore the extended coastline of Alta California. The area's name originated from a romantic novel by Garci Ordóñez de Montalvo in which it meant "earthly paradise." In fact, many of Ordóñez's contemporaries thought that California was a mysteriously long island. An experienced navigator, Rodríguez Cabrillo sailed two caravels northward in 1542, toward upper California in hopes of discovering the elusive Straits of Anián. The Rodríguez Cabrillo expedition sailed northward perhaps as high as point

43° latitude, but, unfortunately, adverse sailing conditions prevented him from discovering the Bay of Monterey, the site of the Golden Gate, or the Bay of San Francisco.[1]

About a quarter of a century later, interest in settlements in California was renewed by the need of a port of call for the Manila Galleons and a base to protect them from pirates and foreign enemies, particularly the audacious attacks of Francis Drake and Thomas Cavendish. Sebastián Rodríguez Cermenho, a Portuguese, was selected to make the necessary survey of the California coast about the close of the century. In command of the Manila Galleon, Cermenho reached the California coast but was able to provide little cartographical information about the hazardous coast and inland bay areas, since his ship, heavy with cargo, wrecked at Drake's Bay.[2]

Of more lasting significance in the development of California settlements was the exploration of Sebastián Vizcaíno. After preliminary explorations in Baja California, Vizcaíno left Acapulco on May 5, 1602, and proceeded up the coast, visiting points charted earlier by Rodríguez Cabrillo and naming them, in spite of orders to the contrary. Skilled cartography coupled with wide circulation of the accounts of Vizcaíno's exploration resulted in the new names, such as San Diego, Santa Catalina, Santa Bárbara, Point Conception, Monterey, and Buenaventura, becoming permanent.[3]

By the third quarter of the eighteenth century the Bourbon reform movement in the northernmost Borderlands had affected far more than New Mexico and Texas. José de Gálvez, the dynamic *visitador general* sent to New Spain by Charles III, never lost sight of his orders to send an expedition to rediscover and establish settlements at the Bays of San Diego and Monterey. Furthermore, he understood that Spain's inactivity in Alta California might well result in the establishment of foreign bases there. The Ports of Loreto in Baja California and San Blas on the southwestern coast of New Spain were bases for the first colonizing attempt into Alta California, namely, the Portolá-Serra expedition. The father-president of the California Franciscans, Fernando Rivera y Moncada, the veteran presidial commander at Loreto, and Gaspar de Portolá, the governor of Baja California, carefully planned every step of the effort. Despite hardships at the port of San Diego, the skillful execution of the plans resulted not simply in exploration but in the occupation of Alta California. Governor Portolá, assigning part of his force to the San Diego settlement, pushed northward with about forty troops, orderlies, and missionaries. By October, 1769, he was beyond Monterey Bay, the planned destination of his northward exploration. He was not to find Monterey Bay until his second attempt in March, 1770. However, the first expedition was not futile; a small scouting party under Sergeant José Ortega, commanded to reconnoiter onward, was the first to see the Bay of San Francisco, a port so conceivably large, noted Fray Juan Crespi, that "not only all the navy of our Most Catholic Majesty but those of all Europe could take shelter there."[4]

In 1773, Viceroy Bucareli reviewed a full report on the Spanish permanent settlements in Alta California. A presidio and mission had been formally inaugurated at Monterey in June, 1770. More than sixty mounted soldiers garrisoned at San Diego and Monterey and parceled out in guard units at each of the missions reflected the presence of the Spanish imperial government. Nineteen friars were at work in five missions, their labors among the Indians resulting in nearly five hundred baptisms. Spain had achieved a promising beginning; however, with few civilians, craftsmen, and farmers, the plans for colonizing Alta California were for the most part still on the drawing board.[5]

Another notable development came in 1773, as a result of Bucareli's interest in California and conversations with Serra during his visit to Mexico City: Juan Bautista de Anza planned his first trip from Sonora to San Gabriel and Monterey. It took place in 1774. The provisioning of Alta California had been done almost exclusively by sea, a slow process that often proved precarious and expensive. Serra had persuaded the viceroy to develop a land route from Sonora to solve the provisioning problems until California became agriculturally self-sufficient. Late in 1773, orders from the viceroy reached Juan Bautista de Anza, the captain at the Tubac presidio in Sonora, to open a trail to California. By 1774, Anza had found a land route to California by way of the Gila and Colorado junction. He returned to Sonora and began to prepare a land expedition in Horcasitas. On September 28, 1775, he ordered his settler party northward to Tubac, where 63 more persons joined the group, raising the company to 240. Tubac, located on Río Santa Cruz south of Tucson, was a fifteen hundred–mile journey to California over a precarious route that included crossing the Colorado River. Anza used 695 horses and mules to move his settlers and was driving 355 head of cattle to sustain them during the journey. In March, 1776, nearly all the settlers safely reached their destination, Monterey. On orders from the viceroy, Anza and Fray Pedro Font selected sites for a presidio and mis-

"Spanish Pioneer Woman," typical of those who arrived in California in 1776 to settle towns. Drawing by J. Cisneros, *Riders across the Centuries* (1980), by permission of Texas Western Press of the University of Texas, El Paso.

sion. Anza then turned the settlers over to Lieutenant José Moraga and headed back to Sonora. On the tip of the peninsula, within site of the Golden Gate, the Sonoran settlers under Moraga founded the outpost of San Francisco on September 17, 1776. Mission Nuestra Señora de los Dolores was laid out a few weeks later.[6] The following year a civil community called San José was established. It was located farther inland, south of the bay and on the banks of the Guadalupe River.

Royal Approval for California Pueblos

The legal groundwork for the establishment of pueblos in Alta California had been laid out three years before Anza's party of 240 settlers arrived in Monterey. The central government in Mexico City had directed Juan José de Echeveste, a member of the Vice-Regal Council, to draw up a set of laws for Alta California that were to serve as a constitution for the province. He completed the regulations by May 19, 1773. They encouraged settlers, carpenters, *vaqueros,* farmers, and muleteers to come and work near the mission centers. They were to bring their families and would receive rations for five years and wages for two. Their presence was expected to assure adequate crops for the support of the missions and to serve as an object lesson in converting the Indians into worthy vassals of the king.[7]

On September 26, 1773, Viceroy Bucareli sent instructions to the commanders of the presidios of San Diego and Monterey indicating that the time had arrived to make explicit provisions for future municipalities in California. The missions were to provide the nuclei for potential towns. The mission pueblos were to have an adequate supply of water for household use and for irrigation. The Indians were to be taught to construct homes and to cultivate grain, vegetables, and fruit trees. Moreover, houses were to be arranged in uniform fashion on wide streets and a large plaza was to serve as a marketplace. The commander of the presidios was authorized to assign the *ejidos* and to distribute land to individual Indians to promote farming and cattle ranching.[8] Soldiers, sailors, and servants or workmen in the service of the crown who decided to remain in California with their families were encouraged to join the proposed pueblo communities in the province. Unmarried men were to be encouraged to marry converted Indian women and remain to populate the new settlements.

Viceroy Bucareli's intentions were noble, but in 1773 there was little to encourage settlers to remain in California, particularly at the mission centers. An additional problem faced Governor Felipe de Neve, who continued to rule the province from Loreto until 1777: the provisioning of the presidios in Alta California. Captain Fernando de Rivera y Moncada had informed him of the scarcity of food and cattle in Baja California, the main grain and livestock center for the presidios in Alta California.[9] Moreover, the cost of clothing, arms, horses, equipment, and food from the mainland had doubled by the time they reached Loreto. By the time they arrived at the presidio in Monterey cost had increased about 150 percent.[10] Dependence on the ships sailing from San Blas further affected presidio personnel in Alta California. Hazardous sailing conditions often delayed ships, causing flour or maize to spoil before reaching California ports. The mission centers had been furnishing limited supplies of food and livestock for the presidios and for ships in port to replenish their supplies. Father Serra indicated that the first time the packet ship *San Carlos* arrived in Monterey, in 1775, the mission provided "sacks upon sacks" of greens, cabbage, lettuce, turnips, and other vegetables for the officers and crew of the ship.[11] Aware of the precarious conditions in which the California forts were supplied by sea, Captain Rivera y Moncada asked Serra in October, 1775, whether the missions could supply grain in the event provisions should run short. Serra's response, although generous, reflected the almost total reliance of military garrisons on the newly established missions. San Gabriel, San Diego, San Luis Obispo, and San Antonio had slaughtered mission livestock and shared their sizable harvests with the soldiers.[12]

Because he needed to free the forts in Alta California from complete dependence on supplies by sea and on mission produce, Governor Neve directed his efforts toward the establishment of towns designed to include diversification of industry and the development and cultivation of farmlands. After examining the topography along the coastline where the missions were being constructed northward as far as San Francisco Salano, Neve reported to Viceroy Bucareli on June 3, 1777, that the tract of land that lay contiguous to Río de la Porciúncula, about forty-two leagues from San Diego and two from Mission San Gabriel, provided an advantageous site for a municipal settlement. A tract of land on the banks of the Guadalupe River about twenty-six leagues north of the Presidio of Monterey, sixteen southeast of San Francisco, and three-quarters of a league from Mission Santa Clara also provided an ideal site for a town. Neve requested permission to proceed with the establishment of towns.[13] He was clearly aware that the central government was attempting to recruit about forty-six settlers in New Spain and to conduct them northward to California. Anxious to relieve the presidios of their heavy reliance on supplies originating at San Blas, Neve did not wait for official confirmation to build towns.[14] Almost immediately he ordered José Moraga, the commander of the Presidio of San Francisco, to recruit nine soldiers experienced in farming, five settlers, and one servant for the establishment of a pueblo on one of the sites proposed in the letter to the viceroy, namely, the great plain of Santa Clara near the mouth of the Guadalupe River.

On November 7, 1777, Lieutenant Moraga left the Presidio of San Francisco with the party of fifteen and their families, sixty-eight persons in all. When they arrived at a site on the east side of the river, Moraga established the town. He marked off the plaza and measured the *solares* that were to serve as the settlers' assigned lots. Moraga then marked off the *suertes,* that is, the farmlands alloted to the settlers. The *suertes* were to be two hundred varas wide, an area that was ordinarily sown by one fanega of maize or two and a half bushels of corn. Each *vecino* of the newly formed pueblo was to receive two *suertes* of irrigable land and two of nonirrigable.[15]

Moreover, each settler was to be provided with farm implements and eight horses, seven mules, twenty-four mares, and twenty-eight she goats. To increase the livestock, the settlers were given as common property one stud horse, one bull, one burro, three she asses, one boar, three sows, three rams, and three billy goats. The settlers immediately began to construct their houses, temporary structures with flat roofs and adobe walls. They then cleared the land for ploughing and planting and started the construction of a dam to divert the river for irrigation. The town was officially founded on November 29, 1777, and named San José de Guadalupe. Governor Neve was hopeful that within two years the town would be able to provision the presidios of Monterey and San Francisco with grain.[16]

José de Gálvez, the implementer of Bourbon reforms in New Spain, played a major role in the initiation of Spanish town settlements in Alta California. On March 6, 1779, he wrote from Mexico City to Teodoro de Croix, commandant general of the Interior Provinces, notifying him that the crown had approved the establishment of San José.[17] Croix communicated the good news to Governor Neve on January 1, 1781.[18] Moreover, he approved an updated code of laws formulated by Neve that was to be the governing instrument during the remaining period of Spanish rule in California. The new laws were to replace the Echeveste regulations.

Although royal approval for the establishment of the town had been received, Neve did not attempt to assign boundaries to Pueblo San José nor to institute the judicial process of providing the settlers with titles to their *solares* and *suertes*. His ambitious plans for the establishment of a pueblo at Los Angeles, the extension of missions, and the reinforcement of the presidios hardly allowed him to turn his attention to San José, a town project that most interested him. His years as governor of the province were numbered. In 1781, while on an expedition to control Yuma Indian mauraders in southern California, Neve, one of the most able governors assigned to Spanish California, was informed by the crown of his promotion to inspector general of the recently reorganized Provincias Internas.

THE BEGINNINGS OF SAN JOSÉ AND LOS ANGELES

In September, 1782, Pedro Fages was made the governor of California. A leader in the province since 1769, when he arrived with a company of Catalonian infantry volunteers, he had served as a military commander in California from 1770 to 1779. On December 1, 1782, Lieutenant Moraga sent the newly appointed governor a copy of a plan for the division of land for farming at San José. Fages sent Moraga orders on December 12 to issue titles to the settlers to assure possession of their property. Moraga was delayed in San Francisco with administrative duties for about a year, but on January 4, 1783, he replied that he would attend to the business at San José.[19]

The procedure implemented by Lieutenant Moraga in laying out the town of San José was essentially similar to the plans used by Captain Almazán in San Antonio and Governor Juan Fernando de Palacio in Laredo. On May 13, 1783, Moraga marked the plaza, the lots for principal public buildings, and the residential lots about the plaza in accordance with the Laws of the Indies. He was accompanied by two soldiers as witnesses, Felipe Tapia and Juan José Peralta, both of whom returned to San José as settlers once their military service was completed. Moraga assigned the common lands of the pueblo, the *ejidos, dehesas,* and *baldío*.[20] Ideally, the *ejidos* were tracts of public land that surrounded the town, designated for the convenience and benefit of the settlers. The *ejidos* were to serve for recreation, the threshing of grain, the grazing of cows and goats, and the tethering of horses. A second tract of public land, lying beyond the *ejidos* and running around the pueblo on all sides, was the *dehesas,* or pasturelands, where much of the livestock owned by the townsmen was allowed to graze freely. Still farther out were the *baldíos,* or uncultivated public land. Like mountains, forests, and water, these pasturelands were held in common by order of the king.[21]

On the next day, Moraga began placing the individual settlers in juridical possession of their *solares* and *suertes.* San José's first landowners were the following settlers: José Ignacio Archuleta, José Manuel Gonzales, José Tiburcio Vásquez, Manuel Amézquita, Antonio Romero, Bernardo Rosales, Francisco Avila, Sebastián Albitre, and Claudio Albírez. In accordance with Neve's regulation, all *suertes* were two hundred varas long and two hundred wide, which extended the size of the original land grants made in 1777. The portion of land between the *suertes,* or town lots, was ten varas. It took until May 18 to complete the measurement of *solares* and *suertes.* When the land was conferred in the name of the king, the titles were drawn up and the documents signed in a ceremony of presentation witnessed by all the pueblo settlers. Archuleta, the *alcalde,* was the first to receive land titles. After the ceremony, the *alcalde* was officially presented with a branding iron for his livestock.[22] The brand was registered and a drawing of it was made on the document that recorded possession of Archuleta's land. On May 19, Moraga marked the *propios,* land belonging to the municipal government and used for its support. In May, 1783, Pueblo San José had not developed sufficiently for the organization of a local government, although the appointment of an *alcalde* was a step in the direction of municipal rule. Moraga apparently assigned *propios* to the pueblo with an eye on the future development of the civil community. The proceedings were recorded in the *Libro Maestro* kept in the archives of the presidio of San Francisco. These records included the measurements and the location of the communal lands and private properties and an account of the land titles and livestock brands of each settler. The original papers were sent to Governor Fages in Monterey. By February 6, 1784, Fages and Don Teodoro de Croix had formally approved the judicial proceedings for the laying out of Pueblo San José.[23]

Almost from its founding San José encountered flood problems from winter rains causing the Guadalupe River and Coyote Arroyo to overflow their banks. To prevent damage to the pueblo and its surrounding farmlands, the floodwaters, particularly those from the Guadalupe River, were harnessed by a dam built in 1778, and then repaired in 1779. In 1784, the year after the settlers were given juridical possession of their homesteads, however, the dam burst again, compelling Pedro Fages to direct the construction of a new one of stone and lime. In 1785, a flood resulting from the spring rains once more destroyed the dam and caused inundations at Pueblo San José and nearby Misión Santa Clara. Heavy rains were to continue to hamper the progress of the town. Twelve years later, Alcalde Marcos Chaboya petitioned the new governor, Diego de Borica, to consider transplanting the pueblo to a nearby elevation within its municipal jurisdiction, namely, a mesa on the opposite side of the Guadalupe River.[24] In May the governor commissioned an experienced engineer, Alberto de Córdoba, to inspect Pueblo San José and to indicate an appropriate area for its transfer. When Córdoba arrived to make the inspection, the settlers claimed that all they wanted was the right to build houses on the mesa across the Guadalupe River so that, in the event of an inundation, they might take refuge in their second homes.[25] The *vecinos* of San José had invested twenty years of labor in building the original pueblo. Understandably enough, they were reluctant to abandon the old town site.

Despite hardships, Pueblo San José managed limited prosperity, particularly under the rule of Governor Fages. Although Father Francisco Palou charged that San José was in a state of decadence, his allegation appears to be more a response to friction generated from boundary disputes between the civil community and Misión Santa Clara. By 1783, the population had grown to about eighty inhabitants. The San Joseans, however, had completed a large wooden granary and had increased their agricultural production to 2,250 bushels of corn and other crops, more than the average harvest of the mission. Moreover, the *vecinos,* allowing sheep to decrease to 600, had increased their cattle and horses from 417 to 980 head. They were also tax-paying citizens, providing the royal treasury with 428 pesos in tithes as early as 1783.[26] Whatever hardships the settlers at San José were called on to bear, their civil community had become, by 1790, a permanent part of the landscape of the Santa Clara Valley.

Governor Felipe de Neve, the indefatigable founder of Pueblo San José in 1777, had been simultaneously laying the groundwork for the founding of La Reina de los Angeles by attempting to pinpoint, as closely as possible, the new pueblo site according to the information he had provided Viceroy Bucareli on June 3, 1777. The new civil community was to be located forty-five leagues north of presidio San Diego, twenty-seven south from the Santa Bárbara Channel, and one and a half leagues west of Misíon San Gabriel. The town site was to be marked near the banks of the Porciúncula River and exposed to the fresh breezes of the south and north winds and free from the danger of floods.[27]

The year he marked out the location of the new pueblo, Neve petitioned Teodoro de Croix to send between 40 and 60 settlers for the establishment of San José and Los Angeles, a request he renewed in September, 1778. Croix had hoped to recruit settlers from Sonora, the province that had provided Anza with 240 pioneers for California three years earlier. However, times had changed. The mining industry in Sonora was drawing on nearly all available manpower. Moreover, farmers in the province were cultivating fertile and well-watered fields that produced abundant crops; hence, they demonstrated no interest in leaving for a remote country about which they knew little. The population was greater near Tepic and Culiacán, an area that had some interest in California because of commerce through the towns of Matanchel, San Blas, and Compostela. The inhabitants, however, informed Croix that they were not interested in going to California, either. They were not even interested in selling horses and mules for use in California, although they would provide cattle, sheep, goats, and pigs.[28]

What effects these objections had on Governor Neve is not known. However, in a letter to Croix dated April 3, 1779, Neve stated that the number of settlers for Los Angeles might be reduced to twenty-four, since San José had already been founded. On December 27, 1779, Croix wrote his instructions to Captain Fernando Rivera y Moncada for the recruiting of twenty-four settlers needed for the proposed pueblo and fifty-nine soldiers for the California presidios.[29] Croix recommended that the recruiting be done from the provinces of Ostimuri and Sinaloa southward as far as Guadalajara. By July, 1781, Rivera y Moncada had enlisted the fifty-nine men, but had fallen short of the required number of settlers, having enrolled only sixteen.

The California expedition was divided into two groups. One traveled by sea, the other by the Anza trail through settlements on the Colorado River.[30] On August 18, 1781, the party that had come by sea under the command of José de Zúñiga arrived at Misíon San Gabriel. The second half of the expedition, under the leadership of Rivera y Moncada, met with disaster. On July 17 and 18, Yuma Indians near the Colorado River rose in unexpected revolt and killed some of the land expedition. Undeterred, the settlers moved on to the place where the new town, La Reina de los Angeles de Porciúncula, was to be established. The settlers

POPULATION OF THE SAN JOSE MUNICIPALITY
DURING THE COLONIAL PERIOD

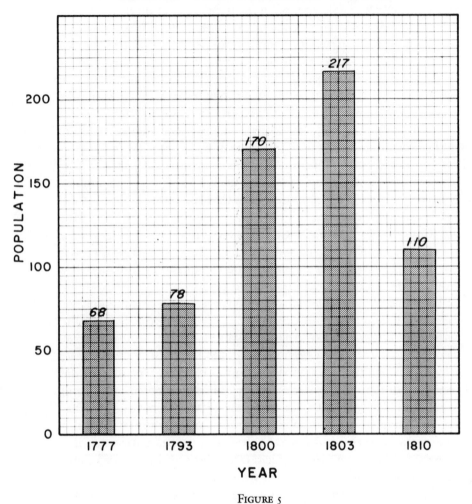

FIGURE 5

and their families consisted of forty-six persons, eleven being heads of family or adult males. In January, 1781, Neve had sent to Misíon San Gabriel 176 head of sheep, 42 cows, 24 calves, and 44 steers to be distributed among the settlers when they arrived. Moreover, each *vecino* was given a plow, a hoe, and an ax. Carts were distributed for common use.[31]

On August 26, 1781, Governor Neve wrote an instruction for the laying out of Pueblo la Reina de los Angeles. The town was to be located near the Porciúncula River on elevated land. The plaza was to be two hundred feet wide by three hundred feet long. The principal streets were to extend from each side of this small plaza and two others were to run parallel to these. Each *vecino* was to receive a *solar*, or town lot, twenty varas wide by forty long and bordering one of the streets. The side of the plaza facing east was selected for the construction of a church and municipal buildings. According to Neve, the four corners of the plaza were to face the cardinal points so that streets would not be exposed to direct winds. The modestly constructed homes of the first settlers had adobe walls and flat roofs and were similar to the original dwellings of the San Joseans. A tract two hundred varas wide was to be left vacant between the emerging town settlement and the *suertes,* or farmlands.

Because one of the main purposes for the establishment of the town was the growth of crops, the distribution of *suertes* was equally important for the *vecinos*. In California each *suerte* consisted of a tract of two hundred varas, an area ordinarily sown by a fanega of maize, or approximately two and one-half bushels of corn. Distributed by lots, four *suertes* were presented to each of the eleven *vecinos*: two *suertes* of irrigable land, two of nonirrigable. One-fourth of the irrigable land within the jurisdiction of the newly established town was to be retained as *baldío,* or uncultivated public lands. Governors were required by the Laws of the Indies to assign *propios* to every municipality to serve as estates for income used to defray town expenses. At Los Angeles, the *propios* were marked off and constituted a tract of land twenty-two hundred varas long from north to south. The rest of the town property was left as a *realengo,* or unappropriated land, of two thousand varas to be distributed free to new settlers.[32]

The Pueblo la Reina de los Angeles de Porciúncula was officially founded on September 4, 1781, but it was not until five years later that Los Angelenos were given formal title to their *solares* and *suertes*. In keeping with the orders issued by Governor Fages, Ensign José Argüello, the royal officer who had officiated at the founding of Los Angeles in 1781, proceeded to assign the *vecinos* juridical possession of their properties.[33] In a formal ceremony witnessed by Corporal Vicente Félix and Roque de Cota, soldiers from the presidial garrison at San Francisco, Argüello presented land titles to the first settler, Félix Villavicencio. Since he was unable to write, Villavicencio made a cross on the document recording the event, and Argüello and the two witnesses signed. A drawing was also made of the branding iron conferred on Villavicencio on the occasion of the ceremony. On the same day, September 4, all heads of family or adult males were given proper titles to their lands, making them the first real estate owners in Los Angeles. The other settlers gaining formal titles to their *solares* and *suertes* were José Venegas, Pablo Rodríguez, Manuel Camero, José Clemente Navarro, José Moreno, Basilio Rosas, Alejandro Rosas, José Francisco Sinova, and Antonio Navarro, who was represented by his son.[34] The ten *vecinos* awarded land titles constituted almost the whole of the original settlers who had arrived in 1781. On September 5, Argüello, accompanied by nine *vecinos*, went on to complete the official boundaries of the lands within the town jurisdiction, namely, the *propios, realengo, ejido,* and *dehesas.* By September 18, Ensign Argüello had entered all the land records from the town in the *Libro de Población,* an archival book at the presidio of Santa Bárbara; the original papers were forwarded to the governor for revalidation.[35]

In the year in which the settlers established Los Angeles, the supply ships from San Blas failed to reach Alta California. Consequently, Los Angelenos required assistance from Misión San Gabriel. The presidio at San Diego was compelled to seek help from Misión San Juan Capistrano, while the soldiers stationed at Monterey were assisted in part by Misión San Luis Obispo. The more promising side of the economic picture in 1781, however, was that the emerging pueblo of San José had harvested a bumper crop of thirteen hundred fanegas of grain and enough foodstuffs to supply all the soldiers quartered in San Francisco and to fill the remaining needs of the presidio of Monterey. The pueblos for the most part were too embryonic to play a major role in the economy of the province in the 1780s; however, Governor Felipe de Neve appeared delighted with the establishment of San José and Los Angeles and with the promise that the presidios would soon be able to depend on a steady supply of grain from the towns.

An ill-fated attempt to establish a third permanent pueblo in 1797, near the presidio of Monterey and Misión Santa Cruz, demonstrated that Spanish efforts to found towns in California were not equally successful. Compelled by English, Russian, and American naval penetration of the coast of the Pacific Northwest, particularly around Nootka Sound, the Spanish imperial government began to reassess its California defenses. The viceroy, the Marqués de Branciforte, became interested in the establishment of an additional town that would increase

POPULATION OF THE LOS ANGELES MUNICIPALITY
DURING THE COLONIAL PERIOD

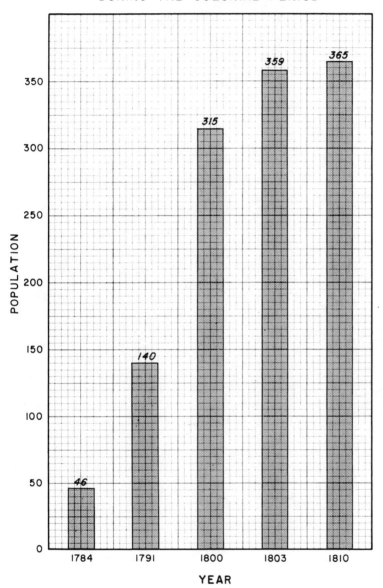

FIGURE 6

Don Miguel de la Grúa Talamanca y Branciforte, viceroy who strengthened the Spanish military presence through California settlements. Courtesy Nettie Lee Benson Latin American Collection, University of Texas, Austin.

the number of settlers in California and serve as a militia center to reinforce the presidial garrisons at San Francisco and Monterey. Planned in accordance with the Laws of the Indies, the new pueblo was elaborately designed by Engineer Alberto de Córdoba, as shown on a map dated September 28, 1797.[36] The map for the proposed new town included a large town plaza, streets, church, curate, quarters, royal government building, a *cabildo* building, a hospital or guest house, and fifty-one town lots for homes located on the plaza. Governor Borica shared Branciforte's intense interest in the new pueblo, hoping to name it, "if the town should succeed . . . in memory and honor of His Excellency the Viceroy."[37]

Almost immediately plans for the new pueblo encountered obstacles. In 1793, Spain entered into war with France and then with England in 1796, the latter not ending until 1802, with the Peace of Amiens. With the arrival of copies of the declaration of war between England and Spain on March 26, 1797, all presidios in California were put on military alert. A state of war prevented soldiers eligible for retirement from settling in the proposed new Villa de Branciforte. An additional problem was to find in Zacatecas, Guadalajara, San Luis Potosí, and other sectors of New Spain, colonists who would voluntarily present themselves for California settlements. As early as October, 1796, Jacobo Ugarte y Loyola, the commandant general, had asked for more settlers in California, but had admitted that the only effective way to get people to go there was to use force.[38] This desperate situation was relieved temporarily when a party of fifteen men, women, and children arrived at Monterey on May 12, 1797. Reaching port poorly clothed, ill-equipped, and in need of medical assistance, the colonists required the governor's attention. He immediately ordered that they be provided with food, clothing, rest facilities, carts, oxen, tools for farming, carpentry, and iron work.[39] They were joined on December 31, 1797, by four married *vecinos* who were much wealthier than the original settlers.[40]

Further misfortunes, however, obstructed the progress of the new pueblo. Most arable land was within the boundaries of Misión Santa Cruz, the *villa* having mostly pasturelands. Moreover, the missionaries objected to the proposed site of the pueblo, which delayed action on the construction of the town until December, 1800.[41] Although the population had increased to 101 inhabitants by December, 1803, it quickly dwindled to 31 persons by the first quarter of the following year. Insufficient arable lands could easily have accounted for the steady decline in population. Its failure to develop eventually made the town the least important civil community in Spanish California.

MUNICIPAL GOVERNMENT IN CALIFORNIA

Established by royal mandate, Pueblo San José and its sister communities represented the Spaniards' proclivities for municipal tradition across the rugged frontier of the northern Borderlands. Their struggle for towns, however, was often thwarted by the economic impact of military hegemony on nearly all town settlements in California, Texas, and New Mexico. The enlightened monarchy, with its renewal policy and plans to protect the vast northern frontier with efficient military force, significantly determined the extent of the mediocre conditions as well as the spirited successes of the municipalities in the Borderlands. Apart from the Bourbon reforms, the limited prosperity of these frontier towns would be difficult to estimate accurately. In 1772, the Royal Regulations for Presidios on the northern frontier further accentuated the importance of a militarily centered economy. The expenditures in the Californias for the presidios at Loreto, San Diego, Monterey, and San Francisco amounted to 55,385 pesos in 1782.[42] In Texas the annual appropriations for the presidio of San Antonio de Béjar alone amounted to 29,580 pesos. The royal treasury also supported Teodoro de Croix, commandant general of the Interior Provinces, who reported an army of "4,686 men—regulars, militia and Indian allies—stationed between Sonora and Texas ready for service."[43]

During the Bourbon reforms, no sizable retrenchment in military expenditures was to be made in favor of the municipalities emerging on the northern frontier. The pueblos in California had been designed primarily as grain-producing centers for the military garrisons quartered in presidios along the West Coast.[44] These military priorities restricted the market for crops harvested by the citizens and even prevented the sale of their surplus horses, colts, and mules.[45] Moreover, all profits were limited according to government-regulated prices. Since specie and virtually all goods imported from New Spain were distributed through government-owned presidios, these centers became essential to all inhabitants residing in nearby towns and missions.

The missionaries opposed the establishment of San José and Los Angeles on economic grounds. They preferred that the presidios depend on trade with the missions.[46] In Texas, government funds from the presidio of San Antonio de Béjar were so important to the economy of La Villa de San Fernando that a dispute arose between mission authorities and the town *cabildo* over the right to sell farm produce to the presidial garrison. On January 4, 1745, the viceroy settled the argument in favor of the missions.[47]

The hidebound and restrictive mercantilistic system and the weight of a monumental bureaucracy also restrained the economic growth of the frontier towns. California settlements were closely guarded against outside contacts, although Yankee skippers and other foreign vessels along the West Coast were anxious to engage in commerce and trade. In French Louisiana, where horses and other livestock from Texas were greatly prized, French entrepreneurs had attempted to establish trade relations with Texas beginning in 1716, when Louis Juchereau de St. Denis first came to Texas. Although Louisiana was ceded to Spain in 1763, the commercial ties with Texas did not significantly improve. With the potential market for crops and goods produced by the citizens of California pueblos restricted to presidios at fixed prices, there was little reason for them to extend themselves in farming and ranching. The consequences of all these circumstances hardly improved the lethargic economic growth of municipalities in the northernmost provinces of the Borderlands.

Despite economic setbacks, the local governments of California pueblos continued to provide law and order. The political hierarchy of California was essentially the same as that in Texas and New Mexico. The governor was the final authority in all civil and political matters, although in Califiornia he delegated considerable authority to presidial officers who were stationed at San Francisco, Monterey, and San Diego. The presidial commander also exercised civil authority and served as a *justicia mayor,* or district magistrate. In civil affairs, the municipalities were generally next in the political hierarchy of the Borderlands, their *cabildos* being the centers of government. In California, a *comisionado* was appointed by the governor to supervise local government and to assist the *alcalde* and the *regidores* in the performance of their duties. Generally a military deputy, the *comisionado* was appointed to oversee local government and to promote peace and harmony among the *vecinos*. The *comisionado's* responsibilities began once the town was established. The first *comisionado* in Alta California was Félix Vicente, who was appointed by Felipe de Neve to supervise the government at La Reina de los Angeles.[48] In the interest of civil order, the *comisionado* assisted local officials in promoting public works. He encourged *vecinos* to fulfill their religious duties and to conduct themselves as Christians. Moreover, he was required to be thorough in his supervision of farming. Every settler was to have two head of oxen, two plows, and farm implements. The *comisionado* inspected *suertes* and saw that each farmer received water to produce adequate crops. If the settlers hired Indian labor, they were to do so through the *comisionado*. He kept records of the provisions, arms, and munitions possessed by the town. He collected taxes or tithes that the *vecinos* were expected to pay to the royal treasury.[49]

The *vecinos* generally elected their *alcaldes* and *regidores* even though the elections were supervised by *comisionados*. Since the towns were small in population, local government officials were elected in a *cabildo abierto*. In 1790, when Mariano Verdugo and Manuel Verdugo both entered their names for the office of *alcalde* at La Villa de la Reina de los Angeles, Don Manuel won the election by a vote of fourteen to five. The *regidores* were elected by the settlers in the same manner as the *alcalde*, that is, by open ballot.[50] San José, shortly after its establishment, implemented a distinct method in the selection of town officials. The outgoing *alcalde* was to name three candidates. If the three *vecinos* were approved by the *comisionado*, they were to cast lots. The winner became the *alcalde* and the other two were named *regidores*.[51] Probably the *comisionado* allowed the selection of town officials by lots since oftentimes the small number of settlers limited the quality of leadership. At any rate, as the population at San José slowly increased, the election of *alcaldes* and other town officials was resumed after 1804.

All pueblos in California were designed to include the public buildings required by the civil community, particularly a church and a municipal government edifice, commonly called a *casa de ayuntamiento*. When Ygnacio Archuleta became *alcalde* of the newly established pueblo of San José, the crown conferred ownership of a *solar* that was appropriately located next to the lot designated for the *casa de ayuntamiento*. Generally, one of the first municipal buildings constructed in California towns was a *juzgado*, or a *cuerpo de guardia*.[52] This building was a guardroom, although it served many other purposes: as a *casa de ayuntamiento*, a prison, assembly and recreational hall, or even a temporary chapel. Moreover, it was the place where decrees were promulgated and public notices were read.

The California *vecinos*, more limited in material wealth than citizens in other towns in the Borderlands, were hardly able to construct parish churches or negotiate for a full-time pastor. Despite these economic problems, however, the settlers at San José petitioned and received permission to construct a chapel in 1802.[53] San Joseans had been attending mass at Misión Santa Clara about three leagues away. When inundations prevented them from reaching their horses in nearby pastures, the settlers walked to church. With approval to construct a chapel next to the town plaza, the 217 *vecinos* in 1803 immediately began construction on the proposed building. By July 12, the elated San Joseans assembled for a formal ceremony in which the cornerstone of the chapel was blessed.[54] In 1804, an earthquake, the formidable challenge with which modern-day Californians also contend, divided their newly built chapel into four parts and left only the major sections of the walls intact.[55] The sacristy apparently was not completely destroyed, because on one occasion in 1808 it was used to store maize. Two events suggest that the settlers probably repaired their chapel. Sympathetic to the settlers' misfortune, José de la Guerra, the presidial commander at Monterey, provided assistance by sending individuals under judicial sentence to work for a month on the municipal chapel. More important, the San Joseans continued to negotiate with the missionaries for the next five years for the celebration of mass in their chapel, particularly for the sake of the sick and elderly.[56]

By 1790, the *vecinos* of Los Angeles had started construction of their chapel. Built on the lot facing east onto the plaza, the chapel was to be twenty varas long and six wide, with walls built about two varas in height.[57] This modest place of worship served for the celebration of mass, although obtaining a priest from Misión San Gabriel, located three and one-half leagues away, continued to pose problems. The pueblo obviously needed a resident pastor. By 1793, there were 131 persons residing in Los Angeles. However, they did not have the means to support a parish priest or even to enlarge their chapel into a church. There was little hope, moreover, that they would receive financial assistance from their bishop, who resided in Sonora, or from the royal treasury. In 1810, the Los Angelenos were doing well to maintain their chapel as a suitable place for religious services.

Regrettably, the limited leadership ability found among the frontier settlers compelled the governors in California to assign a *comisionado* to supervise those who served as *alcaldes* and *regidores* in the new towns of the province. However, the governors at no time intended the co-

misionado to supplant the offices of the *cabildo*. The governors were too versed in Castilian *cabildo* tradition and in the provisions of the Laws of the Indies concerned with town government to suppress indefinitely the offices that reflected the essential political characteristics of Spanish municipalities. Even though the *comisionado* was to serve as a superintendent of local government and as a quasi-municipal judge, he attempted to carry out these duties in conjunction with competent *alcaldes*. In Los Angeles, all civil cases concerned with debts, property titles, theft, and livestock ownership were handled by the *comisionado,* who served as kind of judge of the first instance.[58] Records in civil and criminal cases indicate, however, that a *vecino* alleged to have broken a law was seldom sentenced arbitrarily by a *comisionado*. A court decision rested on due process of law. Accumulation of evidence required days in court, witnesses, depositions from citizens, and virtually all the help a judge could get from a court clerk and municipal officials.[59] The *comisionado,* of course, was delegated judicial authority by the presidial commanders, who were reckoned the district magistrates, and, ultimately, by the governor, but the judicial process was always in essence a municipal endeavor.

Whatever demands the harsh conditions of the untrodden frontier were to make on them, there were enough original citizens in San José and Los Angeles to convert their pueblos into the first municipalities in California. As the sun setting on the Pacific signaled the end of a day, the settlers were reminded of the uncertainties of frontier life by the curfew. In the approaching night the *vecinos* hurried to their homes to prepare the evening meal and for a night's repose. Their towns, long in coming, were indelibly stamped on the soil of California. These were events of a timeless splendor, even though the heroic pioneers heard no golden trumpets sounding. But their exploits were to be recalled by history. These Indo-Hispano town builders are among the finest in American immigrant tradition.

7

The Civilian Settlers
LIFE ON THE NORTHERN FRONTIER

THE PEOPLE OF THE FRONTIER

Two interesting events in New Spain about the time of the Bourbon reforms occurred quite independently of royal proclamation. The first of these *Dei acta* subjected the viceroyalty to a serious agrarian crisis during the third quarter of the eighteenth century. The north-central plateau regions were beset by harsh droughts. In fact, Durango, the capital of Nueva Vizcaya, was unable to cultivate the plains for lack of water. In 1776, its population of nearly ten thousand was short of drinking water.[1] Equally devastating and probably linked to the agricultural problems, were the economic crises suffered in New Spain in the 1760s and in 1785–1786. The agricultural and mining areas were hard hit by a scarcity of jobs, food shortages, and a high cost of living. For many inhabitants, Spaniards, mestizos and mulattoes, it was time to move northward to the frontier Borderlands, "even to such isolated areas as Texas."[2]

The northernmost Borderlands were inhabited by many restive Indian nations. Even so, these frontier provinces attracted a significant flow of settlers from all walks of life from the mining districts of Nueva Vizcaya and Zacatecas. The social structure in Texas shared certain traits with the rest of New Spain, even though the colonization of Central Mexico had already been completed. These similarities were reflected in the municipal, military, and church institutions around which the people rallied as they pushed northward.

Their northward movement and persistent hold on frontier lands were achieved mostly through use of the *cabildo,* presidio, and mission. The frontier municipalities and their local governments played a significant role in the lives of the people, particularly those who were not of the privileged class. Small ranchers, farmers, merchants, clerks, artisans, and their families, along with village curates, constituted the main body of these communities. Moreover, frontier towns were not without their servants, peddlers, vagabonds, and people without land and property. They, too, made up the civil communities and fell under municipal jurisdiction.

Since its founding San Antonio had been the gathering point for migrants who had succeeded in reaching Texas. From San Antonio the trend was toward the settlements at La Bahía and northeast to the Nacogdoches community situated in the piney regions of the province and even as far as Bayou Pierre in Spanish Louisiana. During the Bourbon reforms Teodoro de Croix, commandant general of the Interior Provinces, ordered a census in response to the Royal Order of November 10, 1776. The Croix Census, completed in 1777, indicated that 3,103 inhabitants were residing in Spanish communities in Texas. The most populous center was the San Antonio complex, where 2,060 persons were living. There were 709 Indians dwelling in the mission centers and 1,351 civilian and military inhabitants in the municipal and presidio sectors.[3] In view of the close proximity between the Villa de San Fernando and the San Antonio presidio, no distinction was made between the two localities in the census count. The number of soldiers at the military post fluctuated according to the demands made on them by the frontier. In August, 1759, Colonel Diego Ortiz Parrilla had gathered a military garrison of about 500 men at the presidio for an expedition against the Comanches in the San Sabá area. The number of troops stationed at the presidio for the protection of the San Antonio settlements was generally much smaller. There was a company of only 23 soldiers at the presidio when the number was increased to 80 in 1772. It appears that the more than 1,300 inhabitants registed by the Croix census in the municipal and presidio sectors of San Antonio were mostly civilians.

With a total of 2,060 persons, the mission-presidio-municipal complex in San Antonio was considerably larger than La Bahía and Nacogdoches, the other two main settlements in eighteenth-century Texas. Although neither of these other Texas communities had municipal status, both had civilian residents. Situated near the mouth of the San Antonio River, La Bahía counted a population of 696 persons. There were 515 civilians and soldiers living at the presidio. At nearby Misión del Espíritu Santo de Zúñiga, 181 Indians resided and cared for crops and livestock situated on mission lands. The smallest community was Nacogdoches, the easternmost pueblo in Spanish Texas. According to the Croix census, this settlement had a total population of 347 persons, mostly ranch and farm families of Hispanic and mestizo origins.[4]

San Antonio appeared less impressive when compared to its sister municipalities of the Southwest, since they all claimed larger population, except Laredo, the newest town on the northern bank of the Río Grande. In New Mexico, Santa Fe had 2,324 residents as early as 1776; this count included the 80-man garrison stationed at its presidio. The largest of the four town settlements (San Antonio, Laredo, El Paso, and Santa Fe) was the El Paso complex, consisting of the Pueblo de Guadalupe, its presidio, and five mission centers. When the Marqués de Rubí inspected the El Paso settlements in 1766, he noted a population of around 5,000 people of "every color and complexion."[5] Laredo was the municipality with the smallest population in the northermost Borderlands. Initially settled in 1755, the town was established by four pioneer families under Tomás Sánchez. Twelve years later, Laredo was estimated to have a population of 200. By 1789 the population had reached 700, the increase due in part to a newly constructed presidio and the arrival of the 110 friendly Carrizo Indians from the surrounding area.[6]

These census reports, even though in some cases imperfectly taken, were designed to assist the Bourbon reform movement on the Borderlands frontier. Thus they reflected the need of José de Gálvez and his advisers to know as much as possible about Texas in order to initiate new military, administrative, and economic policies. Although these renewal attempts produced only limited results in the province, the census reports proved to be useful by indicating that the number of people in Texas was not growing; most of the time the population remained stagnant. Increases were due more to a migratory flow from New Spain than to natural growth. Internal migration raised the 1789 population in Texas to 3,210, from fewer than 3,000 during the 1778–1783 period.[7]

The increase in population remained insignificant mainly because life tended to be shorter on the harsh northern frontier. Indian wars, epidemics, and infant mortality were persistent causes for the demographic ebb in the province. Challenging conditions made life very difficult for older people, there being only 161 Spanish and mestizo settlers over fifty years of age in all of Texas in 1793. Epidemics such as smallpox and *matlazahuatl* fever resulted in the loss of many lives, especially among young children. *Matlazahuatl* (from two Aztec words meaning "systemic eruption") fever was a form of typhus imported from Europe, which afflicted Spanish settlers but particularly devastated the Indian population, which had little immunity to the dreaded disease. Life expectancy among the female population appears to have been forty years. Permanent warfare against hostile Indians made life uncertain for the men. As late as 1793, a large part of the population in Texas was less than thirty years old. About two-thirds of the adult population was married and birthrates were high. Even so, because of infant mortality, there was no significant increase in population.

Despite the demographic stagnation, internal migration from New Spain continued to reinforce the existence of the towns and the mission settlements in Texas. Moreover, the flow of new European, mestizo, Indian, and mulatto settlers gave new dimensions to the racial diversification of the province. In a limited but significant sense, the new immigrants increased the heterogeneous population in Texas and contributed to its distinct cosmopolitan and liberal frontier image.

MILITARY MOBILIZATION

The evolution of frontier municipalities during the eighteenth century largely rested on the variations brought about in the Borderlands by the Bourbon reforms. Charles III (r. 1759–1788), the most acclaimed of the Spanish Bourbons, exerted pressure on his ministers to renovate and expand colonial administration.[8] Endowed with determination and foresight, the enlightened monarch dispatched José de Gálvez to supervise a general visitation and to implement changes in the central government of New Spain.[9] A plan was even proposed that would form a new viceroyalty in the frontier provinces of New Spain by changing them into intendancies, that is, uniformly governed districts instead of old kingdoms (*reinos*) and governments.[10] However, this reform proposal was dropped and the existing Provincias Internas, with their jurisdictional structure modified, were strengthened. The government in Texas had been responding directly to the viceroy and members of the Audiencia of Mexico, and in ecclesiastical matters to the archbishop of Guadalajara. By 1776, the reorganization scheme placed government authorities in Texas under the command of the commandant general of the Provincias Internas. To the post of *comandante general* Charles III named Don Teodoro de Croix.[11] During this reform period, the Villa de San Fernando continued to maintain its own *cabildo* and some self-

government. Even so, the Bourbon reforms implemented in the Borderlands emphasized military hegemony on nearly all political and economic matters. In Texas, this martial policy tended to weaken the quality of municipal life and to shackle civil prosperity.

Hostile Indians and border disputes were regarded as the main reasons for the dominance of the military in Spanish Texas. Between 1731
and 1780, ten full-fledged or *ad interim* governors ruled the province. With
the exception of Orobio y Bázterra, who had been a merchant in Saltillo,
and Tomás Felipe Winthuisen and Francisco García Larios, all governors were career military. Only Angel de Martos y Navarrete, a former
naval officer with the rank of *teniente de navío,* was not an army man.
During this period, one general, four colonels, and one captain served
as Texas governor, the average term of office being about four years. By
the last quarter of the eighteenth century the need to mobilize royal
military might on the Borderlands had reached its zenith. Brigadier
Teodoro de Croix, commandant general of the Interior Provinces, was
reported to have had an army of 4,686 men—regulars, militia, and Indian allies—stationed at strategic points all along the northern frontier.[12]

In the meantime, the Spanish crown restricted use of funds to support its two remaining agencies in Texas, the municipalities and missions.
The fruitful labor of the priests at the five mission centers along the San
Antonio River near the Villa de San Fernando started drawing to a close
as secularization became royal policy.[13] The San Antonio municipality
was also affected by changes resulting from royal frontier policy. The Villa
de San Fernando was primarily concerned with its local projects. The
little municipality had seldom received economic assistance from the
crown. With royal policy emphasizing military concerns on the frontier,
the town could expect even less from the royal treasury. Since its founding, the *villa* had been unable to afford the construction of such essential public buildings as a town hall, church, or a suitable jail.[14]

The psychological and economic effects of military hegemony on municipal life in Texas were indeed negative. Military preponderance placed
considerable pressure on the normal functions of municipal government.
Spanish colonial tradition had always reflected the "local versus central
government" concept and stressed the essential difference between town
government and the larger ruling bodies in the colonies. Municipal government was to be indigenous, normally growing out of local conditions, officered by resident landowners, particularly the residents who
had lived longest in the civil community. With no vested interest out-

side its own jurisdiction, the *cabildo* fostered civic pride and promoted local growth. The crown, in efforts to maintain a balance of power, carefully intended to guard the distinctions between local and central government:

> In the administration of the cabildo . . . family ties were favored, strangers were often excluded, and local income was supposed to come from local sources. The attachment of citizens and officers was to the soil. The provincial officers, on the other hand, were supposed to be detached from local ties and local support. The *corregidores* were forbidden to appoint *tenientes* who were natives of the city or property owners. A governor or other provincial officials were forbidden to marry any woman of his district or appoint to office any relative as close as the fourth grade. Under ordinary circumstances, the governor was only to visit the towns of his district once during his term of office. It was the intention of the framers of the Laws of the Indies that their attachment should be to the Crown, the Council, or the Indies and the viceroy.[15]

The martial tone that the presence of the military governor and his troops gave the province hardly promoted the autonomy of local government. Municipal interests were often challenged when the *villa*'s young men who were supposed to attach themselves "to the soil" were called to arms by a trumpet blast from the neighboring presidio. Among the citizens from the San Antonio municipality to serve in the royal armies of the frontier was Francisco Rafael Leal, who was stationed at the Presidio de Santa Rosa. A civilian from the *villa*, a certain Don Joseph Antonio, was persuaded to serve with the king's troops on the frontier by being appointed a lieutenant. Other young men joined as enlisted soldiers. Patricio, the son of Isleños Salvador Rodríguez and María Pérez Cabrera, joined with ten San Antonio volunteers and twenty soldiers from the presidio in a campaign under Rábago y Terán, governor of Coahuila, against hostile Indians. Young Patricio was killed in 1748. Perhaps the most distinguished civilian to serve in the royal armies of the Borderlands was Juan Ignacio Pérez, a descendant of the founding families of the Villa de San Fernando. Born in July, 1761, Pérez reached the rank of lieutenant colonel while in the crown's service.[16]

Charles III had issued the royal regulations of 1772 in the hope that the presidios along the northern frontier of New Spain would attract settlers.[17] Under the protection of the king's troops, these pioneers were to cultivate the land and to introduce essential industry to the Borderlands.

The administrators of the crown's policy experienced only limited success in Texas. Troop movements at the presidio overshadowed municipal activity at the *villa*. While some settlers enlisted in the ranks of the frontier garrison, others became disillusioned with community life, sold their property, and moved away from San Antonio.[18] The majority of the civilian population, however, continued to demonstrate the same determination of the original fifty-nine settlers to maintain their municipal identity. For the citizens of the *villa* life went on as usual. Crops irrigated by the municipal *acequia* had to be tended. Livestock grazing on the town commons required attention. Equally important, the fervor of the *cabildo* had to be maintained, since efficiency in local government assured the flow of community business and the welfare of the town.

THE OPEN TOWN MEETING

The *vecinos* were a hardy group who, albeit lacking formal education, continually sought new opportunities to promote municipal life in the province. Their municipal *fueros*, or chartered rights, created a sense of pride in the *cabildo*, which recognized no superior except the governor. The struggle to maintain the municipal character of the *villa* against enormous odds demanded the collective effort of the citizenry.

The interest of the settlers in town affairs often was reflected in the *cabildo abierto*, an open town meeting where citizens gathered to discuss issues or events of vital importance to all the community. Its roots deeply embedded in the popular *concejos* of medieval Castilian towns, the *cabildo abierto* had reached the New World during the early period of exploration and discovery.[19] The business of administering the affairs of chartered towns ultimately became the responsibility of the *cabildo* and its elected magistrates. However, a share in the determination of local affairs always was vested in an open assembly of citizens. The *cabildo abierto* was

> the only body of a truly popular character that may be said to have existed in the colonial era. . . .[In the *cabildo abierto*] . . . the ordinary *vecino* on occasion voiced his views and opinions on matters of importance affecting the town. In it these views were preserved and nurtured, a residue of the resolute, independent, democratic outlook of the medieval Castilian burgher.[20]

There is little evidence to support the position that the *vecinos* were mandated to attend, for coercion would have limited the usefulness of the *cabildo abierto* as a device to ascertain the will of the citizenry. The number of those present and the nature of the business discussed often determined the location of the open assembly–the main plaza, church-yard, or a prominent citizen's spacious patio frequently being selected. Local matters were best able to generate individual initiative and donations of both labor and money. Matters most frequently discussed were financial drives for local projects or the imposition of royal or local levies. The task of collecting donations or tribute, understandably enough, was greatly facilitated if those who had to pay were consulted in advance. Questions brought before the *cabildo abierto* of large municipalities often concerned the observance of religious holidays or the election of governors *pro tem* and procurators to represent the city before the viceroy or in Spain. Even so, the *cabildo abierto* was regarded more as an extralegal body common to the frontier, since the Laws of the Indies had only three provisions relating to it, directly or by implication.[21] The open town meeting was part of a frontier municipality's larger prerogative from earliest colonial times to redress its grievances and ask the crown for grants and political privileges.

The popular character of the *cabildo abierto* was in keeping with both Hapsburg tradition and Bourbon renewal. During the middle of the eighteenth century municipal governments and the citizenry of New Spain gained a new sense of political importance under Bourbon reforms.[22] On the Texas frontier, however, the new momentum for renewal only confirmed the customary, albeit rustic, democratic character of civil communities, a tradition that persisted despite growing military hegemony. Almost by necessity each *cabildo* meeting was an open assembly, since nearly all the adult male population of the small municipality made up the board of magistrates.

The functions of a *cabildo abierto* were vividly illustrated by the municipal government in San Antonio when the townspeople, local curate, soldiers from the presidio, and other neighbors joined in an open town meeting to plan the construction of a parish church. The settlers had been attending services at Misión San Antonio de Valero and the chapel at the nearby presidio. They now decided with the full support of the governor, to build their own parish church.

On February 17, 1738, the *cabildo,* composed of Manuel de Cruz and Ignacio Lorenzo de Armas as *alcaldes,* and Juan Leal Góraz, Juan Curbelo, Antonio Santos, Juan Leal Alvarez, Vicente Alvarez Travieso, and Antonio Rodríguez as councilmen, reconvened to begin talks on plans for the new town church.[23] The members of the *cabildo* appointed Alvarez Travieso and Francisco Joseph de Arocha as cochairmen of a fundraising campaign for the construction of the church.[24]

The *cabildo* formulated two resolutions during the meetings. First, the new building was to be dedicated and placed under the patronage of Our Lady of the Candlemas and Our Lady of Guadalupe. Second, the church was to be constructed according to the following specifications: thirty varas long and six varas wide with a sacristy and a baptistry similar to the mission of San Antonio de Valero; the main entrance was to face east onto the main plaza of the *villa* and the back door was to face west toward the military plaza of the presidio.[25]

The manner in which the cochairmen went about obtaining subscribers for the fund campaign rested on the *cabildo abierto,* the customary approach in handling public money affairs. The citizens had always concurred on the need for a parish church. Therefore, the main order of business before the general assembly was discussion of the best way to finance the project. Once the opening talks on the importance of the meeting were presented by the local curate and the cochairmen for the campaign, the customary exchange of dialogue by the local townspeople followed.[26] Community support for the project was quickly indicated. The governor of the province, who had lent importance to the meeting by his presence, provided the fund-raisers with a gift of two hundred pesos. Father Juan Recio de León, whose effectiveness as local curate depended on having a church, donated twenty-five pesos. The military officers from the neighboring presidio also endorsed the project. Joseph de Urrutia, the captain of the presidio, led the way with a gift of one hundred pesos. Lieutenant Mateo Peres provided a yearling calf valued at eight pesos; Ensign Juan Galván gave ten pesos; and Sergeant Asencio del Raso donated ten pesos. The enlisted men presented nearly seventy-five pesos to the fund-raisers. Gabriel Castales, the captain of La Bahía presidio, was visiting the governor in San Antonio and contributed twenty-five pesos.[27] Even though the majority of donors were citizens of the *villa,* their offering was less than the total sum originating with the troops. Whereas the number of soldiers in San Antonio was small in 1738 when measured against troop concentrations later during the Bourbon period, the economic hegemony exercised by the military was already in evidence.

Probably the most established citizens from the relatively poor community were cochairmen Alvarez Travieso and José Antonio Rodríguez, a member of one of the founding families of the villa; each donated twenty pesos. Alcalde Ignacio Lorenzo de Armas and several other contributors gave ten pesos each. However, most of the settlers had little money to give, presenting instead livestock and produce that could be converted into money by the fund-raising committee. Juan Leal Alvarez offered ten fanegas, approximately fifteen bushels of corn, which, at two pesos a fanega, equaled twenty pesos. Joseph Leal donated two *fanegas* of corn and a seven-month-old lamb valued at four pesos. Some gave livestock. Martín Lorenzo de Armas, Antonio Jimenes, Bernardo Joseph, and Juan Leal Góraz gave yearling calves and lambs that ranged in value from four to six pesos. Others in the *villa* who had no money to donate devised their own ways to help with the construction of the church. Manuel de Cruz, one of the town *alcaldes,* did not let the shortage of pesos deter him from contributing to the project. Apparently the owner of a sturdy yoke of oxen, Don Manuel offered to bring ten cartloads of construction rock from the town outskirts to the building site. Antonio Rodríguez, motivated by the *alcalde*'s example, offered to do the same, his contribution being twenty cartloads of rock.[28]

On February 25, Alvarez Travieso and Arocha reported to the *cabildo* that there were enough subscribers to begin construction on the church, the first of its kind in Texas. The citizens of the *villa* and their neighbors had donated a total of 642 pesos and two reales, an impressive community effort, considering the modest means of the frontier settlers.[29] Encouraged by the community's favorable response, the *cabildo* proposed that the new building be officially designated as the parish church of the *villa* and its patron saints be approved by a declaration from the local curate. Father Recio de León concurred by announcing the names of the two patron saints for the proposed church. Since Saint Anthony was already the patron of the presidio and the Alamo mission, and Saint Ferdinand that of the *villa,* he thought it fitting that the church be placed under the patronage of Our Lady of the Candlemas and Our Lady of Guadalupe.[30]

With the community firmly supporting the proposed project, the *cabildo abierto* proved to be a major success. First, the townspeople reflected a generous *ésprit de corps* in promoting this public work. The enthusiasm engendered at the open town meeting never diminished. On May 11, 1738, an impressive ceremony took place in which the corner-

stone of the church, blessed by the local curate, was laid. After the ceremony a freewill offering was made by the nearly penniless settlers through
which an additional seventeen pesos and six reales were collected.[31]

Father Recio de León, who spearheaded the project, recommended
to the members of the *cabildo* that, to obtain the additional funds necessary to complete the church, copies of the records of the measures taken
thus far and of the ceremonial dedication be forwarded to the bishop
of Guadalajara and the viceroy. The *cabildo* wrote a formal petition for
aid on June 15, 1738, and presented it to Governor Orobio y Bázterra
who, in turn, forwarded the document along with his own petition for
help in the project to the viceroy in Mexico City.[32]

This action on the part of the Villa de San Fernando suggested two
of the functions of a *cabildo abierto*. First, "the Cabildo, Alcaldes Ordinarios and the community of San Fernando" coordinated their efforts
for the construction of the proposed church. Second, they united to
petition the viceroy for a financial grant. To be sure, the Spanish crown
continued to recognize the municipal right of redress, although with
small frontier *cabildos* the acts of grievance or request for grants were often
directed to the office of the viceroy. In the request for aid in the construction of the church, this seemed to be the case. Through their governor the citizens of the *villa* earnestly solicited royal aid and pressed their
contention that the king should build a church for them. In their petition, the Isleños recalled that Casafuerte, the former viceroy, had directed the settlers to attend worship services at the Valero mission "while
a church was built for them."[33]

It became obvious that the struggling settlers of the *villa* were not
able to raise the funds needed to complete the church. It became equally
evident that repeated appeals to the viceroy and the bishop of Guadalajara were to no avail.[34] Eight years after laying the cornerstone, the *cabildo* learned that the king, as early as April, 1740, had ordered that
twelve thousand pesos be taken from the royal treasury to aid the settlers of the Villa de San Fernando in the construction of the church
but that the viceroy had suspended the order on receipt of misrepre-
sented facts.[35] The news of the forthcoming twelve thousand pesos caused
considerable elation among the citizens of the *villa,* especially since there
had been no hope of getting aid from church authorities, despite the
bishop's promise to use his best efforts to assist.[36]

Taking steps of its own to see that the king's donation for their church
reached San Antonio, the town council sent Vicente Alvarez Travieso,

as accredited representative of the Villa de San Fernando, to Mexico City in 1748 to demand fulfillment of the royal order of 1740.[37] His role was in complete accordance with that of a *procurador,* namely, an attorney authorized to petition the king and Council of the Indies or the viceroy for the correction of grievances or to request grants and favors. For many decades the municipalities in the Spanish colonies had selected *procuradores* to act as their spokesmen and representatives before the crown or the viceroy. These municipal attorneys were occasionally elected by the citizens, although this was not in keeping with the Laws of the Indies. Apparently, the *cabildo* of the *villa* appointed Alvarez Travieso, since this was what the *Recopilación* required.[38]

Alvarez Travieso proved to be an efficient *procurador,* for the viceroy granted twelve thousand pesos to the *villa.*[39] Once the necessary security measures were taken, the money was placed in the hands of Alvarez Travieso and work on the church started again. "With sufficient funds available, the . . . construction . . . must have been carried out more rapidly and the church dedicated two or three years later," although it has been affirmed that the new building was completed as early as 1749.[40] Today, San Antonio's historic San Fernando Cathedral is located on the site of the first parish church in Texas and symbolizes the labor of the early town settlers who established it well over two centuries ago.

The task of constructing public buildings had only started with San Fernando Church. As early as 1749, the municipal government had legislated that tax monies derived from public lands were to be used for the construction of a town hall, courthouse, and city jail.[41] The need for public facilities was further accentuated when the town had increased to fifty-nine stone houses and about seventy-nine homes "of wood of moderate structure."[42] Moreover, San Antonio de Béjar, following transfer of the seat of government from East Texas in 1772, became the capital of the province and the governor's residence. His home initially was built on the east side of Military Plaza. The need for a town courthouse was now doubly important, since it was to meet the needs of both the municipal magistrates and the governor, who was the chief justice of Spanish Texas.

By the last quarter of the eighteenth century San Antonio showed signs of moderate growth. A fairly large settlement of families, termed *agregados,* had developed adjacent to Misión San Antonio de Valero. The settlers were an aggregate of presidial soldiers intermarried with Christian Indians from the mission center, and other families who had settled in San Antonio from East Texas.⁴³ Situated across the San Antonio River southeast from the San Fernando municipality, this settlement formed the town's first suburb and became known as "Villita, meaning little town, [it] was settled by some of the soldiers who came with the . . . army and . . . had intermarried with Indians. . . . The west side . . . was supposed to be residence of the first families [the Isleños] . . . and the descendants of Indians and Spanish soldiers settled on the east side of the river."⁴⁴

Over the centuries, San Antonio's original town site has been modernized but, interestingly enough, La Villita has been preserved and is considered one of the tourist attractions of downtown San Antonio. A feature that attracted settlers to San Antonio was its very scenic site. Even Zebulon M. Pike, the uninvited explorer of the New Mexico and Texas provinces, commented, as he passed through San Antonio in 1807, that "the town is laid out on a very grand plan and . . . one of the most agreeable places that we met in the provinces."⁴⁵

Social Amenities in the Borderlands

Royal influence on the Borderlands extended far beyond military considerations. The Spanish crown effectively spread the social and religious patterns of the people within the empire, including those of frontier settlers, by inaugurating celebrations or special periods of mourning. For example, when King Philip V died, a royal decree that reached the viceroy of New Spain on July 31, 1746, proclaimed a period of mourning throughout the kingdom.⁴⁶ The viceroy, Don Juan Francisco de Güemes y Horcasitas, announced the monarch's death in conformity with the *cédula* and "gave orders for the execution in this capital of the publications, obsequies, funeral rites, mourning, and other demonstrations deemed appropriate for the occasion."⁴⁷

The same proclamation disclosed the order for a period of mourning in Texas. Thus, it was not long before news of the monarch's death reached the colonial institutions in Texas. According to the royal decree, the king's death was to be proclaimed in the following manner: "The governor shall go with the notary, the constable, and the officials on horseback with kettledrums and bugles draped in mourning and playing softly and shall hold demonstrations customary to royal persons." Church bells were to toll at the time of the proclamation "in order that it may be effected with the greatest pomp and solemnity." The inhabitants of the province were to mourn in a manner determined by rank and land ownership. Property owners were to wear black "for a period of six months under the penalty of fifty pesos for Spaniards and of twenty-five pesos for the rest." Because of their poverty, Indian vassals were "excused and exempt from incurring the said penalties." They were not compelled to mourn, although "they may do so voluntarily." Those in religious life were also affected by the decree, since they were "charged to assist with prayers and supplications for the soul of Our King."[48]

Francisco García Larios, governor of Texas, made the proclamation to all settlements on May 22, 1747, ordering that people "proceed with the publication of all its contents and that it be observed, obeyed, and executed exactly as provided."[49] Moreover, the viceroy's decree included an order for a report on the period and ceremonies of mourning carried out in each settlement in the province.

The *cabildo* of the Villa de San Fernando gave a vivid account of the observances commemorating the death of Philip V. San Antonio published the appropriate *autos* obliging all residents to mourn, notwithstanding status. The ceremonies in San Antonio were the most impressive in the province, since they included the participation of members of the municipality, mission, and presidio. "For this purpose, two councilmen were appointed to go to the missions, to invite, in the name of His Lordship, the . . . Father President and the other priests." They were to join "the Cabildo . . . , the entire population, the captain, and the company of this royal presidio in a general expression of grief and sorrow befitting the exceedingly great loss of our Catholic King."[50]

The death of Philip V was significant to the *hidalgos* of the *villa*, because the king had borne the travel expenses to their new homeland and provided them with land, seeds, tools, and livestock with which to start anew. The deceased monarch had honored them *ad perpetuum* with titles of nobility and had covered much of the cost for their church. The benevolent, albeit paternalistic, Philip V had played a very important role in their lives, and his demise was a personal loss. Mourning and funeral services were held also at Los Adaes, according to the governor who at that time was in charge of this East Texas presidio.[51] A report arriving from Captain Joaquín de Orobio y Bázterra indicated that funeral rites for the deceased monarch were held at Misión del Espíritu Santo de Zúñiga and the presidio de Nuestra Señora de Loreto de la Bahía.[52]

Earlier in the year, there had been glad tidings, in contrast to the present sorrow, from the royal court with the proclamation, *"Habemus regem!"* ("We have a king!"). Reflections of the "prestige of the Sun King and the glitter of Versailles" became evident as the new Spanish Bourbon ascended the throne. The *cédula* of January 27, 1747, proclaimed a time for festivities in honor of the new monarch, Ferdinand VI.[53] With the joy of "long live the king!" the citizens of the empire professed their new loyalty. In larger Spanish-American colonial settlements civil and religious celebrations appealed strongly to all classes, the festivities often lasting weeks at a time. The observance of fiestas, while less elaborate in frontier towns, were welcomed and often lightened the landscape, which tended to be harsh and monotonous. Essentially, merrymaking and entertainment provided a pleasant contrast to the austere conditions of the frontier.

In keeping with the patriotic spirit of the royal decree, the *cabildo* authorities sponsored a week of festivities, which contributed gaiety and excitement to the lives of the people in San Antonio. The celebrations in honor of Ferdinand VI began with all the settlers and soldiers displaying festival lights in their homes and in the barracks for three nights. The unfurling of the royal banner followed, a ceremony that played a very prominent part in the life of the king's loyal subjects. To enhance royal prestige, the Bourbon kings encouraged this practice, rooted deeply in Hapsburg tradition. The crown officials and the town magistrates regarded this flag ritual declaring the loyalty of the municipality to the monarch as a significant event, reserved for the annual ceremony and the special ceremonies surrounding the death of a king and the accession of his successor. The festivities began at eight in the morning as the governor and the *cabildo* met "in a house commonly called the palace" and proceeded with a military escort and all the citizens of the municipality to the house of the *alférez*, the royal standard bearer, to have the flag brought to the palace. The office of *alférez* was coveted by socially ambitious citizens. At all public fiestas and ceremonies, the royal standard bearer occupied a prominent place and commanded the envy of his fellow councillors and the admiration of the populace. The royal banner was escorted "with the greatest rejoicing imaginable" amid the plaudits of the masses, and with an honor guard the *alférez*, "astride a spirited charger, bore aloft the royal ensign symbol of the allegiance" due to the Bourbon monarch, and proceeded to the place of celebrations.

When the standard arrived, the governor commanded the notary to read the royal *cédula* in a loud voice that all could hear. When the reading was completed, with much cheering and shouting, accompanied by volleys of artillery and musketry, everyone cried, "Long Live our King!" After the crowd quieted down, the governor exhorted the people, reminding them with pleasing words, of the distinction incumbent on the province to obey their King and Lord; and saying that, since they had always manifested their great loyalty, he hoped that on this occasion they would do their duty as usual. When he had finished, the *alférez* took the standard and performed ceremonies requisite on such an occasion. After this had taken place with much gaiety and rejoicing, the standard was set up and two councilmen and two citizens of the municipality remained guarding it.[54]

"In the afternoon a colorful procession escorted the king's banner to the church, where the priest blessed it. A castle "with four stories and elaborately adorned had been set up" in the center of the plaza and became the place for the forthcoming festivities once the royal ensign was brought and placed there again "with great rejoicing and shouting" of "Long Live the King our Lord." The subjects of Ferdinand VI proceeded to celebrate with an entire week of festivity. On January 28 for example, the populace attended a Thanksgiving mass and afterward enjoyed a medieval pageant that recalled the *moros y christianos* during the Reconquest of Spain. Attired as Castilian knights and Moorish warriors, presidial troops engaged in forays to the delight of the townspeople and their neighbors. On the next four days, January 29 to February 1, there followed an inexhaustible interest in the *corridas*. Bullfights had always been the most popular form of entertainment for citizens of Hispanic municipalities. In colonial times important holidays were celebrated with the *corridas*. The delight that the citizens of the *villa* and their neighbors displayed in attending the bullfights was in keeping with Spain's oldest entertainment tradition.

On February second, another episode recalling the Christian Reconquest unfolded, with "the entire day . . . devoted to fights and skirmishes." On the third, there were more *corridas*. The finale came on the next day, with the soldiers again playing the roles of Christians and the Moors engaged in mock battle, and the actors depicting the Moors ending up as prisoners. "At its conclusion, a magnificent procession carrying the patron saint of the *villa* . . . was formed in the plaza, and marched to the Church, where a Thanksgiving mass was chanted and the statue of San Fernando left in his church."[55]

The festivities ended with a truly Hispanic *comedia*. Since the baroque period, drama had flourished in Spain. Although the title of the dramatic art performed at the *villa* is undisclosed, it is significant to note that the *comedia*, a product of Spain's Golden Age, was universally appreciated in Hispanic America and had even reached a Borderlands municipality.[56]

While fiestas have taken on new features in America over the centuries, their Spanish origins have remained. The development of municipal life and practices in Hispanic Texas is closely linked to the Spanish American empire under the Hapsburg dynasty and the subsequent Bourbon epoch. The ties between Spain and its colonies were so intimate during the eighteenth century that the Borderlands frontier should be studied in the light of its relationship to the Bourbon reforms. In an age when municipal functions were more highly prized, the frontier *cabildo* held on to its rustic democratic traditions and represented the continuum of the independent spirit of the medieval Castilian *ciudad* and, simultaneously, a practical, covert concession by Bourbon authoritarianism to a basic aspiration for local autonomy.

Hemmed in by the adverse circumstances of the frontier, the *cabildo* of the small Villa de San Fernando, although imperfect and oligarchical, kept alive the spirit of individual freedom in Texas and did not cease to enjoy a limited measure of autonomous government.

8

The *Cabildo*
GUARDIAN OF JUSTICE AND SOCIAL ORDER
IN THE BORDERLANDS

Municipal Government in New Mexico

The subject of New Mexico's local government has challenged scholars in view of the slow development of the province during its first half century and because of the sketchy nature of available documentation. Prior to the Pueblo Rebellion of 1680, the *cabildo* of Santa Fe presented the only organized municipal government in New Mexico, as the old San Gabriel settlement was totally abandoned. A relatively simple form of town government had prevailed among the twenty-five hundred Spanish and mestizo settlers in New Mexico. Many of them maintained homes outside the town limits of Santa Fe because of customs peculiar to their hacienda life-style. Even so, the New Mexican settlers, town dwellers by tradition, generally rallied around the Santa Fe *cabildo*. The municipal government served as a power base and gave the civil community the political leverage it required in dealing with other Spanish institutions on the frontier, notably the military governor and the church.

The *cabildo* of the capital was established in keeping with viceregal instructions to Pedro de Peralta, who in 1609 was directed to create a town government "in which he [Peralta] shall allow the citizens to elect four councilmen and two ordinary *alcaldes* each year who shall try civil and criminal cases which may occur in said . . . *villa* and within five leagues around it."[1] Thus, in the provincial capital a regular *cabildo* had existed from the earliest days. The town council consisted of four *regidores,* or councilmen, who were elected annually by the citizens of the *villa*. This council selected two *alcaldes ordinarios,* or municipal magistrates, a procedure the Villa de San Fernando was to follow in Texas about a century later. In addition, the councilmen selected one citizen to serve as *alguacil,* or town constable, a second as *escribano,* or city clerk, and a third as *alférez real,* or royal standard-bearer. A list of members on the Santa Fe municipal council was then sent to the governor of the province for his approval. By the middle of the eighteenth century, the Laredo municipality and the Villa de San Fernando also were petitioning their respective governors for confirmation of newly elected municipal officials.

The *cabildo* of Santa Fe not only administered the internal affairs of the *villa* and its environs within a radius of approximately five leagues but also served as spokesman for all citizens of the province in representations to the governor, the clergy, and even the king's viceroy in Mexico City. The role of the town council in New Mexico's politics was, therefore, a broad and impressive one. As early as the first half of the seventeenth century, the *cabildo* had the special function of serving as an advisory board to the governor of the province,[2] a role not unlike that of Mexico City's *audiencia,* or tribunal of justice, in its relations with the viceroy. This function was unique to the *cabildo* of Santa Fe, however; other town councils in the northernmost provinces of the Borderlands did not seem to deal with their respective governors in the same way. But with this distinct capacity to influence the governor and, as a consequence, the general policies within New Mexico, there arose certain corresponding political hazards for the town council:

> The Santa Fe cabildo . . . exercised a kind of general authority over the entire New Mexican province in the seventeenth and early eighteenth century. Ths wide latitude of its powers and the independent spirit of its members brought the municipal council into frequent conflict with the governor. . . . Friction between the provincial and municipal authorities in the early 1700's was intensified when members of the cabildo joined with factions hostile to the incumbent governors.[3]

Before the destruction of the New Mexican province in 1680 by rebellious Pueblo Indians, a comparatively uncomplicated system of government existed. *Alcaldes mayores* were appointed by the governor to administer different sectors of the province. Only the capital, Santa Fe, and its municipal lands were separate from the jurisdictional powers of these district magistrates. The members of the *cabildo* generally supported policies that were in the best interests of the Spanish and mestizo civil community. In doing so, Santa Fe demonstrated a municipal independence that in some cases placed the civilians in the camp of the incumbent governor while at other times the town joined with the clergy against the governor and his presidial garrisons. This form of municipal independence in promoting what was believed to be the best interests of the civil community actually was in conformity with the citizens' *instrumento de fundación,* or town charter, granted to them by the crown. Even though the municipal corporation of Santa Fe was created by laws from the king, the decisions made by the town council often conflicted with those of the mission establishment, particularly the policies of the incumbent governor. These cases often provoked his anger and compelled him to judge the *cabildo* unfit to exercise political power in the province. Contempt for the Santa Fe town council is reflected in a statement attributed to former Governor López de Mendizábal in 1661 wherein "he considered the cabildo, his mule, and his negress all one."[4]

Undaunted by words, the city fathers continued to pursue municipal autonomy, a process usually joining the members of the *cabildo* with factions hostile to incumbent governors. This demonstration of civil independence proved to be too much during the administration of Governor Juan Ignacio Flores Mogollón, in the first quarter of the eighteenth century. Dark days fell on the town government of Santa Fe. The governor ordered the *cabildo* abolished and the functions normally reserved to municipal officials delegated to an *alcalde mayor,* one of the district magistrates in the province. For about two years, from 1715 to 1716, the citizens persistently clamored for recognition of civil rights lawfully based on their *instrumento de fundación,* compelling Governor Félix Martínez de Torrelaguna eventually to reinstate the members of the Santa Fe *cabildo.*[5]

The successors of the governor, Antonio Valverde y Cossío and Juan Domingo de Bustamante, were not to be so easily persuaded, however. The former was heavily involved in 1720 with coping with raiding Indians from the plains and with threatening French penetrations into New Mexico.[6] Understandably enough, the embattled governor was in no mood to reason with what he considered a recalcitrant town government. Following the precedent of Flores Mogollón, he designated a trustworthy associate to serve as *alcalde mayor* of the municipal district and to conduct the regular business of the *cabildo.* When the governor's successor, Juan Domingo de Bustamante, failed to reestablish the municipal government of Santa Fe, the citizens directed their complaints to the viceroy and claimed that the new governor had made himself absolute master of New Mexico.[7] In the eyes of the viceroy, this allegation was not to be taken lightly. Municipal *fueros* granted by the crown had been by tradition inviolable, but, more important, total usurpation of power in any province was an affront to the king's personal representative in New Spain.

In 1726, the viceroy ordered the governor to reinstate the *cabildo* of Santa Fe and to hold elections for *alcaldes ordinarios*. The tribulations of the town council resulting from decisions made by strong-minded governors led to a demise in its importance, though, and in the years that followed, the town council no longer exerted the influence it had during the seventeenth century. In the Spanish Archives, reference is hardly made to town magistrates of New Mexico at Santa Fe, the *alcalde mayor* assuming almost complete control over the municipal district. The retrogressive tendency of municipal administration in New Mexico has been attributed to an apparent decadence of municipalities in New Spain just before the Bourbon reforms.[8] Conditions peculiar to this northernmost province of the Borderlands would seem to be a more valid reason.

From the advent of the seventeenth century, the chief problem in New Mexico was the restive Indians. The Spaniards had succeeded in neutralizing the Pueblo Indians through use of alliances and the missionary formula, despite periodic flare-ups. However, in the eighteenth century, the Spaniards in New Mexico encountered Indian problems of far larger dimensions when they faced the forceful nomadic Indians of the Great Plains, who had no intention of altering their independent way of life nor their religious practices. The missionary agency of the Spanish imperial government was rejected not only by the Plains Indians, particularly the Comanche nations, but also by Apache nations residing in New Mexico, namely, the Jicarilla and the Cuartelejo. To complicate matters for the embattled governors of New Mexico, Indian resistance was assisted and encouraged by newcomers on the fringe of the Borderlands, the French, after their occupation of the middle Mississippi Valley in 1699.[9]

By the second half of the eighteenth century, conditions for restoring town *cabildos* in New Mexico became more promising. Even though Indian hostility, which had helped give rise to a kind of martial law, did not diminish, two events seem to have helped the regrowth of municipal government. In 1762, France ceded all Louisiana territory west of the Mississippi River to the Spanish crown, thus eliminating French pressure on New Mexico. More important, when José de Gálvez became *visitador general* in 1767, the Bourbon reform movement began to be felt in New Spain, which led to a reinvigoration of municipalities. In New Mexico the introduction of municipal reform became apparent on October 7, 1789, when Pedro de Nava, the commandant general of the Provincias Internas in the west, ordered Fernando de la Concha, the governor of the province, to name *alcaldes ordinarios* for the Villa de Santa Fe and for other communities that warranted civil governments.[10] This was to be done in accordance with the new reform regulations, particularly Article 11 of the important Order of Intendants of 1786.[11] This law, however, gave the governor considerable discretionary power. In a town such as Santa Fe, where for years there had been no regular town council to elect the *alcaldes ordinarios,* the political or military governor was given authority by Article 11 to appoint the municipal magistrates, a function that he felt justified in performing.

No historian has declared that the Santa Fe *cabildo* passed out of existence during the mid-eighteenth century; however, scholars are inclined to agree that municipal government in the capital had reached its nadir, despite its strong *cabildo* tradition. With the turn of the century, the Liberal Reform movement, which climaxed with the Constitution of 1812, provided new regulations for the organization of municipal government. The citizens of Santa Fe, restive at having an *alcalde mayor* arbitrarily appointed over the town district by the governor, were again allowed to elect their own *alcaldes ordinarios* in 1803.[12] Partial restoration of municipal government resulted as the influence of the governor was curtailed. *Alcaldes ordinarios* once more took charge of the internal affairs of their civil community during the Liberal Reform movement. More precisely, the town magistrates resumed their traditional duties of presiding at town meetings, legislating, and sitting as judges in civil and criminal cases within their municipal jurisdiction.

MUNICIPAL COURTS ON THE FRONTIER

A significant function in municipal administration that the *cabildo* brought to the Borderlands and continued to exercise throughout the eighteenth century was the adjudication of legal disputes, both civil and criminal, within its jurisdiction. The *alcaldes ordinarios* also exercised judicial powers of the first instance in their town communities.[13] In Santa Fe, particularly in the nineteenth century, these civil magistrates were called *alcalde de primer voto* and *alcalde de segundo voto.* The former was the senior magistrate and ordinarily presided over the meeting of the municipal government and issued ordinances for the good of the community. The *alcalde de segundo voto* was the junior *alcalde* who, in large measure, restricted his activities to judicial matters.[14] Both *alcaldes* were kept busy making decisions and settling disputes relative to the affairs of town communities. In Texas, starting with the founding of the Villa de San Fernando in 1731, the two civil magistrates generally were called *alcaldes ordinarios,* although the first *alcalde* emerged as principal legislator and town judge.[15] By the middle of the eighteenth century, the term "*alcalde teniente*" was introduced into municipal documents at the Villa de Laredo.[16] An *alcalde teniente* was a magistrate who supervised community affairs in lieu of an *alcalde ordinario.* He was appointed by the governor as chief civil magistrate. The *alcalde teniente* usually was a citizen of the *villa* and his appointment was temporary, *alcaldes ordinarios* approved by the governor being the custom in the Laredo community. The *alcaldes ordinarios* were civil magistrates who exercised judicial powers of the first instance and, as municipal judges, assumed a distinctive role within the *cabildo*'s structure.

Hapsburg respect for the judiciary nature of this office precluded its disposal through sale,[17] and, as the Bourbon era unfolded, the *cabildo* as a whole retained the right to elect yearly two *alcaldes ordinarios.*[18] The framers of Spanish law attempted to guarantee justice on the level of the first instance in towns of the Indies by keeping the office of judicial magistrate apart from economic consideration. With the exception of the right to sell products harvested from his own lands at currently stipulated prices, the *alcalde ordinario* was not to engage in business and commerce.

In *cabildos* of large municipalities, the magistrate held court daily except Sunday, although litigants did not always appear, thus allowing quick adjournment. In frontier town councils the judges convened the court whenever warranted, since, in most cases, the *alcaldes* were busy working their farms and ranches. The law required that justice be administered in the *cabildo* house, popularly known as the *palacio municipal.*[19] Large municipalities often violated this requirement and frontier *cabildos* entirely overlooked it for the simple reason that many of them had no *palacio municipal.*[20] Whenever the *alcalde ordinario* presided at court he had in his possession the *vara,* or staff with a cross on the upper end, which was the Spanish symbol of judicial authority he received when he entered office.[21]

During court sessions, the *alcalde* spent most of his time settling cases involving infractions of city ordinances or legal disputes.[22] In particularly involved cases, the *alcalde ordinario,* especially when his own legal training was not extensive, received legal assistance from the *letrados en leyes,* or lawyers employed by almost every *cabildo.*[23]

A laudable custom established by many *cabildos* during the Hapsburg period was the appointment of a public attorney, generally known as *procurador general,* employed at city expense to defend citizens unable to pay legal fees.[24] Most citizens, therefore, whether rich or poor, were represented fairly well in courts of the first instance. New Mexico, however, had an office in the province that resembled, in some measure, the *procurador general*: the *juez comisionado* or *juez delegado,* actually a public attorney appointed by the governor to examine evidence in cases pending before the courts.[25] In Texas the *procurador general* was involved in municipal courts in cases involving citizens, soldiers, and priests alike. On June 25, 1736, Joseph de la Garza and Juan Resio de León used a power of attorney to collect payment due them from the salary assigned to the priest of the Presidio of San Antonio and the Villa de San Fernando.[26] A distinguished military officer, Joseph de Urrutia, appeared before the municipal court on August 23, 1737, and sought power of attorney to represent himself before the law to "recover, receive, demand, and collect, judicially or extrajudicially, from any and all persons any and all such amounts as they may owe me now or in the future, in currency, gold, silver, grain, . . . fruit, . . . deeds, bonds, charge accounts, bills of lading, memorandums, draft, invoices, commissions, or in any other form."[27] Soldiers often had to use a power of attorney to seek back pay and equipment. On January 24, 1738, for example, soldiers hired a *procurador* to collect "the salary they had earned for the part of two-thirds of the past year."[28]

All *procuradores* had to come before Francisco Joseph de Arocha, secretary of the town council and notary public, to have their papers for power of attorney certified. After this procedure, they were permitted to promote the interests of their clients. The parish priest did not always obtain his salary on time and consequently felt it necessary to go before the secular court to seek justice. Thus, on March 22, 1738, he granted power of attorney for the collection of his salary for 1737–1738.[29] On May 4, 1743, Ygnacio de la Garza Falcón, "a resident but not an original settler of this Villa de San Fernando," granted power of attorney to Juan Antonio de Bustillo y Sevallos to represent him in pending and future lawsuits.[30] Rosa Flores de Valdez protected her rights before the court by granting power of attorney to Juan de Angulo, authorizing him to represent her "in all pending and future claims, litigations, and business."[31]

As the court of the first instance, the *cabildo*'s position as a judicial body remained unquestioned until the middle of the eighteenth century, when Philip V decreed that appeals from the *alcalde*'s decision should proceeds to the governor, *corregidor*, or *audiencia*.[32] With the Bourbon reforms, the intendants abolished the offices of *corregidor* and *alcalde mayor*. Moreover, they created a new office, *alcaldes ordinarios*, endowed with power to collect tribute and to administer justice.[33] These subdelegates, who operated mostly in larger municipalities, hardly, if ever, worked in frontier towns. The Bourbon kings suppressed the old officials and directed the intendants to serve as chief justice of their provinces, but not to interfere with the *alcaldes ordinarios*, who in towns remained judges of the first instance.[34]

Regrettably, the limited resurgence of judicial procedure on the local level under the Spanish Bourbons turned out to be of little use to the Villa de San Fernando. Without resources, the tiny municipality lacked wealthy and learned *alcaldes* with time to pursue judicial responsibilities. Besides this, the *villa* did not at first have a *palacio municipal* in which to hold court. As a consequence, the governor of the province assumed the responsibility of administering justice both to the province and, in collaboration with *cabildo* authorities, to municipalities.[35]

In view of this, it may be valid, since the governor or an *alcalde mayor* conducted most litigations in the court of the second instance, to question the existence of the municipal court of the first instance. Second, what was the *cabildo*'s claim to judicial power, if there was no court before which to bring the majority of legal disputes arising in the municipality? Finally, whence the idea that the *cabildo* of the Borderlands was a bastion of law and judicial procedure?

The *cabildo* rested its claim as guardian of Spanish law and equity on its *fueros*, the legislative and judicial privileges vested in Castilian municipalities by the earliest Christian monarchs.[36] No other colonial institution measured up in the same way. The missions, although protected by the Laws of the Indies, were ephemeral by nature.[37] The presidial garrisons, like wars and the threat of war, came and went. Often misunderstood by mission agencies and overshadowed by military hegemony, the *cabildo*s of the Borderlands stood the test of time during the eighteenth century. Isolated pockets of civil government on the vast northern frontier yet deeply rooted in Castilian municipal history, the town councils on the Borderlands doggedly clung to their role as guardians of individual liberty and justice.

Most frontier municipalities had no *cabildo* courts in which to handle legal proceedings. However, this lack did not invalidate their right to their own tribunals of justice. The Ordenanzas found in Castilian municipal history and the Laws of the Indies granted a *de jure* right to the *cabildo* to serve as a bastion for law and judicial procedure.[38] At the Villa de San Fernando the *de facto* situation accounting for the court of the first instance's functioning in certain cases under the governor at the presidio of San Antonio reflects the harsh frontier circumstances, which prevented the municipality from having a strong court of its own. Nonetheless, royal decrees and the Laws of the Indies had warned higher levels of government for years that the citizen's right to justice began with the *alcalde ordinario* and the tribunals of the local *cabildo*.[39] Moreover, the town council did not forfeit all its judiciary powers to the court of the second instance. The *alcaldes ordinarios* continued to issue ordinances for the good of the *villa*. These municipal laws included punitive measures that indicated the legislators' judiciary powers.[40] For the most part the *cabildo* relegated to the court of the second instance only those judiciary powers that it was unable to put into effect adequately because of its meager resources.

If the *cabildo* at the Villa de San Fernando depended on the governor's court for judicial assistance, it also supported it. Besides an awareness that judiciary power was primarily vested in the municipal courts, the governor also knew that the services of the notary public and secretary of the municipal council were needed in his court, since he had "no royal notary public."[41] In his judicial relations with the citizenry, the governor also utilized the municipal office of *alguacil mayor*. In some cases, the *alguacil mayor*, or town constable, issued a summons to court,[42] in others, he demanded payment on claims brought before the court,[43] and in still others he executed warrants for arrest.[44]

The office of *escribano* was necessary for all judicial functions.[45] The governor, *alcalde mayor*, and *corregidor* could not hold court without an *escribano* to record the proceedings.[46] Required by law to demonstrate the utmost integrity in the line of duty, the *escribano* had the added responsibility of maintaining the records on municipal titles and finances.[47]

More the consequence of Latin temperament than of the peculiarities of the Spanish town legal system,[48] judicial procedure in Spanish courts often produced heated arguments, especially between defense attorneys and the *alguacil mayor* or other arresting officers, who usually served as chief witness and prosecutor. Often, violent disputes took place in and out of the judicial court where the citizens of the Villa de San Fernando sought justice. For example, charging violence before the court, Juan Leal Góraz alleged that Patricio Rodríguez Galano had pulled a knife on him, threatened him with a carbine, and insulted his Hispanic lineage by calling him a "*morisco.*"[49] Manuel de Sandoval, governor of the province, alarmed by the disrespect shown to Leal Góraz, senior councilman of the municipality, immediately conferred with the *alcalde* of the *villa,* Manuel de Nis, about the matter. Both magistrates concluded that the case was criminal in essence, and the *alcalde* quickly carried out the governor's request for the arrest of the impetuous Rodríguez. Unable to justify such misconduct before the court, the defendant quickly ended "a prisoner in the guardroom."[50] However, a week later, Doña María Pérez Cabrera, widow of Salvador Rodríguez, appeared before the governor to plead her son's case "in the best manner and form according to law and . . . her . . . own rights."[51] By then, tempers had cooled and the governor, touched by pity for "a helpless widow" whose "crop . . . was . . . liable to total loss" without her son to harvest it, called for leniency by allowing Patricio Rodríguez to be released under bond. The *alcalde,* moved by the widow's plight, also helped by posting bond and assuming responsibility for the defendant.[52] Interestingly enough, the Spanish court, established for law and order in the province, was alive with human emotion.

COURT CASES IN TEXAS

The dedication of the Hispanic mind to due process of law and the administration of justice in Texas clearly demonstrated itself during the eighteenth century. More specifically, on April 11, 1736, Juan de Barro of Saltillo appeared before the governor's court in San Antonio with power of attorney from Francisco Fernández de Rumayor, a prominent citizen in Zacatecas and a recognized merchant in Saltillo. Barro informed the governor of a promissory note indicating that three citizens of his jurisdiction were debtors of Fernández, who had supplied them with provisions and financial assistance three years previously. Barro alleged that

Doña María Pérez Cabrera, a hardy San Antonio woman left with the care of her family and farmlands after the death of her husband, Salvador Rodríguez in 1734. Drawing by J. Cisneros, *Riders across the Centuries* (1980), by permission of Texas Western Press of the University of Texas, El Paso.

two citizens from the *villa* were in arrears, namely, Juan Curbelo, whose debt was 93 pesos, and Marthin [*sic*] Lorenzo de Armas, with a debt of 215 pesos. Each, besides assuming a personal debt, had countersigned for the other.[53] Joseph Antonio Rodríguez, a resident of the presidio, was the third debtor. Apparently, Fernández had accepted a 400-peso draft from Joseph de Urrutia and drawn on Juan Angulo for Rodríguez. According to the plaintiff's attorney, Rodríguez was responsible for the draft, since it was drawn for him. Barro placed his client's case before the court: "that your Lordship will be pleased for the sake of justice to order the aforementioned debtors to appear before your Lordship, acknowledge said instruments and under oath duly made in conformity with the law declare whether they owe the sum set forth therein and [whether] they are to be paid to my party."[54] Next, Barro stated how he hoped justice would be administered, to wit, that the principal cost occasioned from the maturity of the loan be paid; that the interest (*lucrocesante*) be charged; and that damages caused by nonpayment (*daño emergente*) be included.[55]

On April 11, 1736, Governor Sandoval issued a summons ordering the defendants to appear before the court.[56] On the same day, Curbelo and Armas presented themselves. The former acknowledged the "fact that ninety-three pesos were owed as a balance on a three hundred peso and four reales" loan made on October 4, 1733, while the latter admitted to "the unquestioned fact that he owed two hundred and fifteen pesos as balance on a three hundred and fifteen peso loan made on October 4, 1733."[57] The following day Rodríguez appeared in court and "acknowledged the draft for four hundred pesos for which he was being held responsible."[58]

The submissive posture of the defendants underscored the fact that statements of debt and credit were entered in the cash books of the Villa de San Fernando. These municipal records left little room for debate, at least to the mind of the governor, who was presented with the accounts.[59] Eight days later, Sandoval, after studying the case, commanded Vicente Alvarez Travieso, the *alguacil mayor*, to notify the three defendants "to pay immediately Juan del Barro the principal sums of money and the costs owed by each."[60] Next, the governor directed the municipal constable that in the event of default, the force of the law was to be applied. First, he was to take possession of the property, movable and immovable, of the defendants and to place it under custody. Next, the *alguacil mayor* was to inform the defendants to "appear within thirty days to make a declaration regarding the justice thereof." Finally, if he did not find property of sufficient value, the constable was to imprison the defendants in the guardhouse of the presidio.[61]

The governor quickly convinced the defendants that they needed to take immediate action toward the payment of their debts. On the same day, Curbelo, whose balance on the loan was the smallest, appeared in court to present a draft of 112 pesos. The plaintiff's attorney accepted the draft as payment on the principal of 93 pesos and on the cost of the loan, 19 pesos. Curbelo had paid his debt to the satisfaction of the court and in keeping with the demands of the litigant from Saltillo.[62]

Armas, however, was not so fortunate. When the constable appeared at the defendant's home, he was unable to pay the debt. Alvarez Travieso, in accordance with the governor's orders, took possession of the defendant's property by preparing an inventory before three witnesses, *testigos de asistencia*. The list of Armas' possessions suggests something about the life and social history of the early Spanish settlers:

Eight cows that bear calves
Six yearlings
One ox and one bull
One work horse [*cabayo de entrega*]
One gentle mare
One gentle saddle mule
One white pine chest about one and one-half varas long, with a lock, key, and lock bolt
One chest made in Periban [*peribana*] one vara long, with its lock, key, and lock bolt
Two more chests made in Periban, about three *quartas* long, with their keys, locks, bolts, and having one small *manto* inside
One used dress skirt [*basquina*] of black ribbed silk, with silver galloon around the bottom
One coat [*casaca*] of ribbed silk of the aforementioned color, adapted to women's wear
Several used olive-colored pekin [*piquín*] underskirts
One used man's coat, military style, made of *caro de oro* [gold ornamentation] and lined with *coleta* [cloth made of hemp]
One used satin jacket [*chupa*] lined with ribbed silk
Several [pairs of] short shag breeches with silver buttons, cut English style
Four used Leonese bedsheets
Two used wool mattresses covered with *contense* [burlap]
One ordinary used bedspread
One ordinary cowboy saddle with its ironwork [*erage*] and stirrup [*estribera*]
One ordinary, short firelock with its case made in San Miguel [*sanmigeleña*] on which a *tinbre* [probably *timbre*, or emblem] is embroidered with *agave* [century plant] thread
Several used saddle pads [*coginillos*]
One used *axadón* [*sadón*; hoe]

One used rega [*reja*, plowshare]
One small used iron comal
One used *metate* with pestle
One used medium-sized *caso* [possibly a copper saucepan with iron handle]
One used copper *olla* [kettle]
One hundred pesos for the stone having that value [which is] intended for building to the house a room seven varas long
Eight small rectangular pieces of Michoacán about three *tersias* long[63]

Recalling that the principal on Don Marthin's loan was 215 pesos, one would estimate the value of the entire inventory to be enough to pay the debt. In fact, with 100 pesos deducted for the stone set aside for building purposes, the defendant's livestock easily should have covered the remainder. However, even by including all household furnishings and family wardrobe, the total was not met, so either money was hard to come by on the frontier or the value of the peso ran high in the eighteenth century.

The municipal constable informed Armas that since his goods did not cover the loan he was to go to prison in the guardhouse of the presidio. Manuel de Nis, bonded by the court, was made custodian of the attached goods.[64]

Alvarez Travieso proceeded to Rodríguez's home and ordered him to pay his debt as commanded by the governor. When the defendant was unable to meet the payment on the loan, the constable transferred his property to the claimant with a list of possessions made before three witnesses, as in the former case:

Fifteen gentle pack mules
Nine pack saddles
Six gentle bridle horses
One gentle, extra-good milk cow
Eight *petacas* [cases] of Huastecan [*guasteco*] *piloncillo* [a unit of brown sugar, probably candy], 160 *piloncillos* in each *petaca*
One parcel [*tersio*] of salt from Colima weighing six *arobas* [*arroba*; 25 pounds]
Twenty strings of Coahuila [*quaguileño*] *chile ancho*, each twelve and one-fourth *varas* long
Ten new mottled, tanned bison skins with hair left on
Thirty tanned deer hides with hair left on

Two chests made in Periban [*peribanas*] about five *quartas* in length, with their lock, keys, and lock bolts

One pine chest of the same size

One *vaquero* saddle [with] a *tinbre* of parchment [de *pergamo*] and having all the saddle straps [*ariseses*] and the stirrup, all used

Several saddle pads [*coginillos*] with the *tinbre* also used

One new case made in San Miguel [*sanmigeleña*] and embroidered with silk and *agave* thread

One ordinary firelock

One excellent new bridle with spurs [*espuelas*], reins, small chains, and handstalls

One *pollera* [hooped skirt] of black ribbed silk with a fine gold fringe two fingers [*dedos*] in width with sharp hooped petticoat around the bottom

One new *pollera* made of narrow ribbon [*melandre*] and trimmed around the bottom with silver Milan galloon [braid trim of worsted silk and rayon tinsel, or even of gold or silver] two fingers in width

One new *denge* [dress] trimmed with silk tissue [*tisu*], ribbon and faced around the bottom with thin cloth of tableland plateau

One long cloak *con sus puntas de sinco en corte* [possibly with its design of five stitches]

One yellow satin jacket [*chupa*] lined with Chinese silk and interlined with *mitán* [linen]

One used *tapapié* of pearl-colored ribbed silk, lined with linen and trimmed around the bottom with lace and embroidered ribbon [*listón*] [possibly a decorative blanket used to cover the feet during cool weather]

One fashionable, bright red *paño de reboso* [rebozo] made of narrow ribbon [*melandre*] and trimmed with silver fringe and galloon.

One used yellow *aqustador* [*ajustador*] made of gold and silver brocade [possibly a woman's petticoat, or a ring guard used to prevent large rings from slipping]

One used iron *comal* [flat dish used for cooking, especially tortillas]

One used medium-sized copper *caso* [or *vaso*, a tumbler or vase]

One used *metate* made in Puebla [*poblano*] with pestle

One used wool mattress covered with *cotense*

Two used bed sheets of *morlas* [loosely woven linen]

One new bedspread made in San Miguel [*sanmigileña*]

Two used wool pillows [*almuedas,* or *almohadas*] with pillow cases of Brittany cloth.

One broadsword [*espada ancha*] five *quartas* long with silver hilt, hook and scabbard [*contera*][65]

After placing Rodríguez in prison and assigning Mateo Carabajal [*sic*] as custodian of the attached goods, Alvarez Travieso went before the court to give an account of his actions.[66] On April 20, 1736, Armas appeared before the governor and appealed for release from confinement in order to find a way of repaying Fernández. Furthermore, he offered a bondsman, a *fiador a cárcel segura,* as security for his person.[67]

The court, aware of Don Marthin Lorenzo's need to find a way to pay the debt, informed the plaintiff's attorney of his petition and requested that Barro take the matter into consideration and forward his opinion to the governor as soon as possible.[68] On April 21, 1736, Barro communicated to the court that he favored the release of the prisoner. His response suggested justice tempered with civility: "I ask your Lordship kindly to command that the action requested by the petitioner be taken so that I may realize said principal sum, since [it] is in accordance with justice [and] since by such actions I shall receive kindness and mercy."[69] The cost, interest, and damages incurred by the debt, however, were part of the suit. Although he showed clemency, Barro made it clear that he expected all expenses to be covered along with the payment of the principal.

Apparently the presiding judge concurred with the recommendations of the plaintiff's attorney for, on the same day, the *alguacil mayor,* in compliance with court orders, issued a statement naming Antonio Rodríguez Maderos as bondsman for Armas. The municipal constable acquainted Rodríguez with his obligations as bondsman, namely, to return Armas to jail within thirty days or any time the order was given by a competent judge, or on days the defendant should have to appear in court.[70]

The court's prudent efforts to promote justice began to produce results. Barro and Curbelo reached a mutual settlement on April 23, 1736, and came before the governor and petitioned that the defendant's case be legally closed. Assured that justice was done, the presiding judge ordered that the papers declaring the case officially settled be drawn up. In the document both litigant and defendant stated that whereas Curbelo had delivered to Barro a draft of 112 pesos, which covered the debt of 93 pesos and the balance of 19 pesos for other costs in the case, the litigant considered the entire debt satisfied and paid.[71] In keeping with the legal nature of this document, the governor included the following stipulations: first, that henceforth both parties would have canceled any right or claim whatsoever that might appertain by reason of this case;

second, that in the event of fraud, the debtor was to remit payment and present it "as a pure and perfect donation *inter vivos*"; third, that both parties waived the laws of royal Ordenamiento de Alcalá de Henares;[72] fourth, that the failure to comply with the terms of the document made either party liable to a fine; and finally, that "they gave powers to His Majesty's justices and judges especially those of these provinces of Texas . . . [over] . . . themselves and their property . . . [waiving] . . . the law *si combenarit de yurisdicione omnium yudicum* and the *pragmatica* regarding *sumiciones.*"[73]

About a week later, Juan Antonio Rodríguez was able to work out a settlement with Fernandez's attorney. He and Juan Barro went before the court to petition the dismissal of the case.[74] Before the presiding judge had acted on the Rodríguez case, Don Marthin Lorenzo obtained the money to pay his debt in full. Thus, on May 8, 1736, Juan Barro once more appeared before the governor, this time accompanied by Armas, the third defendant, and requested dismissal of the final case.[75] As in Fernández versus Curbelo, the governor studied both cases and, convinced that justice had been done, declared, in the same manner as in the Curbelo case, the cases of Rodríguez and Armas legally dismissed.[76] The court further ruled that both defendants were to retrieve all their property. On April 30, 1736, Matheo Carabajal delivered Rodríguez's property "to the entire satisfaction of the latter and in accordance with the same list." On May 9, Manuel de Nis presented Armas' property to him and obtained a release (*finiquito*) with "the delivery of said property . . . accomplished."[77]

An Overview of Municipal Administration

The *cabildo*'s role in administering justice on the frontier consisted of far more than collaborating with the governor's court. Its reach extended into the economic level of municipal life, where it attempted to prevent and to punish malpractice and thus to introduce a higher concept of business in the marketplace, particularly through the office of the *fiel executor*.[78] Charged with the general enforcement of municipal ordinances dealing with trade and commerce, the ownership of municipal and private property, and sundry phases of economic life within the community, this office functioned under the *alcalde*. The *fiel executor*, at times called *fiel de pesos y medidas* or *fiel y medidor,* was elected to take charge of checking weights and measures used by merchants and shopkeepers.[79] In some *cabildos,* the *fiel executor* surveyed plots of land within the town and its vicinity. In Mexico City, the responsibility for enforcement of various ordinances passed by the *cabildo* for control of economic transactions within its town limits ultimately fell on the office of the *fieles executores.* In fact, the *fiel executor* became a sort of ambulatory court.[80] Accompanied by the *escribano de número,* or official accountant, on the daily rounds of the public market, he possessed authority to impose fines for the violation of market regulations, with the *escribano de número* making record of the proceedings. Appeals, if not over thirty ducats, came before the *cabildo,* and, if above this sum, to the *audiencia,* the tribunal of justice in Mexico City.[81] The *alguacil mayor,* who usually accompanied the *fiel executor,* generally collected the fines on the spot. In the large municipalities of New Spain, assuring a plentiful supply of bread, meat, and produce at fair prices often required the services of two or three *fieles executores.*[82]

The *cabildos* on the Borderlands did not let this important office go unattended. In 1799 the town council of the Villa de San Fernando declared in a report to Juan Bautista de Elguezábal, governor of the province, that the third *regidor* was carrying out the duties of the *fiel executor.*[83] By taking charge of the weights and measures, he guarded consumers against fraud in the sale of goods. Apparently, the *fiel executor* worked very closely with the other council members, for although little is said about his office, records indicate that the *cabildo* as a whole kept watch over trade and market prices. Hardly any citizen escaped scrutiny. In 1745, the *cabildo* issued an affidavit confirming a statement alleging that Don Juan Francisco de Espronceda was guilty of business practices both disreputable to his clerical state and detrimental to the common good of the community: "We state that it is true that the señor priest [Espronceda] . . . sells *aguardiente,* salt, soap, tobacco, *piloncillo,* and that he charges higher prices for goods he sells than is the custom and practice of the region."[84]

Six years after the misguided cleric was reprimanded, with the expansion of trade in the community, other opportunities presented themselves for people in the municipal markets to engage in illicit trade. Thus, on April 29, 1752, the *cabildo,* determined to check unfair business practices in the Villa de San Fernando, issued a decree for the inspection of all commercial weights and measures:

Whereas great irregularity is being practiced in this villa in weights and measures, which each individual uses willfully, without heeding the orders given in the past to the effect that nothing should be sold by anyone [using] measures that had not been marked and stamped by the *cabildo,* therefore we hereby order all the *vecinos* residing permanently or temporarily without exception who use the vara, scales, and measures to report on the next Thursday, the fourth of May [1752], each one bringing the measures that he uses; varas, scales, cuartillo, medio cuartillo, cuarta, almud, medio almud, *cuartilla,* and *media [cuartilla]* to have them checked and stamped, as [is] usual and customary in the capital of Mexico. Whoever shall not bring them [the measures] to have them checked and stamped shall be punished by having them broken.[85]

The decree concluded by reminding the citizenry that the ordinance would be supported by the *cabildo's* judiciary powers. Scheduled to be tacked to the door of the church for all to see at Sunday morning mass, the decree was to go into effect on the day promulgated. To be sure that the *cabildo's* instructions were taken seriously, potential violators were told that they would be prosecuted and fined twenty-five pesos in common gold, "to be applied for public works."[86]

Strict municipal measures to promote fair business practices in the civil communities of the Borderlands lasted into the early part of the nineteenth century. Suspecting that avaricious merchants were gouging citizens, municipal authorities at the Villa de Laredo appointed Manuel Dovalina as *procurador* for the town council with orders to stop unjust prices for produce and merchandise offered for sale to the people of the town. Dovalina issued a decree that "as one of the primary considerations for the government . . . is to guard the equity and economy of the body politic and with particular attention to those in needy circumstances and the poor," the sale of all important food commodities was to be regulated and the price, weight, and measures of such articles were to be standardized. "The price of meat was fixed at five pounds for one real, wax for candles at four ounces for one-half real, and bread, after it was taken from the oven, at twelve ounces for one-half real. Cornering of the market on any one commodity was prevented by requiring all peddlers to offer their goods at retail in the public plaza for three days before a deal at wholesale could be made."[87]

The enactment of a curfew law in 1779 apparently had lessened civil disturbance in the evenings. However, daytime morals within the community also concerned the Laredo city fathers. The *cabildo* began deliberations regarding regulations on mixed bathing along the banks of the Río Grande. The custom, in practice as early as 1784, apparently had moral shortcomings, according to the local curate, who unsuccessfully attempted to prevent this popular social pastime. On May 3, 1784, Santiago de Jesús Sánchez, the lieutenant *alcalde,* issued a decree against the practice. Claiming that it set a poor example for children and was offensive "to both Majesties, God and King," he decreed that women should bathe at sunset and men after the ringing of the Angelus. Violations of the new ordinance exacted a penalty of ten days in jail and a fine of six pesos. The manner of promulgating the municipal law received equal attention. At a time when the largest number of people were at the town square, Sánchez drew their attention by the roll of the kettledrum and then ordered the decree recited, directing those in attendance to comply with the new ordinance and to inform those citizens not present to do the same.[88]

In retrospect, the *cabildo*'s legislative, judicial, and police functions examined in this chapter pertained to the citizens of the civil communities in the Borderlands and the demands made upon these people by a frontier society. In Hispanic Texas, the interaction between the governor's court and that of the *cabildo* was an arrangement welcomed by both institutions in view of the harsh conditions found on the frontier. Thus, the governor's court offered its assistance to the municipal government whenever it was needed. On May 18, 1735, for example, Alcalde Juan Leal Góraz of the Villa de San Fernando petitioned the judge of the court of the second instance for help in a case in which he had arrested three citizens for failing to heed his citations. He informed the governor: "I . . . first-ranking *alcalde* . . . state that I have initiated [a case without success] . . . against . . . three citizens concerning their repeated disobedience of my administration of justice . . . therefore I ask and entreat Your Lordship to be so good as to admit in your court the writs in this case and prosecute same to their conclusions."[89]

All the same, the Texas *cabildo* jealously guarded its autonomy and the right to administer civil justice. When a captain from the military presidio of San Antonio rashly attempted to meddle in the town's internal affairs, the *cabildo* quickly cited the viceroy's decree of February 13, 1744:

[Said captain] . . . under penalty of removal from office is not to vex nor molest the Isleños; but on the contrary, is to respect and make his officers respect the exemptions and privileges that have been conceded to them. He shall not meddle with the administration of justice of the said settlers and *vecinos agregados* of the said villa of San Fernando which should be in charge of the ordinary *alcalde*.[90]

On the whole, the municipal governments of the Borderlands functioned as viable institutions during the eighteenth century, particularly at the Villa de San Fernando and the town of Laredo. The *alcaldes ordinarios,* outranking the *regidores* in prestige and authority, presided at town councils, enacted laws for the common good, and assured the administration of justice. The *procuradores,* aware of their legal responsibilities to clients, played a vital part by exacting justice before Hispanic tribunals. The *escribano*'s fastidious method of keeping the records of the court accentuated the importance of justice in the lives of Spanish settlers in the Borderlands. Assigned to execute the orders of the court magistrates, the *alguacil mayor* was responsible for the police activities that the little municipalities required for their material, economic, and social development.

Determined to maintain their autonomy against the tour de force generated by both presidio and mission establishments, and armed with their coveted *fueros,* deeply rooted in Castilian municipal tradition, the town governments of the Borderlands served as bulwarks of justice and civic freedom in the wilderness of the northern frontier of New Spain. Further, these municipal governments reassured the early Hispanic settlers of a social and moral structure in which the rights of life and property would be guaranteed in the normal activities of citizens. These frontier *cabildo*s, through their court systems, reminded people of Spain's deep sense of civil justice by serving as bastions for law and judicial procedure in the former Spanish provinces of the northern frontier.

9

Spanish Municipalities in North American History

To secure the northern frontier Borderlands, the Spanish imperial government implemented three colonial institutions—the mission, the presidio, and the town settlement. These institutions had distinct functions, but their larger goals were similar, namely, to implant on an enormous part of the North American continent Spanish linguistic, social, religious, and political values.[1] Spanish town councils added distinct dimensions to the influence that New Spain once exerted over the American Southwest. By means of these *cabildos*, Spain introduced municipal law and order, patterns of local government, a rough democracy, and the concept of justice based on law. Municipal governments were implanted in the Borderlands *ex mandato regis Hispaniensis*. These civil governments assisted Spanish town settlers in conquering and subduing the land, and even in settling and Christianizing it for their king. Over the centuries, they preserved in New Mexico, Texas, and California the distinctive cultural, social, and language patterns characteristic of the present-day Southwest.

These frontier town settlements, even more than the presidios and missions, have withstood the test of time. Spain's colonization efforts brought to North America the basic concepts of municipal development and the *cabildo* institution. By the eighteenth century, New Spain had grown into the prosperous child of the mother country, and its sons, recalling the valor of the knights of the Reconquest, joined in the roles of *adelantados* by pushing farther northward the frontiers of the vast Borderlands. These early Spanish explorers mapped out the new lands and, accompanied by the zealous missionaries, principally the loyal sons of Saint Francis, they laid claim to the land and brought to it Christianity and other aspects of Western civilization. Municipalities were one of these contributions in the Southwest. By the first half of the eighteenth century municipal life on New Spain's northern frontier centered largely around the varied activities of four permanent town settlements: Santa Fe and El Paso del Río del Norte of the former colony of Nuevo México; and Laredo and San Antonio of present-day Texas. On the West Coast, during the last quarter of the same century, the permanent civil communities of San José and Los Angeles joined their sister towns of the northern Borderlands.

The citizens of these frontier towns, at times left entirely to their own devices for survival on the Borderlands, kept alive the concept of government by open assembly and promoted the democratic process for their security and welfare. Influenced by the Bourbon reforms, which gave additional hegemony to the presidial institutions in New Mexico, Texas, and California, the *cabildos* nonetheless attempted to maintain their real, albeit limited, sense of autonomy. Moreover, they retreated not a single inch from the position that as municipalities officially established by the order of the Spanish crown they were independent civil institutions. Invested with the traditional *fueros* of Castilian municipalities, these Borderland towns enjoyed, at least legally, an institutional status that neither the presidio nor the mission could approximate.

With no special interest outside their own jurisdiction, the *cabildos* fostered civic pride and promoted the welfare of the citizenry. In this context, the Borderland municipalities projected a notable quality that was in keeping with the best in Castilian municipal traditions. With each year, their local governments, controlled by the crown's grateful subjects, became more indigenous to the new homeland. Newly created, these civil governments—whether on the New Mexico landscape, the coastal plains of South Texas, or California's Pacific shores—began to reflect distinct characteristics resulting from local conditions and problems. *Cabildo* officers were the resident landowners. They might be few in number and have limited income; nonetheless, they, as proud *hidalgos,* highly prized their respective offices on the town council.

Not all municipal authority resided in the town council, however. The concept of the *cabildo abierto,* with its roots deeply implanted in the *concejos* of medieval Castilian towns, manifested itself in the varied activities and discussions particularly in El Paso and at the Villa de San Fernando. The leading citizens along with their neighbors united with the *cabildo* in a common effort to promote what they believed to be the

"Entierro de un Angel," by Theodore Gentilz. A funeral for a young child was all too common an occurrence in Borderlands communities, where epidemics and harsh conditions kept the death rate high. Courtesy Alamo Library of the Daughters of the Republic of Texas, San Antonio.

common good. At the Villa de San Fernando the townspeople united to build a needed community building, the parish church. The project, spearheaded by the local curate, promoted by the town council, and supported by generous donations from the citizenry, resulted in the beginnings of San Fernando Church. The San Joseans and Los Angelenos demonstrated, in large measure, an identical civic spirit in attempts to construct modest chapels in their pueblos.

El Paso del Río del Norte also contributed to the municipal character of New Spain's northern frontier. There were many similarities between the El Paso and San Antonio de Béjar civil settlements. First, in both cases the Franciscan padres were responsible for the selection of the site.

Although missionary work took place around the El Paso district before 1659, the actual founding of the mission of Nuestra Señora de Guadalupe by Father García de San Francisco y Zúñiga may be regarded as the cornerstone for the establishment of El Paso, Texas, and particularly the city of Juárez, Chihuahua. Second, just as hostile Apache and Comanche warriors continually harassed the Villa de San Fernando, so also the El Paso settlement maintained incessant vigilance on the unpredictable movement of aggressive natives who dwelled in the interior of New Mexico, as well as the Apaches from Texas. Third, both San Antonio and El Paso played an important role by serving as vital way stations between the towns in New Spain and outposts on the northern frontier during the eighteenth century. Settlers and supplies needed in the Spanish settlements of Santa Fe, Santa Cruz de la Cañada, and Albuquerque in Central New Mexico came from as far south as Durango and Zacatecas. The journey between the New Mexican settlements and their supply centers in central Mexico was long and tedious. Geographically situated almost equidistant between the points, El Paso served as a haven and rest center between these two points in New Spain. The San Antonio community offered the same services. Commerce, trade, and the flow of supplies from Saltillo, Monclova, and Allende in Coahuila to the Spanish settlements of easternmost Texas had to be maintained. San Antonio de Béjar supported the colonial effort by being an important way station for the towns of Coahuila and the Texas settlements of Los Adaes, Nacogdoches, and the Bahía del Espíritu Santo.

The impact of the Bourbon reforms on the Spanish Borderlands of North America affected the social life of the frontier townspeople and their neighbors at the presidios and nearby missions. Religious processions, fiestas, bullfights, *comedias,* and prescribed periods of mourning for deceased Spanish royalty varied the panorama of colonial living amid harsh conditions. A product of Bourbon genius, municipal life in Spanish Texas manifested both the austere and regimented tone of royal dominance and the merrymaking and fiestas that the crown often encouraged and, in fact, promoted.

The manner in which the city councils protected citizens and their property rights constituted one of the major accomplishments of the Borderland *cabildos.* Despite meager resources, these municipal governments stood firm in their role of enforcing local law and maintaining order. In sharp contrast to the frequent lawlessness common in many frontier communities in the Trans-Mississippi West of North America

"El Convite para el Baile," by Theodore Gentilz. Invitations to dances and feasts signaled the occasion for festivities in frontier social life. Courtesy Alamo Library of the Daughters of the Republic of Texas, San Antonio.

in a later period, the Spanish *cabildo*s maintained law and justice in the eighteenth century. Preventing the spread of exaggerated individualism and disregard for established legal tradition, the *cabildo*s on the Borderlands provided the early settlers with a social structure in which the rights of life and property were secure for all citizens.

Historians, placing emphasis on the important, albeit romantic, role of Spanish soldiery and accentuating the heroic part that missionaries played in the Borderlands, have neglected to give the municipal institution due credit. The contributions of the towns and their collective memory as an institution constituted a third pillar in the colonial experience of the Borderlands.

With the advent of the nineteenth century new concepts of the rights of men and of democratic government found expression in Europe and gradually reached the northern provinces of New Spain. Yet these concepts – individual freedom, respect for the law, and protection of property rights in a well-ordered society – for all their worth actually had been attained in Nuevo México, Texas, and California in large measure by the end of the eighteenth century. The first *cabildos* of the Spanish Borderlands struggled for years to make many of these achievements possible. Dedicated to the goals of preserving the basic human rights of Spanish citizens within their respective jurisdictions, frontier town settlements, proud of their Castillian *fueros* and municipal traditions, achieved what no other colonial institution was equipped to do: they kept aglow the torch of justice, equity and civil freedom on the northern Borderlands frontier.

Appendix A

VICEROYS OF NEW SPAIN THROUGH 1813

1535–1550	Antonio de Mendoza
1550–1554	Luis de Velasco
1566–1567	Gastón de Peralta, Marqués de Falces
1568–1580	Martín Enríquez de Almanza
1580–1583	Lorenzo Suárez de Mendoza, Conde de la Coruña
1584–1585	Pedro Moya de Contreras, archbishop and *visitador*
1585–1590	Alvaro Manrique de Zúñiga, Marqués de Villa Manrique
1590–1595	Luis de Velasco, Marqués de Salinas
1595–1603	Gaspar de Zúñiga y Acevedo, Conde de Monterrey
1603–1607	Juan de Mendoza y Luna, Marqués de Montesclaros
1607–1611	Luis de Velasco, Marqués de Salinas
1611–1612	Fray García Guerra, archbishop of Mexico
1612–1621	Diego Fernández de Córdoba, Marqués de Guadalcázar
1621–1624	Diego Carrillo de Mendoza y Pimentel, Marqués de Gelves y Conde de Priego
1624–1635	Rodrigo Pacheco Osorio, Marqués de Cerralvo
1635–1640	Lope Díaz de Armendáriz, Marqués de Cadereyta
1640–1642	Diego López Pacheco Cabrera y Bobadilla, Marqués de Villena, Duque de Escalona
1642	Juan de Palafox y Mendoza, Bishop of Puebla
1642–1648	García Sarmiento de Sotomayor, Conde de Salvatierra, Marqués de Sobroso
1648–1649	Marcos de Torres y Rueda, Bishop of Yucatan
1650–1653	Luis Enríquez de Guzmán, Conde de Alba de Liste, Marqués de Villaflor
1653–1660	Francisco Fernández de la Cueva, Duque de Albuquerque

1660–1664	Juan de Leiva y de la Cerda, Marqués de Leiva y de Ladrada, Conde de Baños
1664	Diego Osorio de Escobar y Llamas, bishop of Puebla
1664–1673	Antonio Sebastían de Toledo, Marqués de Mancera
1673	Pedro Nuño Colón de Portugal, Duque de Veragua, Marqués de la Jamaica
1673–1680	Payo Enríquez de Rivera, archbishop of Mexico
1680–1686	Tomás Antonio de la Cerda y Aragón, Conde de Paredes, Marqués de la Laguna
1686–1688	Melchor Portocarrero Lazo de la Vega, Conde de la Monclova
1688–1696	Gaspar de la Cerda Sandoval Silva y Mendoza, Conde de Galve
1696–1697	Juan de Ortega Montáñez, bishop of Michoacán
1697–1701	José Sarmiento Valladares, Conde de Moctezuma y de Tula
1701–1702	Juan de Ortega Montáñez, bishop of Michoacán
1702–1711	Francisco Fernández de la Cueva Enríquez, Duque de Albuquerque
1711–1716	Fernando de Alencastre Noreña y Silva, Duque de Linares, Marqués de Valdefuentes
1716–1722	Baltasar de Zúñiga, Marqués de Valero, Duque de Arión
1722–1734	Juan de Acuña, Marqués de Casafuerte
1734–1740	Juan Antonio de Vizarrón y Eguiarreta, archbishop of Mexico
1740–1741	Pedro de Castro y Figueroa, Duque de la Conquista y Marqués de Gracia Real
1742–1746	Pedro Cebrián y Agustín, Conde de Fuenclara
1746–1755	Juan Francisco de Güemes y Horcasitas, Conde de Revilla Gigedo
1755–1760	Agustín de Ahumada y Villalón, Marqués de las Amarillas
1760	Francisco Cajigal de la Vega
1760–1766	Joaquín de Monserrat, Marqués de Cruillas
1766–1771	Carlos Francisco de Croix, Marqués de Croix
1771–1779	Fray Antonio María de Bucareli y Ursúa
1779–1783	Martín de Mayorga
1783–1784	Matías de Gálvez
1785–1786	Bernardo de Gálvez, Conde de Gálvez
1787	Alonso Núñez de Haro y Peralta, archbishop of Mexico

1787–1789	Manuel Antonio Flores
1789–1794	Juan Vicente de Güemes Pacheco de Padilla, Conde de Revillagigedo
1794–1798	Miguel de la Grúa Talamanca y Branciforte, Marqués de Branciforte
1798–1800	Miguel José de Azanza
1800–1803	Félix Berenguer de Marquina
1803–1808	José de Iturrigaray
1808–1809	Pedro Garibay
1809–1810	Francisco Javier de Lizana y Beaumont, archbishop of Mexico
1810–1813	Francisco Javier Venegas, Conde de la Reunión de la Nueva España

Appendix B

1691–1692	Domingo Terán de los Ríos
1693–1716	Texas unoccupied but included in Coahuila
1716–1719	Martín de Alarcón, governor of Texas and Coahuila
1719–1722	Joseph de Azlor, Marqués de San Miguel de Aguayo, governor of Coahuila and Texas
1722–1726	Fernando Pérez de Almazán
1727–1730	Melchor de Media Villa y Ascona
1730–1734	Juan Antonio Bustillo y Zevallos
1734–1736	Manuel de Sandoval
1736–1737	Carlos Benites Franquis de Lugo
1737	Fernández de Jaureguí y Urrutia, governor of Nuevo León, governor extraordinary, and *visitador*
1737–1740	Prudencio de Orobio y Bázterra, governor *ad interim*
1741–1743	Tomás Felipe Winthuisen
1743–1744	Justo Boneo y Morales
1744–1748	Francisco García Larios, governor *ad interim*
1748–1750	Pedro del Barrio Junco y Espriella
1751–1759	Jacinto de Barrioso y Jaureguí
1759–1766	Angel de Martos y Navarrete
1767–1770	Hugo Oconor, governor *ad interim*
1770–1778	The Baron de Ripperdá
1778–1786	Domingo Cabello
1786	Bernardo Bonavia appointed July 8, but apparently did not serve
1787–1790	Rafael Martínez Pachecho
1788	The office of governor was ordered suppressed and the province put under a presidial captain

1790–1799(?)	Manuel Muñoz
1798(?)	Josef Irigoyen, apparently appointed but did not serve
1800(?)–1805	Juan Bautista de Elguezábel
1805–1810	Antonio Cordero y Bustamante
1810–1813	Manuel de Salcedo

Appendix C

GOVERNORS OF SPANISH NEW MEXICO THROUGH 1814

1598–1608	Juan de Oñate
1608	Pedro de Peralta
1621–1628	Felipe Zotylo
1629	Manuel de Silva
1640	Fernando de Argüello
1641	Louis de Rosas
1642	———— Valdez
1643	Alonso Pacheco de Heredia
1645	Fernando de Argüello
1647	Luis de Guzmán
1650	Hernando de Ugarte y la Concha
1653–1654	Juan de Samaniego
1656	Enrique de Avila y Pacheco
1660	Bernardo López de Mendizábal
1661–1664	Diego de Peñalosa Briceño
	Fernando de Villanueva
	Juan de Medrano
	Juan de Miranda
1675	Juan Francisco de Treviño
1679–1683	Antonio Otermín
1683–1686	Domingo Jironza Petriz de Cruzate
1686–1688	Pedro Reñeros de Posada
1689–1691	Domingo Jironza Petriz de Cruzate
1691–1697	Diego de Vargas Zapata Luján Ponce de León
1697–1703	Pedro Rodríguez Cubero
1703–1704	Diego de Vargas Zapata Luján Ponce de León
1704–1705	Juan Páez Hurtado, acting

1705–1707	Francisco Cuervo y Valdez, *ad interim*
1707–1712	José Chacón Medina Salazar y Villaseñor, Marqués de la Peñuela
1712–1715	Juan Ignacio Flores Mogollón
1715–1717	Félix Martínez de Torrelaguna, *ad interim*
1717	Juan Páez Hurtado, acting
1717–1722	Antonio Valverde y Cosío, *ad interim*
1721	Juan de Estrada y Austria (?), *ad interim*
1722–1731	Juan Domingo de Bustamante
1731–1736	Gervasio Cruzat y Góngora
1736–1739	Enrique de Olavide y Micheleña, *ad interim*
1739–1743	Gaspar Domingo de Mendoza
1743–1749	Joaquín Codallos y Rabal
1749–1754	Tomás Vélez Cachupín
1754–1760	Francisco Antonio Marín del Valle
1760	Mateo Antonio de Mendoza, acting
1761–1762	Manuel Portillo Urrisola, acting
1762–1767	Tomás Vélez Cachupín
1767–1778	Pedro Fermín de Mendinueta
1778	Francisco Trebol Navarro, acting
1778–1789	Juan Bautista de Anza
1789–1794	Fernando de la Concha
1794–1805	Fernando Chacón
1805–1808	Joaquín del Real Alencáster
1807–1808	Alberto Mainez, acting
1808–1814	José Manrique

Appendix D

GOVERNORS OF SPANISH CALIFORNIA THROUGH 1814

1768–1770	Gaspar de Portolá, governor of Las Californias, Alta and Baja
1770–1775	Felipe de Barri, governor of Las Californias, residing at Loreto
1775–1782	Felipe de Neve, governor of Las Californias
1782–1791	Pedro Fages
1791–1792	José Antonio Roméu
1792–1794	Jose Joaquín de Arrillaga
1794–1800	Diego de Borica
1800–1814	José Joaquín de Arrillaga

Notes

ABBREVIATIONS

AGI-UC   Archivo general de las Indias, Bancroft Library, University of California, Berkeley

AGI-UT   Archivo general de las Indias, Eugene C. Barker Texas History Center, University of Texas, Austin

AGN-UC   Archivo General de la Nación, Bancroft Library, University of California, Berkeley

AGN-UT   Archivo General de la Nación, Eugene C. Barker Texas History Center, University of Texas, Austin

ASF   Archivo de San Francisco el Grande, Eugene C. Barker Texas History Center, University of Texas, Austin

ASJ   Archivo de San José, Bancroft Library, University of California, Berkeley

BA   Bexar County Archives, Eugene C. Barker Texas History Center, University of Texas, Austin

C-A   Archives of California, Bancroft Library, University of California, Berkeley

LA   Laredo Archives, Eugene C. Barker Texas History Center, University of Texas, Austin

NA   Nacogdoches Archives, Eugene C. Barker Texas History Center, University of Texas, Austin

SANM   Spanish Archives of New Mexico, Coronado Special Collection Center, University of New Mexico, Albuquerque

WBS   W. B. Stephens Collection, Eugene C. Barker Texas History Center, University of Texas, Austin

CHAPTER I

1. C. H. Haring, *The Spanish Empire in America*, pp. 69–147, 166–94; Herbert E. Bolton, *The Mission as a Frontier Institution*, p. 1.

2. Roger Bigelow Merriman, *The Rise of the Spanish Empire in the Old World and in the New*, I, 7–9. See also Modesto La Fuente, *Historia general de España*, I, 7, 158; Rafael Altamira y Crevea, *A History of Spain*, p. 22.

3. Jaime Vicens Vives, *Approaches to the History of Spain*, pp. 17–21; La Fuente, *Historia*, I, 57; C. H. V. Sutherland, *The Romans in Spain*, p. 53; Altamira y Crevea, *History of Spain*, p. 52.

4. Vicens Vives, *Approaches to the History of Spain*, pp. 22–27; Altamira y Crevea, *History of Spain*, p. 78. The term *urban* is used throughout this volume more in the historical sense than in the contemporary sense, which would include connotations of the metroplex and the life-styles of twentieth-century municipalities. The derivation of the word (*urbs, urbis,* gen.) is Latin, a language in use in Spain when it was Hispania, a province of the Roman Empire. The *urbs* was a walled town or city with a distinct municipal character. The city of Rome was the principal *urbs* of the empire, and a common phrase among Romans was to be at or near Rome (*ad urbem esse*). In literature, Cicero talked about building a city (*urbem aedificare*), and Virgil, in using the word, referred to dwellers in the city when describing the town people as buried in sleep and wine (*urbs somno vinoque sepulta*).

5. Florencio Janer, *Condición social de moriscos de españa: causas de su expulsión y consecuencias que esta produjo en el orden económico y político*, p. 17.

6. Stanley Lane-Poole, *The Moors in Spain*, p. 129. See also Altamira y Crevea, *History of Spain*, p. 130.

7. John Huxtable Elliot, *Imperial Spain, 1469–1716*, pp. 81–82. See also José Antonio Maravall, *El concepto de España en la edad media*, p. 249; Ramón Menéndez Pidal, *Historia de España*, VI, 260.

8. "While the nobility, Church, monastic organizations and military orders were chief beneficiaries of the Christian Reconquest, in the long run, little could be achieved without the people *en masse*. In order to encourage the populating of newly acquired lands, the monarch and the chief beneficiaries granted rights and privileges to communities along the frontier and elsewhere in the kingdom. These prerogatives granted by the crown and privileged classes to the common man were embodied in a charter called a *carta* or *fuero*" (Martin A. S. Hume, *Spain, Its Greatness and Its Decay*, p. 18). See also Ernesto Mayer, *Historia de las instituciones sociales y políticas de España y Portugal*, II, 126; Charles E. Chapman, *A History of Spain*, p. 162; Altamira y Crevea, *History of Spain*, pp. 146, 181; *Las siete partidas*, p. 275; Luis G. Valdeavellano, *Historia de España*, p. 90.

Alcaldes ordinarios were the town mayors who, besides presiding at municipal councils, had certain legislative and juridical powers; the *regidores* were town councilmen; the *alguaciles* were the town constables responsible for law and order; the *escribanos* were the city clerks who kept the minutes of the municipal council and the city records. For more detailed information, see chapter 4, "First Municipal Government in Texas."

9. Rafael Torres Campos, *Carácter de la conquista y colonización de las Canarias,* pp. 24–35.

10. This element of self-government, according to some scholars, was not as effective throughout the Spanish American empire after the Comunero Revolt, protests that indicated the great extent of municipal power in Spain. But even though the Hapsburg kings, after the revolt, began encouraging viceroys and governors to watch the affairs of *cabildos* in the New World, frontier town councils continued to demonstrate significant freedom in the management of their internal civil affairs.

11. Haring, *Spanish Empire,* p. 158; John Preston Moore, *The Cabildo in Peru under the Hapsburgs,* p. 61.

12. Bernal Díaz del Castillo, *The Discovery and Conquest of Mexico, 1517–1521,* p. 31.

13. Francisco López de Gómara, *Cortés: The Life of the Conqueror by His Secretary,* p. 11.

14. Roberto Ricard, *La conquista espiritual de México,* p. 515.

15. "Cortés . . . directed that the aqueducts should be restored, and the city cleared of the dead so that within two months it might be inhabited as before. The palaces and houses he ordered to be repaired and pointed out that part which was to be inhabited by the natives, and that which was to be reserved for Spaniards" (Bernal Díaz del Castillo, *The True History of the Conquest of Mexico,* p. 321).

16. López de Gómara, *Cortés,* p. 323.

17. Arthur Scott Aiton, *Antonio de Mendoza: The First Viceroy of New Spain,* pp. 17–18. With its elevation to the status of viceroyalty, New Spain was formed into a cartographical quilt, with the viceregal empire divided into *audiencias, gobernaciones,* and municipal districts of different shapes and sizes, namely, *ciudad, villa,* pueblo, and, in the central mining plateau region, the *real de minas.*

18. Aiton, *Mendoza,* p. 18. Cortés had established the first town settlement in New Spain as early as July, 1519, at Veracruz. He "took most of his men ashore . . . and in the name of the King founded a city which he gave the name of Villa Rica de la Veracruz" (Andrés de Tapia, "Chronicle of Andrés de Tapia," p. 24). According to Salvador Madariaga, Cortés, despite indifference shown him at the court, demonstrated deep faith in the crown, was in accord with the colonization of New Spain, and planned to live in Mexico the rest of his life (*Hernán Cortés,* pp. 642–59). Henry R. Wagner presents a more cautious acceptance of the conqueror's achievements and his concern for Indian welfare and questions the degree of loyalty that Cortés had for the king (*The Rise of Fernando Cortés,* pp. 458–61). For a speculative study of the lives of the conquistadors, consult John Francis Bannon, ed., *The Spanish Conquistadores: Men or Devils?*

"On the day Cortés was appointed governor and captain general, the central government assigned by the king took over management of the finances. Once the crown's officials . . . began to supervise the affairs of New Spain, it became apparent that Spanish colonial policy meant to keep the military arm of the empire under political control (ibid., p. 24).

19. Hubert Howe Bancroft, *History of Mexico,* II, 321. The abuses of the first *audiencia* led to its replacement in 1530 by a new corps of judges, of whom the president was the noted Sebastián Ramírez de Fuenleal. The *oidores* Vasco de Quiroga, Alonso Maldonado, Francisco de Ceynos, and Juan de Salmerón attempted to re-

form the government in New Spain but were unable to cope with all the problems resulting from the first *audiencia* and the *encomienda* system (Aiton, *Mendoza*, pp. 22–30).

20. Aiton, *Mendoza*, p. 34.

21. *Actas de Cabildo de la Ciudad de México,* August 20, 1535, Libro 3, 121; August 25, 1535, Libro III, 123; October 2, 1535, Libro 3, 129.

22. Ibid., November 12, 1535, Libro 3, 131.

23. Ibid., November 17, 1535, Libro 3, 131–32; April 28, 1536, Libro 4, 19; December 12, 1536, Libro 4, 56. See also Donald Eugene Smith, *The Viceroy of New Spain,* pp. 191–92.

24. *Actas de Cabildo, México,* September 15, 1536, Libro 4, 35. Ibid., September 18, 1536, Libro 4, 37 relates to the laws whereby the *cabildo* was to function. For city regulations regarding the use of arms in the city, the practice and sale of medicine, meat regulation, and the distribution of city lots, see ibid., October 13, 1536, Libro 4, 43; October 20, 1536, Libro 4, 44; and October 24, 1536, Libro 4, 45. Regarding the *cabildo*'s authority to grant town lots and determine citizenship, see ibid., August 25, 1536, Libro 4, 34; October 20, 1536, Libro 4, 44; October 24, 1536, Libro 4, 45.

25. Ibid., September 15, 1536, Libro 4, 35–36.

26. Aiton, *Mendoza*, p. 55.

27. Irving A. Leonard, *Baroque Times in Old Mexico,* pp. 73–74. During the colonial period, city streets were far more than thoroughfares. Many had stories of origin rooted in Indian, early conquest, or ecclesiastical traditions (Artemio de Valle-Arizpe, *Historia, tradiciones y layendas de calles de México,* p. 25.

28. Business thrived in the capital on weekdays and even on Sundays until church authorities prevailed in a controversy forbidding commerce on Sundays and feast days (*Actas de Cabildo, México,* August 25, 1542, Libro 4, 298; August 31, 1545, Libro 5, 108).

29. Bancroft, *History of Mexico,* III, 7–8; Conde de Revilla Gigedo, *Instrucción que dio a su sucesor en el mando, Marqués de Branciforte sobre el gobierno de este Continente en el tiempo que fue su virrey,* Art. 268, p. 64.

30. Smith, *Viceroy,* pp. 167–68.

31. Revilla Gigedo, *Instrucción,* Arts. 228, 245, 246, pp. 52, 57.

32. Ibid., Arts. 285–86, pp. 68–69; Arts. 292, p. 71; Arts. 299–303, pp. 73–74.

33. *Actas de Cabildo, México,* March 28, 1590, Libro 10, 87.

34. Bancroft, *History of Mexico,* II, 383.

35. Revilla Gigedo, *Instrucción,* Art. 306, p. 75.

36. Aiton, *Mendoza*, p. 67.

37. Robert C. West, *The Mining Community in Northern New Spain: The Parral Mining District,* p. 1.

38. J. Lloyd Mecham, "The Real de Minas as a Political Institution," p. 45; Alexander von Humboldt, *Political Essay on the Kingdom of New Spain,* III, 107, 119.

39. Robert West provides a technical explanation of the metallurgical processes involved in smelting and amalgamation (*The Mining Community,* pp. 9, 24–46). See also D. A. Brading, *Miners and Merchants in Bourbon Mexico, 1763–1810,* pp. 131–33. Tabulations on the amount of mercury and other reagents used in the amalgama-

tion process during the second half of the colonial period are summed up in Humboldt, *Political Essay*, III, 251–85. An impressive historical assessment of the amalgamation process in Zacatecas is found in P. J. Bakewell, *Silver Mining and Society in Colonial Mexico: Zacatecas, 1546–1700*, pp. 132–34.

40. "Spanish law and custom claimed that the crown was to retain title to all mineral wealth in the empire. Private individuals operated mines under concessions from the crown . . . the royal government maintained legal monopoly over blasting powder needed for hard rock mining and charged fees for mining, minting, assaying, and stamping the metal and finally added a stiff export duty" (Charles Henry Cumberland, *Mexico: The Struggle for Modernity*, pp. 86–87). Another general estimate deducted from scanty records suggests a total silver production of two billion pesos up to 1803. Actually, there are few records on the costs and profits in silver mining prior to 1690. Some historians are just now attempting to understand the financial aspects of mining through archival research; others tend to base their conclusions on sales in silver mining on the estimations of Alexander von Humboldt, which treat mostly the later colonial period.

41. Philip Wayne Powell, *Soldiers, Indians and Silver: The Northward Advance of New Spain, 1550–1600*, pp. 32–54. "Matched against the fierce Chichimeca for almost fifty years before pacification took hold, Spaniards seriously considered a war of extermination as a solution and might have followed through had not churchmen in the capital and Franciscan missionaries strenuously opposed the strategy" (John Francis Bannon, *The Spanish Borderlands, Frontier, 1513–1821*, p. 29). See also John Horace Parry, *The Audiencia of New Galicia in the Sixteenth Century: A Study in Colonial Government*, pp. 17–18.

42. Elías Amador, *Bosquejo histórico de Zacatecas*, p. 188; Bakewell, *Silver Mining*, p. 221.

43. Amador, *Bosquejo histórico*, pp. 246–47, 315–16; Herón E. Domínguez, *Zacatecas: una recopilación sintetizada de datos históricos, geográficos, económicos . . . del Estado de Zacatecas en ocasión del IV centenario de la fundación de su capital*, pp. 77–78.

44. Amador, *Bosquejo histórico*, p. 269.

45. Powell, *Soldiers*, pp. 17–19.

46. "El mas formidable bastión prehispánico frente a los bárbaros fue la gran ciudad arqueológica de la Quemada. Igual papel jugó Zacatecas desde que, descubiertos sus minas en 1546, fue punto de partida de la colonización del norte, que recorrían amenazadores bandas de nomadas. Esas minas riquísimas – que aseguraron la estabilidad del poblamiento hispánico en México – atrajeron en 1549, a caravanas de aventureros, e indujeron a abrir el camino entre Querétaro y Zacatecas, gracias al cual surgió la 'zona intermedia' la más equilibradamente mestiza, mediadora desde entonces Norte y Sur, y cuna, más tarde, de la independencia" (Wigberto Jiménez Moreno, *Estudio de historia colonial*, pp. 99–100).

47. Zárate Salmerón, "Relaciones de Nuevo México," pp. 271–72.

48. Bancroft, *North Mexican States*, III, 103.

49. John Lloyd Mecham, *Francisco de Ibarra and Nueva Vizcaya*, pp. 122–24.

50. Ibid.

51. Bancroft, *North Mexican States*, III, 305–306.

52. Mecham, *Ibarra*, p. 209–31.

53. George P. Hammond and Agapito Rey, *The Rediscovery of New Mexico, 1580–1594: The Explorations of Chamuscado, Espejo, Castaño de Sosa, Morlete, and Leyva de Bonilla and Humaña*, p. 5.

54. Amador, *Bosquejo histórico*, pp. 209–11; Francisco Javier Alegre, *Historia de La Compañía de Jesús en Nueva España*, II (Libro 5), 58; II (Libro 10), 50. "The Pioneer Jesuit of Nueva Vizcaya was Gonzalo de Tapia, of eternal fame. With one companion in 1591 he crossed the perilous Sierra Madre. His precise destination was San Felipe, on the Sinaloa River, then the very last outpost of European civilization in northern New Spain. San Felipe became and long continued to be the Jesuit capital on the Pacific coast" (Herbert Eugene Bolton, *Rim of Christendom: A Biography of Eusebio Francisco Kino, Pacific Coast Pioneer*, p. 14).

CHAPTER 2

1. "There was no building activity on the present site of the city of Santa Fe before the spring of 1610. It is true that the proposal to move the colony from San Gabriel to a new site had been made long before Don Juan de Oñate, in August of 1607, tendered his resignation as governor but instructions to Peralta show nothing had been done, or even decided, up to that time" (Lansing B. Bloom, "When Was Santa Fe Founded?" pp. 188–89). The actual name of the *villa* is debated. Ralph Twitchell proposes that the capital city of New Mexico was called the Villa de Santa Fe de San Francisco (*Old Santa Fe: The Story of New Mexico's Ancient Capital*, p. 17); other scholars, such as Myra Ellen Jenkins, former chief of the Historical Services Division of the State of New Mexico Records Center and state historian, claim that the *villa* was simply named Villa de Santa Fe.

2. Amador, *Bosquejo histórico*, p. 188.

3. Francisco Peña, *Estudio histórico sobre San Luís Potosí*, pp. 6–7.

4. See France V. Scholes and Eleanor B. Adams, eds., "Copia de los advertimientos que el virrey Don Luis de Velasco dejo al Conde de Monterrey para el gobierno de la Nueva Espana," pp. 45–46 (SANM). Actually, it was the Conde de Monterrey, the successor to don Luis de Velasco, who gave Oñate's expedition final approval (idem, "Copia de los advertimientos generales tocante al gobierno de la Nueva España que el virrey Conde de Monterrey dejo al Marqués de Montecarlos," pp. 83–85).

5. Bannon, *Spanish Borderlands*, pp. 35–36.

6. George P. Hammond and Agapito Rey, eds., *Don Juan de Oñate, Colonizer of New Mexico, 1595–1628*, I, 311; Gaspar Pérez de Villagrá, *History of New Mexico*, p. 99.

7. The history of Santa Fe begins, in large measure, with the valor of the 129 soldiers who for months safely escorted friars, settlers, supply wagons, and livestock northward to the district of the river *pueblos* of the upper Rio Grande Valley, 750 miles by horse and oxen over the newly staked Chihuahua trail. Gaspar Pérez de Villagrá, Oñate's captain provides a penetrating view into the lives of the Spanish soldiers in New Mexico during Oñate's rule. The hardships, battles, and privations,

including the menial tasks of carpentering, cooking, sewing, and tilling the soil, temper Quixotic notions of their lives. As a result of the efficiency of the soldiers, on April 30, 1598, Juan de Oñate, first governor and captain general of New Mexico, took possession of the province in the name of Philip II, King of Spain (Pérez de Villagrá, *History,* pp. 177–83). For the route taken by the expedition, see Max L. Moorhead, *New Mexico's Royal Road, Trade and Travel on the Chihuahua Trail,* pp. 7–27; Hammond and Rey, *Juan de Oñate,* V, 329.

8. For detailed inventory and census of settlers proposed by Oñate, see Hammond and Rey, *Juan de Oñate,* V, 199–308; Charles W. Hackett, ed., *Historical Documents Relating to New Mexico, Nueva Vizcaya and Approaches Thereto, to 1773,* I, 280–83.

9. "In March a band of ten Franciscans, eight priests and two lay brothers, headed by Fray Padre Alonso Martinez, moved up to join the larger company. It was early May before the party reached the ford of the Rio Grande, El Paso del Rio Norte" (Bannon, *Spanish Borderlands,* p. 36).

10. Hackett, *Historical Documents,* I, 267.

11. Twitchell, *Old Santa Fe,* p. 17.

12. George P. Hammond, *Don Juan de Oñate and the Founding of New Mexico,* p. 100. "There is controversy regarding the location of San Gabriel. Professor Bolton, relying on a contemporary map, places it on the right bank of the Chama, while Twitchell insists on the left bank of the stream, holding that the map is in error. He bases his contention on ruins found there and on traditions of the Indians. But it should be noted that the map referred to has a pueblo on the left bank of the Chama and tradition may have readily confused the two as regards the location of Oñate's headquarters during those first years in New Mexico" (ibid., p. 384).

Herbert E. Bolton, *Spanish Explorations in the Southwest, 1542–1706,* p. 203 n.1, says: "Until as late as March, 1599, Oñate's headquarters were at Pueblo San Juan. In June, 1601, and also in December of the same year, they were at Pueblo de San Gabriel. The contemporary map of Oñate's journey to Quivira . . . shows San Gabriel to the west of the Rio Grande, below the junction with Chama. In April, 1605, Oñate's headquarters were still at San Gabriel." Florence Hawley Ellis is also investigating these locations.

13. Hammond, *Don Juan de Oñate,* p. 178. The viceroy failed to approve the *cabildo's* decision because Don Cristóbal was too young and did not possess the wealth necessary to develop the province.

14. Pérez de Villagrá, *History,* p. 263.

15. Hammond and Rey, *Juan de Oñate,* I, 484.

16. Hackett, *Historical Documents,* I, 244–45.

17. Hammond and Rey, *Juan de Oñate,* VI, 746–60; V, 420–24; VI, 1012–31.

18. Ibid., VI, 1052–45.

19. Hammond, *Don Juan de Oñate,* p. 179.

20. Juan de Torquemada, *Monarquía indiana,* Libro 21, chap. 9, p. 626; Gerónimo de Mendieta, *Historia eclesiástica indiana,* Libro 4, chap. 10, p. 400; Libro 5, chap. 45, p. 674.

21. Historic Santa Fe Foundation, *Old Santa Fe Today,* "The only organized municipal settlement was the headquarters at San Juan de los Caballeros in 1598 which was moved across the river to San Gabriel in 1599, then to the site of the new Villa

of Santa Fe established in 1610. Whatever the formalities, Spanish families settled in the Rio Grande Valley from the region around Socorro as far north as the valley of the Taos, the area around Santa Fe, and the Galisteo Basin. Land was irrigated for farming, livestock was grazed, and many sizable haciendas were constructed. The leading families in the outlying regions had dwellings in Santa Fe" (Myra Ellen Jenkins, "Spanish Land Grants in the Tewa Area," p. 116).

22. Lansing B. Bloom and Ireneo L. Chaves, ed. and trans., "Instruction to Peralta by Vice-roy," pp. 178, 179, 181. For more detail on town foundings, see Dora P. Crouch, Daniel J. Carr, and Axel I. Mundigo, *Spanish City Planning in North America*, pp. 74–75.

23. Ibid.

24. Zelia Nuttal, "Royal Ordinances Concerning the Laying Out of New Towns," p. 745. See also Crouch, Carr, and Mundigo, *Spanish City Planning*, pp. 3–4; Marc Simmons, "Spanish Irrigation Practice in New Mexico," p. 138.

25. Hackett, *Historical Documents*, III, 399.

26. Marc Simmons, *Spanish Government in New Mexico*, p. 159. Because the *Actas de Cabildo* of the Villa de Santa Fe were lost in the Pueblo Rebellion of 1680, there are no municipal records or local documentation. According to France V. Scholes, only two small documents remain of the pre-1680 records: documents #2 and #3 (photostatic copies), SANM.

27. Simmons, *Spanish Government*, p. 159.

28. "The Santa Fe cabildo . . . exercised a kind of general authority over the entire New Mexican province in the seventeenth and early eighteenth centuries. The wide latitude of its powers and the independent spirit of its members brought the municipal council into frequent conflict with the governor. . . . Friction between the provincial and municipal authorities in the early 1700's was intensified when members of the cabildo joined with factions hostile to the incumbent governors" (ibid., p. 194).

29. France V. Scholes, "Civil Government and Society in New Mexico in the Seventeeth Century," pp. 76–78.

30. Historic Santa Fe Foundation, *Old Santa Fe Today*, p. 13.

31. Twitchell, *Old Santa Fe*, p. 81.

32. J. Manuel Espinosa, trans., *First Expedition of Vargas in New Mexico, 1692*, pp. 79–80, 94.

33. Twitchell, *Old Santa Fe*, p. 96; Espinosa, *First Expedition of Vargas*, p. 108. There are two in-depth studies on Indo-Spanish relations before and after the Pueblo Rebellion of 1680. See Charles Wilson Hackett, "The Uprising of the Pueblo Indians of New Mexico, 1630–1682"; and Oakah L. Jones, Jr., *Pueblo Warriors and the Spanish Conquest*.

34. "Entrada en la Villa de Santa Fe del Governador y Capitán General" (Diego de Vargas Zapata y Luján Ponce de León, journal of conquest . . . report to the viceroy, December 27, 1692–January 8, 1693), microfilm, roll i, frame 927–28 (Twitchell 53), SANM.

35. Historic Santa Fe Foundation, *Old Santa Fe Today*, p. 13; Twitchell, *Old Santa Fe*, p. 47.

36. Peter P. Forrestal, trans., *Benavides' Memorial of 1630*, p. 8; France V. Scholes, "Problems in the Early Ecclesiastical History in New Mexico," pp. 42, 62; Historic

Santa Fe Foundation, *Old Santa Fe Today,* pp. 58–59; Angélico Chávez, *La Conquista-dora, the Autobiography of an Ancient Statue,* pp. 69–75.

Santa Fe was influenced perhaps more than other Borderlands towns by the technical aspects of urban organization originating in colonial Mexico. For background reading on civil-religious architecture in the building of towns in the early colonial period, refer to George Kubler, *Mexican Architecture of the Sixteenth Century.*

37. Angélico Chávez, trans., *The Missions of New Mexico, 1776: A Description by Fray Francisco Atanasio Domínguez with Other Contemporary Documents,* p. 13.

38. Ibid., p. 33; A. Von Wuthenau, "The Spanish Military Chapels in Santa Fe and the Reredos of Our Lady of Light," p. 176; Eleanor B. Adams, ed., "Bishop Tamaron's Visitation of New Mexico, 1760," pp. 204–205.

39. Adams and Chávez, *The Missions,* pp. xv, 12–24. Situated beyond the Santa Fe River, on the south side of the *villa,* "el barrio de Analco," the capital's first suburb, was founded by Tlaxcalans who had followed the Spanish settlers into New Mexico immediately after Oñate's *entrada.* These dutiful Indians from central Mexico are reported to have built the main structure of San Miguel Church, a chapel centered in the Analco neighborhood, probably shortly after Santa Fe was officially founded as the Spanish capital of New Mexico. This chapel served the Tlaxcalans and native converts and was considered an extra church conveniently located for those who worked and tilled the land along the slopes of the Santa Fe River. When Popé, the rebellious shaman from San Juan Pueblo, engineered a plot to overthrow the Spaniards in 1680, a torch was set to the wooden sections of the Hermita de San Miguel, the tiny chapel that symbolized, for restive Pueblo Indians, a center of Spanish repression. In 1692, Vargas ordered that repairs to San Miguel Church be made, declaring that with the heavy, solid walls of the chapel still in place, only the wooden structure needed to be replaced. At the turn of the century, San Miguel was rebuilt through the efforts of an association, the Confraternity of St. Michael, devoted to the patron saint of the chapel (Adams and Chávez, *The Missions,* p. 37; France V. Scholes, *Troublesome Times in New Mexico, 1659–1670,* p. 11; Historic Santa Fe Foundation, *Old Santa Fe Today,* p. 30).

40. France V. Scholes, "The Supply Service of the New Mexican Missions in the Seventeenth Century," p. 93.

41. Ibid., p. 95; Moorhead, *New Mexico's Royal Road,* pp. 7–27.

42. Jenkins, "Spanish Land Grants," p. 117.

43. Forrestal, *Benavides' Memorial,* pp. 23–24.

44. Adams, "Tamaron's Visitation," p. 205. Tamarón's assessment of Santa Fe's population in the 1760s is better known by scholars; however, a detailed report on the settlements in New Mexico attributed to its governor, Don Tomás Vélez Cachupín, indicates that the population in the town of Santa Fe in 1752 consisted of 605 people–130 heads of families, 162 arms-bearing men, and 365 children. See Robert Ryal Miller, trans. & ed., "New Mexico in the Mid-Eighteenth Century: A Report Based on Governor Vélez Cachupín's Inspection," pp. 176–77. Perhaps the highest figure for the population of Santa Fe was given in 1765, when it was reported that 2,324 inhabitants resided in the town.

Donald C. Cutter, trans., "An Anonymous Statistical Report on New Mexico in 1765," p. 351).

45. Adams and Cháves, *The Missions,* p. 15.

46. Hackett, *Historical Documents,* III, 108.

47. Adams and Chávez, *The Missions,* p. 15.

48. Alfred Barnaby Thomas, "Antonio de Bonilla and Spanish Plans for the Defense of New Mexico, 1772–1778," pp. 183–209.

49. Social and cultural conflict have been put forth as primary causes of the Pueblo Revolt that exiled Spaniards from New Mexico for fourteen years. However, most of the reasons for the revolt are linked, in some measure, with the economic conditions of pre-1680 New Mexico. The Indian rebellion of 1680 resulted from the failure to stimulate adequate trade and the commercial growth required by the civilized and sedentary Indian populace dwelling along the Río Grande. The shaky *pax hispaniensis* in New Mexico crumbled for reasons far broader than the inability of neophyte minds to appreciate Christianity or the persistent use of the anachronistic *encomienda.* Even the failure of the administration to provide for the inhabitants during drought and the religious syncretism implemented by friars of the "one true church" suggest an ailing economy. Actually, the preindustrial economic system used in New Mexico prior to 1680 was simply inadequate to foment the commercial development demanded by the population centers clustered in the land of the river pueblos. This outdated economic framework needed to be discarded for municipalities characterized by intense internal differentiation based on variations in wealth, economic specialization, and industrial growth. The crown provided New Mexico with the vital political organization it required to regulate human behavior and to integrate society through law and order; however, its policy of forming the province into a missionary utopia converted Santa Fe more into a large catechetical center than a viable urban community characterized by mobility, busy marketplaces, and enthusiastic merchants.

50. Oakah L. Jones, *Los Paisanos: Spanish Settlers on the Northern Frontier of New Spain,* pp. 114–17; Jenkins, "Spanish Land Grants," p. 115; Miller, "New Mexico in the Mid-Eighteenth Century," pp. 176–77.

51. Marc Simmons, *Albuquerque: A Narrative History,* pp. 81–94; Richard E. Greenleaf, "Land and Water Rights in Mexico and New Mexico, 1700–1821," p. 95; Miller, "New Mexico in the Mid-Eighteenth Century," pp. 176–77.

52. Lansing B. Bloom, "Early Weaving in New Mexico," p. 229.

53. Bloom, "Weaving," pp. 230–31.

54. Nemesio Salcedo, Chihuahua, regarding request for economic information by the *consulado* of Veracruz, August 28, 1803, microfilm, roll 15, frames 86–91 (Twitchell 1670A), SANM; Bloom, "Weaving," pp. 239–40.

55. Thomas, "Bonilla," p. 194.

56. Wines, olive oil, linens, vinegar, and various condiments of European and Asiatic origin imported from Spain were available at these marketplaces. Luxury foods from Central Mexico included sugar, brown sugar, candies, molasses, preserves, chocolate, and rice. Lemons, oranges, and other fruits from the Sinaloa coast and the sierra canyons were also available. An estimated 600,000 pesos' worth of merchandise was sent annually from Mexico City to the town of Parral (West, *The Mining Community,* pp. 49–60, 80).

57. Scholes, "Supply Service," p. 115; West, *The Mining Community,* p. 63. One

of the original aims of Spanish colonization in New Mexico, of course, was the development of the mining industry, a goal never attained to the extent it was achieved in Nueva Vizcaya. For a study on the Spanish search for silver in New Mexico, see Leona Davis Boylan, "A Study of Spanish Colonial Silver in New Mexico."

58. Jacobo Ugarte y Loyola, Chihuahua, regarding the improvement of New Mexican commerce, December 18, 1789, microfilm, roll 12, frame 238 (Twitchell 1072a), SANM; Bloom, "Weaving," pp. 231–32. For an impressive study on the success of the fur industry in also stimulating the economy in northern sectors of New Mexico, see David J. Weber, *The Taos Trappers: The Fur Trade in the Far Southwest, 1540–1846.*

CHAPTER 3

1. Jack D. Forbes, *Apache, Navajo and Spaniard,* pp. 3–28; idem, "Unknown Athapaskans: The Identification of the Jano, Jocome, Jumano, Manso, Suma, and other Indian Tribes of the Southwest," pp. 99–100. See also Cleve Hallenbeck, *Alvar Núñez Cabeza de Vaca: The Journey and Route of the First European to Cross the Continent of North America, 1534–1536,* pp. 202–15.

2. Jack D. Forbes, "The Janos, Jocomes, Mansos and Sumas," pp. 320–23; George P. Hammond and Agapito Rey, *Expedition into New Mexico Made by Antonio de Espejo 1582–83, as Revealed in the Journal of Diego Pérez de Luxan,* pp. 58, 69; Herbert E. Bolton, "The Jumano Indians in Texas, 1650–1771," pp. 66–74; C. L. Sonnichsen, *Pass of the North: Four Centuries on the Rio Grande,* p. 19.

3. Ibid.

4. Hammond and Rey, *Oñate,* p. 315.

5. Ibid., pp. 329–36.

6. George P. Hammond and Agapito Rey, "The Rodríguez Expedition to New Mexico, 1581–82," p. 239; idem, *Antonio de Espejo,* pp. 59, 64, 71.

7. Forrestal, *Benavides' Memorial,* p. 8.

8. Ibid.

9. Agustín de Vetancurt, *Teatro mexicano: descripción breve de los sucessos exemplares de la Nueva-España en el nuevo mundo occidental de las Indias,* IV, 22, pp. 18–19.

10. Ibid.; Sonnichsen, *Pass of the North,* p. 21.

11. Vetancurt, *Teatro mexicano,* IV, 22, p. 18.

12. Vina Walz, "History of the El Paso Area, 1680–1692," p. 12.

13. Scholes, "Supply Service," Part II, 139.

14. Vetancurt, *Teantro mexicano,* IV, 22, p. 18.

15. Walz, "El Paso," p. 113; Vetancurt, *Teatro mexicano,* IV, 22, pp. 18–19.

16. Anne E. Hughes, *The Beginning of Spanish Settlement in the El Paso District,* p. 305.

17. Ibid., p. 305–306. See also A. Alcázar de Velasco and Cleofas Calleros, *Historia del Templo de Nuestra Señora de Guadalupe* p. 88.

18. Alcazar de Velasco and Cleofas Calleros, *Historia,* p. 91.

19. Vetancurt, *Teatro mexicano,* III, 27, pp. 264–65.

20. France V. Scholes, trans., "Documents for the History of the New Mexican

Missions in the Seventeenth Century," p. 197. "The document, printed here in translation, is the official notification of the dedication drawn up by order of the custodio, Fray Juan de Talaban and sent to the members of the Franciscan order in Mexico City. The original and a copy are in the National Library in Mexico City in Manuscritos para la Historia del Nuevo Mexzico, legajo 1, nos. 30, 31. Its title is: *Testimonio del estado que tiene la conversión de los Mansos y dedicación de su iglesia*" (ibid., p. 195).

21. Ibid., p. 200.

22. Ibid., p. 196.

23. Ibid., p. 198.

24. Ibid., p. 199.

25. Ibid., pp. 197–200.

26. Vetancurt, *Teatro mexicano* III, 27, p. 265.

27. Hughes, *El Paso District*, p. 310.

28. Sonnichsen, *Pass of the North*, p. 24.

29. Scholes, *Troublesome Times*, p. 253.

30. Walz, "El Paso," p. 23.

31. Not all of the Indians around El Paso were favorably disposed toward foreign religious practices and the regimented life that the missionaries had in store for them. One tribe north of the pass resisted nearly all forms of missionary persuasion, their tough chieftain, Chiquito, causing much unrest even among converted Mansos. Certain Sumas also were dissatisfied with the Spanish interpretation of "peace and religion." In both Indian uprisings—Manso and Suma—Spanish military might was nearby in sufficient force to reassure native El Pasoans of the wisdom of conversion. The hanging of two Indian rebels in 1667 by Captain Andrés de García, the *alcalde mayor* of the El Paso district, settled the problem of insurrection at least for the time being. For an interesting study on the challenge awaiting the Spanish imperial government with regard to Christianizing friendly Indians and controlling bold nomadic natives in the Big Bend area and southeast almost as far as Saltillo, see James M. Daniel, "The Advance of the Spanish Frontier and the Despoblado."

32. Scholes, "Documents for New Mexican Missions," pp. 197–99.

33. Walz, "El Paso," p. 23.

34. Ibid., p. 24.

35. Hughes, *El Paso District*, p. 321.

36. Charles Wilson Hackett and Charmion Clair Shelby, eds. and trans., *Revolt of the Pueblo Indians of New Mexico and Otermin's Attempted Reconquest 1680–1682*, I, lxxviii.

37. Ibid., I, cix. Four days later, after having registered the amount of provisions in the wagons and having returned from the monastery of Guadalupe, where he had gone for the same purpose, Otermín drew up a report to the effect that in those two places there were four hundred bushels of shelled corn and four hundred head of cattle and sheep, all of which Father Ayeta said might be distributed to the people when they arrived. To prevent shortages, Otermín sent out foraging parties to Casas Grandes, Taraumares (eighty leagues distant), and elsewhere to buy all the corn and meat possible and bring them to El Paso (Charles Wilson Hackett, "The Retreat of the Spaniards from New Mexico in 1680, and the Beginnings of El Paso," p. 263).

38. Hackett and Shelby, *Revolt,* I, 184–88.

39. Ibid., I, 215, II, 88.

40. Ibid., II, 204–205, 214; Hughes, *El Paso District,* p. 388. Fray Ayeta felt compelled to provide the distraught refugees with additional aid in the fall of 1681. In order that their hunger might be relieved, a second *entrada* might go on, and the missionary activity in New Mexico might continue, he offered the New Mexicans another two thousand fanegas of maize and two thousand head of cattle for the period of October 1, 1681, to April 30, 1682 (Hackett and Shelby, *Revolt,* II, 88).

41. Hackett and Shelby, *Revolt,* II, 371; Hughes, *El Paso District,* p. 322.

42. Walz, "El Paso History," p. 54.

43. Ibid., p. 119.

44. Ibid., pp. 104–13.

45. Hughes, *El Paso District,* p. 389.

46. Ibid., pp. 330–33.

47. Ibid., p. 389.

48. Ibid., p. 367.

49. Ibid., p. 382.

50. Ibid., p. 384.

51. Walz, "El Paso History," p. 190.

52. Hughes, *El Paso District,* p. 387.

53. Walz, "El Paso History," p. 210.

54. Hughes, *El Paso District,* p. 387.

55. John L. Kessell, *Kiva, Cross and Crown: The Pecos Indians and New Mexico, 1540–1840,* pp. 222–24.

56. Walz, "El Paso History," p. 147.

57. John Leddy Phelan, *The Millenial Kingdom of the Franciscans in the New World: A Study of the Writings of Gerónimo de Mendieta (1525–1604),* p. 11.

58. Since the second half of the sixteenth century, the Spanish religious mission to America had been the idea of Fray Gerónimo de Mendieta, the author of *Historia ecclesiástica indiana,* who had portrayed Hernán Cortés as the Moses of the New World. Fray Juan de Torquemada, also connecting the secular and religious history of Spanish America, in his *Monarquía indiana* pushed Mendieta's concept, stating that the Spanish crown had an obligation to exploit the spiritual mines of the New World — the souls of the Indians. The Messiah of the New World, in theory at least, was supposed to be the king of Spain, and his Indian Commonwealth in America a prosperous millennial kingdom. With these religious ideals, it was almost unthinkable that Franciscans would ever leave the Pueblo Indians alone.

59. Walz, "El Paso History," p. 33.

60. Hughes, *El Paso District,* p. 322.

61. Walz, "El Paso History," pp. 80–81.

62. Hughes, *El Paso District,* p. 327.

63. Walz, "El Paso History," p. 146.

64. Hughes, *El Paso District,* pp. 372–73.

65. Ibid., pp. 386–87.

66. Walz, "El Paso History," pp. 193–94.

67. Ibid., pp. 206–20.

68. Scholes, "Civil Government," p. 95.
69. Hughes, *El Paso District*, p. 366.
70. Hackett and Shelby, *Revolt*, II, 57; Jones, *Los Paisanos*, p. 120. Jones provides a very good demographic outline of the people that made up the larger El Paso community during the first half of the eighteenth century. See especially chapter 6.
71. Miller, "New Mexico in the Mid-Eighteenth Century," p. 170.
72. Ibid., p. 179.
73. Adams, "Tamaron's Visitation," p. 193.
74. Ibid., pp. 193–94.
75. Bloom, "Weaving," pp. 234, 237.
76. Hughes, *El Paso District*, pp. 391–92.

CHAPTER 4

1. The War of Spanish Succession was precipitated by the demise of the Spanish Hapsburg dynasty. In the last years of Hapsburg rule, the Spanish kings provided no leadership for the empire as the Spanish branch of the House of Austria ended its reign. Political decadence affected parts of the empire, and economic stagnation was widespread in the seventeenth century during the reign of Charles II, Philip IV's son and successor and last of the Hapsburg kings. His poor health, limited intelligence, and accession to the throne at the age of four contributed nothing to Spanish rule. Without a direct heir, Charles II transferred Spain's political fate to the royal house of France, designating Philip, Duke of Anjou, grandson of Louis XIV and Maria Theresa, his sister, as his successor. See Altamira, *History of Spain*, p. 398; R. Trevor Davies, *Spain in Decline, 1621–1700*, p. 109; Harold Livermore, *A History of Spain*, pp. 318, 321.

2. Principally with sea fights and attacks on ports such as San Agustín, Puerto Rico, Antigua, and the mines of Santacruz de la Cana in Darién (eastern Panama and Apalache in New Spain), the English caused so much alarm and havoc that the French and Spanish retaliated by landing a party at the Bahamas that took prisoners and captured large supplies of armaments. Even after the War of Spanish Succession terminated, sporadic fighting continued against English pirates and smugglers in the Caribbean and the Pacific. See Altamira, *History of Spain*, p. 486; John Horace Parry, *The Spanish Seaborne Empire*, p. 271; Herbert E. Bolton, "Defensive Spanish Expansion and the Significance of the Borderlands."

3. Laureano de Torres y Ayala, respuesta de, September 16, 1699. Da Quenta a V.M. el Governador de la florida de las diligencias que ha hecho enviando a Rebisitar la bahía del Espíritu Santa y Ascensión Con motibo de aver Yntentado los Yngleses para ocuparla, AGI-UT, Audiencia de México (61–6–22), Dunn transcripts.

4. Carlos E. Castañeda, *Our Catholic Heritage in Texas, 1519–1936*, II, 7–11.

5. Laureano de Torres y Ayala to His Majesty, March 19, 1699, El Governador de la florida de a quenta a V.M. de aber estado zinco nabios de francia sobre la Baya . . . contres testimonio de cartas, AGI-UT, Audencia de México (61–6–22), Dunn transcripts.

6. Bannon, *Spanish Borderlands*, pp. 92–107.

7. Herbert E. Bolton, *The Spanish Borderlands: A Chronicle of Old Florida and the Southwest*, pp. 219–20.

8. Consulta de Guerra de Indias, August 1, 1702, Pone en noticia de V.M. los que se han recuido de la orden que han dado su Xistianisima para que preocupen sus Armas, AGI-UT, Audiencia de México (61-6-22), Dunn transcripts.

9. Robert S. Weddle, *Wilderness Manhunt: The Spanish Search for La Salle*, pp. 15–75; William E. Dunn, "Spanish Search for La Salle's Colony on the Bay of Espíritu Santo," pp. 365–69.

10. John Anthony Caruso, *The Mississippi Valley Frontier: The Age of French Exploration and Settlement*, pp. 225–40; John G. Clark, *New Orleans 1718–1812: An Economic History*, pp. 7–16, 21, 22, 40–42; Nellis M. Crouse, *Lemoyne Iberville: Soldier of New France*, pp. 226–41; Agnes C. Laut, *Cadillac, Knight Errant of the Wilderness*, p. 54; and Ross Phares, *Cavalier in the Wilderness: The Story of the Explorer and Trader Louis Juchereau de St. Denis*, pp. 111–24.

11. Bannon, *Spanish Borderlands*, p. 102.

12. Ibid.; Herbert E. Bolton, *Texas in the Middle Eighteenth Century: Studies in Spanish Colonial History and Administration*, pp. 1–4.

13. Juan Agustín Morfi, *History of Texas, 1673–1779*, I, 31.

14. Castañeda, *Heritage in Texas*, II, 16; Bolton, *Texas in the Middle Eighteenth Century*, pp. 67–70. The boundary between Texas and Louisiana was unsettled as late as 1753. It was generally accepted by Spanish officials that "the Red River was the true boundary," even though there was evidence that since 1736 Arroyo Hondo or Gran Montaña had been the accepted limit. See ibid., pp. 70–73.

15. Sidney B. Brinckerhoff and Odie B. Faulk, *Lancers for the King: A Study of the Frontier Military System of Northern New Spain, with a Translation of the Royal Regulations of 1772*, p. 81.

16. Bolton, *The Mission as a Frontier Institution*, p. 5.

17. Ibid., p. 6.

18. Brinckerhoff and Faulk, *Lancers for the King*, p. 81. According to Marion A. Habig, there is no historical evidence that the missionaries and mission guards used force or deception to bring the natives to the missions and to hold them prisoner. To support his claims, Habig quotes Isidro Espinosa, the Texas missionary who on March 23, 1728, brought Brigadier General Pedro de Rivera, the viceroy's inspector of the frontier province, to account for alleging the use of arms at mission centers in the conversion of the Indians: "[Rivera] labors under manifest misapprehension. It is one thing for missionaries to have an armed guard in order to insure the respect of the savages, and another thing to impart the faith by force of arms. This latter no one has even dreamed of" (Marion A. Habig, *San Antonio's Mission San José: State and National Historic Site, 1720–1968*, p. 4). Interestingly enough, Brinckerhoff and Faulk find no need to elaborate on what constitutes the force needed to compel "heathens into a receptive attitude." Habig, moreover, is well armed with the sword-pen of Fray Isidro de Espinosa. If General Rivera was already beginning to suspect inherent weaknesses in mission centers designed to reduce restive Texas Indians at royal expense and was reporting his impressions to Mexico City, certainly Fray Espinosa's defense of the Texas mission system is understandable.

19. Brinckerhoff and Faulk, *Lancers for the King*, p. 81.

20. Castañeda, *Heritage in Texas*, II, 22.

21. Isidro de Espinosa, *Espinosa's Diary of 1709*, I, 3.

22. Ibid., p. 5.

23. Clark, *New Orleans*, p. 12.

24. When the Spanish imperial government refused to trade with the French, who were hoping to bring their merchant ships to Veracruz, the governor of Louisiana capitalized on a letter sent to him by the Spanish missionary Fray Francisco Hidalgo inquiring about the welfare of the Indians in East Texas and asking the governor's help in establishing missions in the area. The governor sent St. Denis to Texas ostensibly in response to the request. Actually, the French wanted to establish trade relations with population centers in New Spain. St. Denis asserted that he had eighteen thousand pesos' worth of merchandise in Mobile for this purpose. See Resumen general de los autos sobre . . . la necesidad de poblar la región entre Texas y la Mobila, Mexico, November 30, 1716, ASF, Provincias Internas, p. 153.

25. Domingo Ramón to Viceroy, Informes del Capitan Ramón sobre la buena conducta de Luis de San Denis y armas encontradas entre los indios, July 26, 1716, ASF, VIII, 62.

26. Relación de los empleos, méritos y servicos de D. Martín Alarcón, Mexico, January 3, 1721, ASF, IX, 1, 19.

27. Francisco Céliz, *Diary of the Alarcón Expedition into Texas, 1718–1719*, pp. 23–25.

28. Ibid., p. 23.

29. Clark, *New Orleans*, pp. 1–20; Bolton, *The Spanish Borderlands*, p. 226.

30. Morfi, *History of Texas*, I, 193.

31. Eleanor Claire Buckley, "The Aguayo Expedition into Texas and Louisiana, 1719–1722," pp. 32–60. Aguayo quickly reestablished the six abandoned missions in East Texas. He also strengthened the presidio of Dolores and added a fort at Los Adaes. There were now ten missions, four presidios, and four settlement centers: Los Adaes, Nacogdoches, San Antonio, and La Bahía del Espíritu Santo. See Morfi, *History of Texas*, I, 193. During this time Fray Antonio Márgil de Jesús, president of the first group of missionaries from the College of Zacatecas and founder of San José in 1720, established the four missions that helped Spain maintain sovereignty in East Texas: Nuestra Señora de Guadalupe de Nacogdoches (1716–1773), Nuestra Señora de los Dolores de los Ais (1717–1773), San Miguel de Linares de los Adaes (1717–1773), and Nuestra Señora del Espíritu Santo de Zúñiga, near Lavaca Bay (1722–1830). See Habig, *San Antonio's Mission San José*, pp. 3–19.

32. Buckley, "The Aguayo Expedition," p. 61.

33. Castañeda, *Heritage in Texas*, II, 268–74.

34. Satisfaciendo a la orden de V.M. con ques se servio Remitir tres Cartas . . . , March 27, 1719, AGI-UT, Audiencia de México (61–6–38), Dunn transcripts.

35. Castañeda, *Heritage in Texas*, II, 268.

36. Cédula Real, April 22, 1719, in ibid., p. 321.

37. Cédula Real to Marqués de Valero, March 18, 1723, AGI-UT, Audiencia de Guadalajara, (67–1–37).

38. Cédula Real, April 22, 1719, Historia, Vol. 298, 321, UT Archives; Cédula Real to Juan Montero, Intendant of Canary Islands, July 24, 1723, AGI-UT, Audiencia de Guadalajara (67–1–37), Dunn transcripts.

39. Cédula Real to Governor of Yucatán, May 10, 1723, AGI-UT, Audiencia de Guadalajara (67–1–37), Dunn transcripts.

40. Cédula Real, April 22, 1719, AGI-UT, p. 321, Dunn transcripts.

41. Juan Montero to Marquis of Grimaldo, September 19, 1723, AGI-UT, Audiencia de Guadalajara (67–1–37), Dunn transcripts.

42. Joseph Patino to the Duje Arion, July 3, 1727, AGI-UT, Audiencia de Guadalajara (67–1–37), Dunn transcripts.

43. Cédula Real, February 14, 1729, *Historia,* Vol. 298, pp. 412–13, University of Texas Archives.

44. Castañeda, *Heritage in Texas,* II, 274.

45. Pedro de Rivera to Casafuerte, January 16, 1730, AGI-UT, Audiencia de Guadalajara (67–4–38), Dunn transcripts.

46. Juan de Oliván Rebolledo to Marqués de Casafuerte, July 17, 1730, AGI-UT, Audiencia de Guadalajara (67–4–38).

47. Castañeda, *Heritage in Texas,* II, 280.

48. Official roll by order of the viceroy, September 9, 1730, Cuatitlán, AGN-UT, *Historia,* vol. 84.

49. Juan Antonio Almazán to Marqués de Casafuerte, July 11, 1731, Hatcher translation.

50. Moore, *The Cabildo in Peru under the Hapsburgs,* p. 45.

51. "11. Auviendo [*sic*] Hecho la Eleción del sitio adonde se ha de hazer la población que como esta dicho, a de ser en lugares lebandtados, a donde aya sanidad, fortaleza, fertilidad y copia de tierra de labor y pasto, lena y madera y materiales, aguas dulces, gente natural, comodidad, acarretos, entrada y salida, que este descubierto de viento norte . . . " (Real Ordenanzas para Nueva Poblaciones, Philip II, July 3, 1573; in Nuttall, "Royal Ordinances," p. 745).

52. Auto de Fundación de la Villa de San Fernando, Marqués Juan Acuña de Casafuerte, November 28, 1730, BA, Hatcher translation. Auto de Fundación, Casafuerte, November 28, 1730).

53. Auto de Fundación, Casafuerte, November 28, 1730. Actually, the basic measure of length used by the Spaniards evolved into a unit of approximately eleven inches. It was distinct from the Roman pes, which became known as the linear foot. "The *vara,* an iron or wooden bar, commonly used as a three-foot measure varied in length throughout the provincias. The decrees of Philip II in 1573 and in 1581 designated the Castilian *vara* as the official Spanish standard and in 1801 Charles IV ordered its use in all his overseas possessions. At that time the established length of the *vara* was between 834 and 835 millimeters, or slightly less than 32.9 inches" (Virginia H. Taylor Houston, "Surveying in Texas," pp. 204–205).

54. Castañeda, *Heritage in Texas,* II, 303.

55. Almazán to Casafuerte, July 11, 1731, BA.

56. Ibid. The distribution of municipal lots at the Villa de San Fernando became the first recorded survey in Texas. These records were placed in the chest of the *cabildo* to serve as the permanent representation of the rights of each family (Houston, "Surveying in Texas," pp. 206–207).

57. *Recopilación de leyes de los reynos de las Indias mandadas imprimir y publicar por la magestad católica de Rey Don Carlos II,* libro 4, título 12, ley 4.

58. For details on the distribution of residential lots, see Frederick Charles Chabot, *With the Makers of San Antonio,* p. 146.

59. Auto de Fundación, Casafuerte, November 28, 1730.

60. Almazán to Casafuerte, July 11, 1731, BA.

61. "This ground was used for a great variety of purposes. It contained the pound for stray cattle as well as the public threshing floor, and a place where the villagers might winnow their grain in the open air. It contained the public rubbish heap and the village slaughter pen. Upon it the farmer might unload the crops brought in from the fields or might keep his hives of bees. Parts otherwise unoccupied served for play grounds and loafing places. No building might be constructed upon this land, nor might it be cultivated" (G. N. McBride, cited in Eyler N. Simpson, *The Ejido: Mexico's Way Out,* pp. 11–12).

62. Acta de la General Visita, Notification to the Surveyors, Laredo, June 20, 1767, LA.

63. Alamazán to Casafuerte, July 11, 1731, BA.

64. Ibid.

65. Ibid.

66. Moore, *The Cabildo in Peru under the Hapsburgs.*

67. Ibid.

68. Castañeda, *Heritage in Texas,* II, 306.

69. Alamazán to Casafuerte, July 11, 1731, BA.

70. Almazán, Títulos de Regidores to Casafuerte, Presidio de San Antonio, July 20, 1731, AGN-UT, Provincias Internas, 32, Bolton transcripts.

71. Austin, "Municipal Government," p. 321.

72. Ibid.

73. Almazán, Título de Alguacil-mayor, to Casafuerte, July 20, 1731, AGN-UT, Provincias Internas, 32, Bolton transcripts.

74. *Recopilación de leyes,* libro 5, título 12, ley 4.

75. Ibid.

76. Hatcher, "Municipal Government," p. 318.

77. Almazán, Título de Escribanos de consejo y ppco., to Casafuerte, July 20, 1731, AGN-UT, Provincias Internas, 32, Bolton transcripts.

78. *Recopilación de leyes,* libro 4, título 10, ley 21.

79. Moore, *The Cabildo in Peru under the Hapsburgs,* p. 111.

80. Chabot, *With the Makers of San Antonio,* p. 167.

81. Moore, *The Cabildo in Peru under the Hapsburgs,* p. 112.

82. Libro de Cabildo, Minutes, June 28, 1745–April 10, 1749, vol. I, NA.

83. Chabot, *With the Makers of San Antonio,* p. 170.

84. Castañeda, *Heritage in Texas,* II, 309.

85. Moore, *The Cabildo in Peru under the Hapsburgs,* p. 77.

86. Auto de Elecciones, by Almazán, August 2, 1731, AGN-UT, Provincias Internas, vol. 32, Bolton transcripts.

87. Castañeda, *Heritage in Texas,* II, 309.

88. Moore, *The Cabildo in Peru under the Hapsburgs,* p. 79.

89. *Recopilación de leyes,* libro 4, título 5, ley 10.

90. Auto de Eleciones, by Almazán, August 2, 1731, AGN-UT, Provincias Internas, vol. 32, Bolton transcripts.

91. Ibid.

92. Ibid.

93. Moore, *The Cabildo in Peru under the Hapsburgs,* p. 80.

94. Auto de Eleciones, by Almazán, August 2, 1731, BA.

95. Castañeda, *Heritage in Texas,* II, 309.

96. *Recopilación de leyes,* libro 5, título 3, ley 12.

97. Moore, *The Cabildo in Peru under the Hapsburgs,* p. 101.

98. Decrees of Alcalde Juan Leal Góraz, April 14, 1735, vol. VI, McLean translations, BA.

99. Hatcher, "The Municipal Government," p. 314.

100. Decree of Alcalde Juan Joseph Montes de Oça, February 6, 1745, vol. XVII, Hunnicut translations, BA.

101. Samuel M. Buck, *Yanaguana's Successors,* p. 62.

102. Instruction of Casafuerte to Almazán concerning the Canary Islanders, November 28, 1730, Vol. I (September 30, 1699–November 28, 1730), Miller translation, BA.

103. Félix Díaz Almaraz, Jr., *Tragic Cavalier: Governor Manuel Salcedo of Texas, 1808–1813,* pp. 5–11.

104. Morfi, *History of Texas,* II, 419.

105. Almaraz, *Tragic Cavalier,* p. 7.

106. Morfi, *History of Texas,* I, 92–93. Morfi, who had little use for the Isleños, could hardly be expected to demonstrate much respect for the small number of Hispanic settlers in their efforts to hack a municipality out of the wilderness of Central Texas.

107. Ten years after Morfi's appraisal, an associate of Pedro Vial, the peripatetic French frontiersman in the service of the Spanish government in the Louisiana–Texas–New Mexico salient, upon arriving in San Antonio expressed delight with the tiny *villa* and described its dwellings as "more of wood of moderate structure."

108. Isaac Joslin Cox, "The Early Settlers of San Fernando," p. 152.

109. Casafuerte to Almazán, December 31, 1731, Vol. II (December 25, 1731–June 25, 1733), Miller translations, BA.

110. Ibid.

111. Cox, "The Early Settlers of San Fernando," p. 150.

CHAPTER 5

1. "Instrucciones que han de observar Don José Tienda de Cuervo y Don Agustín López de la Cámara Alta, para el recognicimiento de la Costa del Seno Mexicano, cuya conquista y reducción está a cargo de Don José de Escandón," pp. 5–10; Isaac Joslin Cox, "The Southwest Boundary of Texas," pp. 88–89.

2. Alejandro Prieto, *Historia geográfica y estadística del Estado de Tamaulipas,* pp. 227–48.

3. "Relación de los méritos de Don José Escandón," II: 303–307.

4. "Puso en quietud a la Ciudad de Querétaro, en la sublevación que hizo la plebe. . . . [Escandon] reprimió la violencia, arrestó a los cabecillas y se les impuso el castigo correspondiente. . . . Libertó el Nuevo Reino de León y las Fronteras de Pánuco, Tampico, Villa de Valles, Guadalcázar y Charcas de los insultos, hostilidades y excesos que los bárbaros chichimecos cometían" (ibid., pp. 305–306). See also Lawrence Francis Hill, *José de Escandón and the Founding of Nuevo Santander*, p. 21.

5. "Relación de los méritos de Don José Escandon," II: 304–305.

6. Ibid.

7. "Reconosimiento del Seno Mexicano hecho por el Escandón," AGN-UT, Provincias Internas, 179, pp. 167–68.

8. Hill, *Escandón*, pp. 58–68.

9. "Reconosimiento del Seno Mexicano hecho por el Escandón, AGN-UT, Provincias Internas, 179, pp. 168–74.

10. "Descripción o mapa de las fundaciones hechas por el orden del Excellentísimo Señor Conde de Revillagigedo, con sus nombres, misiones, distancias . . . consecuentes a la consulta de 1747," I: 12–43.

11. Ibid.

12. Florence Johnson Scott, *Historical Heritage of the Lower Rio Grande*, p. 14.

13. Ibid., p. 27.

14. Prieto, *Historia*, pp. 155–59.

15. "Diario que hizo el Padre Fray Simón del Yerro en el Seno Mexicano año 1749," AGN-UT *Historia*, vol. 29, pt. 2 (Mexico), pp. 282–83. See also Scott, *Lower Rio Grande*, p. 28.

16. Scott, *Lower Rio Grande*, p. 28.

17. *Estado General*, I: 379–86.

18. Prieto, *Historia*, p. 154.

19. *Estado General*, I: 429–30.

20. Ibid., pp. 407–18.

21. Ibid., pp. 412–13.

22. Cox, "Southwest Boundary," p. 89.

23. Ibid.

24. Bolton, *Texas in the Middle Eighteenth Century*, p. 296.

25. Ibid.

26. There were two types of land grants made to the settlers raising livestock in the Río Grande area during the Spanish period: the *sitio de ganado mayor*, about forty-three hundred acres land assigned for raising cattle and horses; and the *sitio de ganado menor*, about nineteen hundred acres for the raising of sheep and goats. Once the land was granted, however, it was further divided and eventually used lands to graze all livestock.

27. Florence Johnson Scott, *Royal Land Grants North of the Rio Grande, 1777–1821*, p. 9.

28. Many Mexican Americans in the Lower Rio Grande Valley proudly trace their lineage to these first settlers. These pioneers of the middle eighteenth century, mostly from New Spain's provinces of Coahuila and Nuevo León, included José María de la Garza Falcón, José Florencio Chapa, Manuel de Hinojosa, and Miguel

Martínez, who were the founders of Camargo and Mier; Vicente Guerra and Antonio Tabares, founders of Revilla (now Guerrero); Carlos Cantú, a founder of Reynosa; Blas María de la Garza Falcón and Nicolás de los Santos Coy, founders of the first ranch settlements on the northern banks of the Rio Grande near Carnestolendas, present-day Rio Grande City; and Tomás Sánchez de la Barrera y Gallardo, founder of Laredo.

29. Rogelia O. García, *Dolores, Revilla and Laredo: Three Sister Settlements*, pp. 2–4.

30. *Estado General*, I: 437–41.

31. Ibid., I: 436, 439.

32. Captain Tienda de Cuervo was commissioned by Viceroy Marqués de Amarillas to serve as *juez inspector* of the settlements near the Gulf of Mexico in 1757. He was assisted by Agustín López de la Cámara Alta (ibid., I: 437–41).

33. Ibid., I: 444.

34. Ibid., II: 123–24.

35. Herbert Eugene Bolton, trans., "Tienda de Cuervo's Ynspección of Laredo, 1757," p. 188.

36. Castañeda, *Heritage in Texas*, III, 173.

37. Ibid.

38. *Estado General*, I:445.

39. The lands that constituted the town commons (*ejidos* or *propios*) were approximately fifteen square leagues, at about 6,642 acres per league; the fifteen leagues thus equalled over 99,000 acres.

40. *Estado General*, I:445; Seb S. Wilcox, "Laredo during the Texas Republic," p. 86.

41. Kathleen De Camara, *Laredo on the Rio Grande*, p. 13.

42. Bolton, "Cuervo's Ynspección," p. 194.

43. Ibid., p. 190.

44. Ibid., pp. 191, 200.

45. Ibid., p. 198.

46. De Camara, *Laredo*, pp. 12–14.

47. Bolton, "Cuervo's Ynspección," p. 192.

48. De Camara, *Laredo*, pp. 12–14.

49. Bolton, "Cuervo's Ynspección," pp. 196–98.

50. Ibid.

51. "Acta de la General Visita al Pueblo de San Agustín de Laredo by Juan Fernando and Don José de Ossorio y Llamas, Laredo, June 1767," 108–10.

52. Scott, *Royal Land Grants*, p. 12.

53. Scott, *Lower Rio Grande*, p. 62.

54. "Acta de la General Visita," pp. 71–74.

55. Ibid.

56. Ibid., pp. 80–84.

57. Ibid.

58. Ibid., pp. 100–10.

59. Ibid.

60. Ibid.

61. Ibid.

62. Castañeda, *Heritage in Texas,* III, 174–75.

63. Bolton, "Cuervo's Ynspección," pp. 190–91.

64. Castañeda, *Heritage in Texas,* III, 176.

65. Margaret Kenny Kress, "Diary of a Visit of Inspection of the Texas Missions Made by Fray Gaspar José Solís in the Year 1767–68," p. 74. According to Castañeda, a priest took charge of church duties on or before December 26, 1759. The priest arrived from Boca de Leones, Nuevo León, after Bishop Martínez de Tejada accepted the offer of the settlers to contribute 150 pesos a year for the support of a parish priest and to construct a church. Apparently this arrangement was temporary, since in 1767 the settlers had no church and were still petitioning for a permanent pastor (Castañeda, *Heritage in Texas,* III, 176).

66. Juan Fernando de Palacio to Joseph M. de Soto, August 31, 1769, LA 1-5-2.

67. Census Report of Miguel Ponce Borrego, lieutenant *alcalde,* Laredo, January 28, 1789, LA 4-4-41.

68. "Acta de la General Visita," pp. 109–10.

69. Ibid., pp. 110–18.

70. Ibid.; Scott, *Lower Rio Grande,* pp. 71–76.

71. Scott, *Lower Rio Grande,* pp. 71–76.

72. Bolton, "Cuervo's Ynspección," pp. 197–99.

73. Scott, *Lower Rio Grande,* pp. 71–76.

74. Don José Ossorio to Señores Capitán, Cabildo, y Apoderados de Laredo, April 8, 1768, LA 1-6-24.

75. Seb S. Wilcox, "The Spanish Archives of Laredo," pp. 348–49.

76. Governor Vicente Gonzales de Santianes, San Carlos, July 5, 1770, to Tomás Sánchez, LA.

77. Decree of Chief Justice Tomás Sánchez, Laredo, July 9, 1774, LA 1-20-13.

78. Decree of Chief Justice Tomás Sánchez, Laredo, May 5, 1779, LA 1-15-25.

79. Austin, "Municipal Government," p. 314.

80. Decree of Alcalde Juan Joseph Montes de Oça, Villa de San Fernando, February 6, 1745, vol. XVII, Hunnicut translation, BA.

81. Census Report of Miguel Ponce Borrego, lieutenant *alcalde,* Laredo, January 28, 1789, LA.

82. Ibid.

CHAPTER 6

1. Hubert Howe Bancroft, *History of California,* I, 69–81. Rodríguez Cabrillo's expedition left the port of La Navidad in New Spain on June 27, 1542, a dangerously late date after which adverse winds and currents were prevalent. He entered what is now San Diego Bay on September 28, 1542. After resting six days, the two vessels sailed northward and reached Catalina Island on October 7. Continuing the journey northward, they visited the sites of what are now San Pedro, Santa Monica, and Ventura. The fleet passed Point Conception on October 18. As the northward voyage continued, heavy storms and intense fog made it hazardous to examine the coastline closely and to locate the vital rivers and bays that the Indians had told

them about. Some authorities believe that the expedition might have gone as far as latitude 42° 30″, where the Rogue River enters the Pacific. Rodríguez Cabrillo explored some eight hundred miles of coastline, located and named scores of places (many of which were renamed), and laid claim to a vast territory for Spain. However, the Spanish imperial government reserved approval of these achievements because it failed to discover either the legendary straits or wealthy Indian kingdoms. Bartolomé Ferrelo succeeded Rodríguez Cabrillo, who died from an injury on the journey. See Richard F. Pourade, "Juan Rodríguez Cabrillo: Discoverer of California"; Herbert E. Bolton, *Spanish Explorations,* pp. 150–71.

2. Although never large, the Manila Galleon had a definite influence as an incentive for establishing settlements in California. Sailing from Acapulco and carrying bullion, the ships made the westward journey in two or three months. On the return voyage, silk, spices, and other items from the Far East were carried to be sold in the mining centers of Mexico and Peru, and even shipped on to Spain. The profits to be made on luxury goods were enormous. Consequently, space aboard ship was at a premium and supplies of water and food were inadequate. The crew suffered accordingly. Thus, there was a constant interest in a port of call where inbound ships could stop, men could recover their health, the ships' stores could be replenished, and necessary repairs could be made. Although Spain was beset for almost 150 years by domestic trouble, problems with international rivals, and the difficulties faced in administering its far-flung empire, the Philippine trade encouraged the settlement of California and prevented it from being ignored by Spanish policymakers. (Bancroft, *History of California,* I, 69–81).

A successful merchant, despite his losses when Cavendish captured the Spanish galleon in 1587, Cermenho was able to recoup his fortune in other areas. The most northerly point reached by his expedition was probably 41° latitude, although some claim it went as far as the forty-third parallel (Henry R. Wagner, "The Voyage to California"; Robert F. Heizer, "Archeological Evidence of Sebastián Rodríguez Cermenho's California Visit").

3. Bancroft, *History of California,* I, 98–109; Bolton, *Spanish Explorations,* pp. 52–103.

4. Bannon, *Spanish Borderlands,* pp. 157–59.

5. Ibid., pp. 160–61; Herbert E. Bolton, *Fray Juan Crepsi, Missionary Explorer on the Pacific Coast, 1769–1774,* pp. 29–38.

6. Bannon, *Spanish Borderlands,* pp. 162–64. José Joaquín Moraga, commander of the presidio, is well known as a founder of missions, presidios, and the civil settlement of San José during the 1770s. His military career is equally significant in the development of Spanish California. For an interesting study, see Donald C. Cutter, "Moraga of the Military: His California Service, 1784–1810."

7. Francisco Palou, *Historical Memoirs of New California,* III, 17–18, 42–93. The purely civic colonies of California were called pueblos to distinguish them from missions or presidios. The term "pueblo," in its most extended meaning, may embrace towns of every description, from a hamlet to a city and, consequently, might apply equally well to the missions, with their adjacent Indian villages, to the small villages springing up around the presidios, or to the regularly settled colony. However, in its special significance, a pueblo means a corporate town, with certain rights of juris-

diction and administration. In Spain the term "*lugar*" was usually applied to towns of this nature, but Spanish Americans prefer and persistently use the term "pueblo." The word may be used in several distinct ways, each of which may be entirely correct. It had a political significance when it was applied to the jurisdiction of all the legal voters within a certain territory; it also applied to the judicial jurisdiction represented by an *alcalde* of the pueblo, which did not always coincide with the political jurisdiction; and the pueblo had a proprietary existence defined by the rights to certain lands given by the grant. When complete it had a town council (*ayuntamiento*), composed of councilmen (*regidores*), judges (*alcaldes*), and a mayor (Frank W. Blackmar, *Spanish Institutions of the Southwest*, p. 153).

8. Antonio Bucareli to Julián de Arriaga, Mexico, September 26, 1773. No. III Remite copia de las instrucciones que dió al Comte. de los Presidios de Sn. Diego y Monterey en la California, AGI-UC, Guadalajara, 514; Jones, *Los Paisanos*, pp. 212-13.

9. Florian Francis Guest, "Municipal Institutions in Spanish California, 1769-1821," pp. 81-84. Father Florian Guest, O.F.M., is one of the most noted authorities on California municipalities during the colonial period.

10. Ibid., p. 83.

11. Antoinine Tibesar, ed., *The Writings of Junípero Serra*, II, 269.

12. Ibid., p. 365.

13. From the very moment when Governor Don Felipe Neve entered Monterey he was anxious about how to support the inhabitants of these new establishments. He thought in the beginning that increased agriculture in the missions, if the crops were good, could furnish the three presidios with the surplus. He was informed that this could not be done at once, for as the crops increased the consumers also increased because of new Christians being created. He agreed to found a pueblo in a good place. The new pueblo would be made up entirely of Spaniards and mestizos, to be employed exclusively in raising every kind of grain and crop, so that all the presidios might be provided from them, especially if barks did not come or if they should suffer some disaster (Palou, *Historical Memoirs*, IV, 66).

14. Frederick Hall, *The History of San José*, pp. 14-15.

15. Palou, *Historical Memoirs*, IV, 166-68.

16. Guest, "Municipal Institutions," pp. 99-100.

17. Bucareli to Croix, Mexico, July 15, 1778, AGN-UC, Provincias Internas, 121; Bucareli to Neve, Mexico, July 22, 1778, C-A, 52.

18. Croix to Neve, Chihuahua, September 3, 1778, AGN-UC, Provincias Internas, 121.

19. Moraga to Fages, San Francisco, December 1, 1782, C-A, 2; Fages to Moraga, Monterey, December 12, 1782, C-A, 23; Moraga to Fages, San Francisco, January 4, 1783, C-A, 52.

20. José Moraga, Concesión de tierras a varios individuos, May 13, 1783, C-A, 52; Fr. Tomás de la Peña to the viceroy, Miguel de Anza, College of San Fernando, July 27, 1798, C-A, 52. The town was first located about a mile and a quarter north of the old market street plaza on which the City Hall now stands. The old town was located on the Alviso Road, or First Street, where it crosses the first bridge on the outskirts of the present town. As the Santa Clara Mission was located at that

time somewhat east of the present situation of the old mission church, which now stands within the precincts of Santa Clara University, the pueblo and the mission were not far apart; the latter was very nearly west of the former. The proximity of the mission to the town gave rise to much contention, and the governor concluded that the respective properties of the two settlements were too near each other. Another, more potent, reason for the change of site was that the town site was located on low ground and was subject to frequent floods. In the winter of 1778–79, water stood nearly three feet deep in the houses of the Santa Clara Mission and in the new pueblo, and a circuitous path of three leagues was the only safe route between the two places (Blackmar, *Spanish Institutions,* p. 178).

21. Guest, "Municipal Institutions," pp. 38–45.

22. William F. James and George H. McMurray, *History of San José, California,* pp. 15–30; O. Garfield Jones, "Local Government in the Spanish Colonies as Provided by the Recopilación de Leyes de los Reynos de las Indias," p. 88.

23. Pedro Fages, Sobre punto del gobierno de la Península de California e inspeción general de sus tropas, Monterey, February 26, 1791, C-A, 6.

24. Marcos Chaboya to Diego de Borica, San José, January 10, 1797, C-A.

25. Guest, "Municipal Institutions," p. 111.

26. James, *San José,* p. 22.

27. Croix to José de Gálvez, Arispe, February 28, 1782, AGI-UC, Guadalajara, 267. For a comprehensive treatise on the life and activity of the great pueblo founder in California, see Edwin A. Bielharz, *Felipe de Neve, First Governor of California.*

28. Guest, "Municipal Institutions," p. 114.

29. Neve to Croix, Monterey, April 3, 1779, AGI-UC, Guadalajara, 278; Croix to Rivera, Arispe, December 27, 1779 [Instrucciones para la fundación de un presidio en el canal de Santa Bárbara y de tres misiones y del pueblo la Reina de los Angeles], C-A, 1.

30. The settlers were to receive a salary of ten pesos a month plus daily rations for three years, counting from the day of their admission into the company of the expedition. Each settler was to be given two cows, two oxen, two mares, two horses, one mule, two sheep, two she-goats, and tools and implements necessary for farming. For all the aid in livestock mounts, equipment, and clothes, the settlers had to repay the Real Hacienda. No reimbursement was required, however, for aid given in salary and rations, for fruits and seeds for planting, or for the offspring of the livestock (Guest, "Municipal Institutions," p. 116).

31. Neve to Croix, Monterey, January 2, 1781, C-A, 22; Padrón del vecindario el que tiene el pueblo de la Reina de los Angeles, San Gabriel, November 19, 1781, C-A, 52; Harry Kelsey, "A New Look at the Founding of Old Los Angeles," p. 331. Kelsey claims that there were eleven families but only forty-four individuals who completed the hazardous journey.

32. Neve, Instrucción para la fundación de Los Angeles, San Gabriel, August 26, 1788 [should be 1781], transcript, Bancroft Library.

33. Pedro Fages to José Argüello, Monterey, August 14, 1786, C-A, 3.

34. Guest, "Municipal Institutions," p. 127.

35. Pedro Fages, Repartición de solares y suertes de tierra de regadio y secadel, Monterrey, August 14, 1786, C-A, 52.

36. Plan que manifiesta la idea de una población nueva en la alta California con el distingidisimo nombre de Branciforte, . . . Expediente sobre erección de la villa de Branciforte en la Nueva California, 1796–1803, WBS (hereafter Branciforte Expediente, WBS). With almost all the documents original, the Stephens Collection includes a complete record of the founding of the settlement near the site of present Santa Cruz.

37. Borica to Branciforte, Monterey, September 23, 1796, Branciforte Expediente, WBS; Royal Fiscal, Mexico City, December 29, 1796, in ibid.

38. Jacobo Ugarte y Loyola to Branciforte, Guadalajara, October 24, 1796, AGN-UC.

39. The settlers who came to Branciforte were all volunteers: José Vicente Mojica, his wife, Victoria Luna, and five children; José Barbosa, his wife, Felipa de Estrada; Josef Silvestre Machuca, his wife, María Cirila Argüello; Josef María Arceo, unmarried; Fermín Cordero, unmarried; Josef Antonio Robles, unmarried; Josef Agustín Narváez, unmarried (Borica to Viceroy, Monterey, May 12, 1797, Branciforte Expediente, WBS; Borica to Viceroy, July 24, 1797, in ibid.).

40. The heads of families who joined in December were Marcelino Brabo, with thirty-two cattle, eight oxen, twenty horses, eleven mares, and one burro; Macario Castro, with thirty-six cattle; Apolinario Bernal, with twenty cattle, eight horses, eighteen mares, and one burro; and Juan Pinto, with eighteen cattle, four horses, twenty-two mares, one mule, one burro, and two oxen. By the end of the year the population at the Villa de Branciforte numbered forty (Gabriel Moraga, Villa de Branciforte, December 31, 1797, in Branciforte Expediente, WBS).

41. Guest, "Municipal Institutions," pp. 188–90.

42. Neve to Croix, Monterey, December 19, 1782, AGN-UC, Provincias Internas, 121, C-A, 22.

43. Brinckerhoff and Faulk, *Lancers for the King*, pp. 19, 84.

44. Guest, "Municipal Institutions," pp. 188–90.

45. Guest, "Municipal Institutions," p. 199.

46. Guest, "Municipal Institutions," p. 128.

47. Morfi, *History of Texas*, II, 22.

48. Theodore Grivas, "Alcalde Rule: The Nature of Local Government in Spanish Mexican California," *California Historical Quarterly* 40 (1961): 11–12.

49. Grivas, "Alcalde Rule," pp. 12–13.

50. Felipe de Goycoechea to Fages, Santa Barbara, July 6, 1790, C-A, 5; Felipe de Goycoechea to [?], Santa Barbara, December 31, 1801, C-A, 50.

51. Macario de Castro to Ygnacio Castro, Pueblo San José, October 30, 1804, ASJ, vol. III, transcripts; José de la Guerra to Macario de Castro, Monterey, December 5, 1804, in ibid. When the *vecinos* did not elect able town magistrates the *comisionado* appointed one of his choice. Such was the case in 1783, when José Domingo, *comisionado* at San José, appointed Manuel González, an Apache Indian, as *alcalde*. González, a natural leader, showed vigor and precision in the observance of the regulations and skill in directing the work required in the fields (Guest, "Municipal Institutions," p. 203).

52. Felipe de Goycoechea to [?], Santa Bárbara, December 31, 1789, C-A, 50.

53. Macario de Castro to Raymundo Carillo, San José, April 30, 1802, C-A, 11; Raymundo Carrillo to José Joaquín de Arrillaga, Monterrey, May 3, 1802, C-A, 11.

54. Fray José Viader, San José, July 12, 1803, Acta de la colocación de la primera piedra de la capilla del pueblo, ASJ, vol. III, transcripts.

55. Macario de Castro to [?], San José, January 1, 1805, C-A, 50.

56. Ibid. Both San José and Los Angeles had granaries by 1789. The temporary storge of maize in the chapel sacristy may have been necessitated by repairs on the granary.

57. Felipe de Goycoechea to [?], Santa Bárbara, December 31, 1789, C-A, 50. The actual construction of a parish church to replace the small chapel started in 1819, when Father Mariano Payeras, president of the missions, offered to assist the citizens of Los Angeles. With permission from the viceroy to build a church, the *vecinos,* ably assisted by Father Payeras, collected 575 pesos, 6½ reales from the sale of *aguardiente* supplied by the missions. Part of this money was used to pay Indian laborers from Mission San Luis Rey at one real a day plus their board and lodging. The inhabitants of the pueblo, who numbered eight hundred, bore the largest burden by cutting and carrying the timber for the new church. By 1821, they had constructed the walls as high as the closing of the arches of the windows. Although Los Angelenos had incurred a church debt amounting to about 2,000 pesos by 1821, they were not able to complete their church until after the Mexican Revolution (Guest, "Municipal Institutions," pp. 237–38).

58. Guest, "Municipal Institutions." pp. 218–27.

59. The *alcalde* also used his authority in criminal cases. On November 19, 1815, the *alcalde* at San José, Felipe Talamantes, arrested Guillermo Soto and his son José María for aggravated assault on Eugenio Valdez. The *alcalde* handed over the assailants to the *comisionado.* At the trial, Don Felipe made a deposition depicting the intoxicated and belligerent mood of the defendants. Since Eugenio Valdez recovered completely from a wound suffered in the assault, the defendants were released from jail on March 5, under the proviso that they abstain from drinking (ibid.).

CHAPTER 7

1. Bannon, *Spanish Borderlands,* p. 174.

2. Alicia V. Tjarks, "Comparative Demographic Analysis of Texas, 1777–1793," pp. 291–94.

3. Ibid.

4. Ibid.

5. Vito Alessio Robles, *Nicolás de la Fora, Relación del viaje que hizo a los presidios internos situados en la frontera de la América Septentrional pertenecientes al Rey de España,* p. 89.

6. Census Report of Miguel Ponce Borrego, Lieutenant Alcalde, Laredo, January 28, 1789, LA.

7. The estimates on Texas population during the last quarter of the eighteenth and the advent of the nineteenth century fluctuate and are doubtful. Croix gave

an approximate total of 4,000 inhabitants in 1780. Vicente Riva Palacio reported that the population of Texas was 3,394 at the turn of the century. Juan Bautista de Elguezábal, governor of the province in 1803, estimated a population of 4,800–2,500 of whom dwelled in San Antonio. In 1809, according to Tjarks, Governor Manuel de Salcedo reported a total population of 3,122 persons. A year later Texas was estimated to have a total of 3,334 inhabitants, according to the works of Fernando Navarro y Noriega (Tjarks, "Demographic Analysis," p. 300).

8. Herbert Ingram Priestly, *José de Gálvez, Visitor-General of New Spain, 1765–1771*, pp. 25–30; Lillian Estelle Fisher, *The Intendant System in Spanish America*, p. 8; Bancroft, *History of the Northern Mexican States*, II, 450.

9. Fisher, *Intendant System*, pp. 8–16.

10. The Bourbon reforms in the 1760s "provided among other things for the creation of a government *comandancia general,* and a *superintendencia de hacienda,* entirely independent of the viceroyalty of New Spain, in the *provincias internas,* so called, including Nueva Vizcaya, Sonora, Sinaloa, and two Californias, together with Coahuila, Texas, and New Mexico; the new governor was to have also the *patronato real* . . . a final arrangement was made under royal decrees of the 23rd and 24th of November 1792, with the organization of a *comandancia general de provincias internas,* comprising Sonora, Nueva Vizcaya, New Mexico, Texas, and Coahuila, independent of the viceroy. The two Californias, Nuevo Leon, and the colony of Nuevo Santander were attached to the viceroyalty of New Spain" (Bancroft, *History of the Northern Mexican States,* II, 450–51).

11. Bolton, *Texas in the Middle Eighteenth Century,* p. 8.

12. Brinckerhoff and Faulk, *Lancers for the King,* pp. 80–88. In 1786, Juan de Ugalde, "comandante of the eastern Interior Province, greatly enhanced his fighting reputation, and to a degree carried out Croix's plans, by uniting with the Comanche, Taovayas, Wichita, and Tawakoni, and inflicting a severe defeat upon the Apache at Arroyo de la Soledad west of San Antonio" (Bolton, *Texas in the Middle Eighteenth Century,* p. 127).

13. Castañeda, *Heritage in Texas,* V, 40.

14. Alcalde Antonio Rodríguez y Mederes, decree, October 2, 1745, BA, vol. 17 (January 16, 1745–July 31, 1746), Hunnicut translations.

15. Jones, "Local Government," pp. 88–89.

16. Chabot, *With the Makers of San Antonio,* pp. 151–79.

17. "#1 With the justified aim that protection by well regulated presidios will foment settlements and commerce in the frontier area, and that the strength of the presidios likewise be augmented by a great number of inhabitants I order . . . on no pretext to impede to dissuade people of good reputation and habits from entering and settling in their district. . . . I order . . . to distribute and assign lands and towns lots to those who ask them, with the obligation that they cultivate them.

#2 I . . . prohibit the molesting of merchants selling goods . . . or artisans who wish to work" (Royal Regulations of 1772, in Brinckerhoff and Faulk in *Lancers for the King,* p. 35).

18. "Juan Leal Alvarez . . . renounced his office of *regidor perpetuo,* March 28, 1742, owing to the deplorable situation in San Antonio, and removed with his family to the Presidio de Santa Rosa, an important base of supply for the colonists (and

which later became the capital of all Eastern Provinces), where he stated he could find greater advantages; or where at least, he might have found fewer disadvantages" (Chabot, *With the Makers of San Antonio,* p. 149; Castañeda, *Heritage in Texas,* III, 90).

19. The *cabildo abierto* originated on the American mainland at Veracruz, where it elected Hernán Cortés captain and *justicia mayor* (July, 1519), and at Santiago, Chile, where Pedro de Valdivia was elected governor of the province (June, 1541) (Jean Hippolyte Mariejol, *The Spain of Ferdinand and Isabella,* p. 286; Moore, *Cabildo in Peru under the Hapsburgs,* p. 126).

20. Francisco Xavier Tapia, *El cabildo abierto colonial,* pp. 6–7.

21. *Recopilación de leyes,* libro 4, título 10, ley 3; libro 4, título 11, ley 1; libro 4, título 11, ley 2.

22. Robert Butler, "The Cabildo and the Intendant," p. 29; Fisher, *The Intendant System,* pp. 31–32.

23. Auto de Cabildo, Villa de San Fernando, February 17, 1738, Vol. I (November 26, 1731–January 12, 1747), NA, p. 74.

24. Ibid., February 18, 1938, NA, p. 69.

25. Ibid., pp. 69–70.

26. Report on the fund campaign by cochairmen to the Cabildo, Villa de San Fernando, February 25, 1738, NA, p. 74.

27. Ibid., February 18, 1738, NA, pp. 71–74.

28. Ibid.

29. Ibid., February 25, 1738, NA, pp. 71–74.

30. Ibid.

31. Ibid., p. 71.

32. Ibid., pp. 77–78.

33. Ibid., July 15, 1738, NA, p. 81.

34. Alcalde Antonio Rodrigues y Mederos, decree, Villa de San Fernando, October 2, 1745, BA, vol. 17 (January 16, 1745–July 31, 1746), p. 81.

35. Opinion of the Fiscal, Mexico, January 15, 1748, BA, vol. 19 (January 15, 1748–July 19, 1749), p. 2.

36. Castañeda, *Heritage in Texas,* II, 101.

37. Opinion of the Fiscal, Mexico, January 15, 1748, BA, vol. 19, pp. 1–3.

38. *Recopilación de leyes,* libro 4, título 11, ley 2.

39. Opinion of the Fiscal, Mexico, January 15, 1748, BA, vol. 19, p. 3. It was customary for the crown to provide funds for municipal churches in view of relations existing between the crown and the Catholic church. Through the Real Patronato the crown dominated and directed the church in Spanish America. By means of this prerogative, the monarch nominated church officials and supervised ecclesiastical revenues (J. Lloyd Mecham. *Church and State in Latin America,* pp. 10–22; W. Eugene Shiels, *King and Church: The Rise and Fall of the Patronato Real,* p. 11).

40. The deep faith of the Isleños motivated them to construct a church even though they had only meager resources. The following suggests that they had a parish ministry from the time of their arrival: Fathers José de la Garza (1731–1734), Juan Recio de León (1734–1743), Juan Francisco de Esproncede (1743–1746), and

Francisco Manuel Polanco (1746–?) were their first four priests (Sam Woolford, ed., *San Antonio, a History for Tomorrow,* pp. 2–3; Castañeda, *Heritage in Texas,* III, 101).

41. Auto de Cabildo, Villa de San Fernando, January 12, 1742, NA, vol. I (November 26, 1731–January 12, 1747), pp. 90–91.

42. Noel Loomis and Abraham P. Nasatir, *Pedro de Vial and the Roads to Santa Fe,* p. 356.

43. Inventory of San Antonio de Valero, Legajo Núm. 7, 1793–1797, Exp. Núm. 440, Año 1797, Saltillo Archives, Vol. V (Mexican Photo Print Company, UT Archives), pp. 223–34; Castañeda, *Heritage in Texas,* V, 38.

44. María J. Rodríguez, *Rodríguez Memoirs of Early Texas,* pp. 37–38.

45. Elliot Coues, ed., *The Expeditions of Zebulon Montgomery Pike to the Headwaters of the Mississippi River, through Louisiana Territory, and in New Spain, during the Years 1805–6–7,* II, 783–84.

46. Cédula Real, July 31, 1746, BA, vol. 17 (January 16, 1745–July 31, 1746), pp. 101–102.

47. Decree of Viceroy Juan Francisco de Güemes y Horcasitas [Revilla Gigedo], Mexico, December 27, 1746, BA, p. 103.

48. Proclamation of Governor García Larios, Presidio of N. S. del Pilar de los Adaes (May 22, 1747), VOL. 17 (January 16, 1745–July 31, 1746), BA, p. 106.

49. Report from Cabildo, Villa de San Fernando, January 15, 1747, Vol. 17 (January 16, 1745–July 31, 1746, BA, pp. 140–41.

50. The "garrison stationed at this said presidio . . . [marched] . . . in formation through its streets . . . to the sound of war drums draped in mourning and with bells tolling . . . the exequies, funeral rites, and chanted mass were celebrated in church in which . . . had been previously prepared a covered tumulus with crown and scepter . . . lighted by 100 wax candles" (Report of Governor Larios, Los Adaes, May 26, 1747, Vol. 18, BA, p. 110).

51. Report of Joachin de Orobio Bázterra, Captain of the royal presidio of N.S. de Loreto and Bahía del Espíritu Santo, February 4, 1748, BA, vol. 18, p. 132.

52. Report from Cabildo, Villa de San Fernando, January 27, 1747, BA, vol. 18, p. 141.

53. Ibid.

54. Ibid., p. 144.

55. Ibid.

56. Leonard, *Baroque Times in Old Mexico,* p. 104.

CHAPTER 8

1. "Instructions to Peralta by Vice-Roy," p. 178.
2. Scholes, "Civil Government," pp. 76–78.
3. Simmons, *Spanish Government,* p. 194.
4. Ibid., pp. 193–94.
5. Ibid., p. 194.
6. Bannon, *Spanish Borderlands,* pp. 124–42.
7. Simmons, *Spanish Government,* p. 194.

8. Ibid.

9. Bannon, *Spanish Borderlands*, pp. 124–42.

10. Simmons, *Spanish Government*, pp. 196–97.

11. Fisher, *The Intendant System*, p. 106. These new laws, Charles III's Ordinance for New Spain, consisted of a preamble and 306 articles. There was also a 60-page index and appendix showing supporting legislation. A translation of the Ordinances of 1786 on the Intendancies of New Spain is included in Fisher. The intendancies provided systematization in the colonies "by erecting them into uniformly governed . . . districts . . . in place of old provinces, kingdoms (reynos), and governments" (ibid., p. 8).

12. Simmons, *Spanish Government*, p. 198.

13. *Recopilación de leyes*, libro 5, título 3, ley 1.

14. Simmons, *Spanish Government*, p. 198.

15. See chapter 3.

16. Wilcox, "Archives of Laredo." Other terms used to indicate the principal municipal magistrate were chief justice and acting *alcalde*.

17. John Horace Parry, *The Sale of Public Office in the Spanish Indies under the Hapsburgs*, p. 2.

18. *Recopilación de leyes*, libro 5, título 3, ley 1.

19. Cédula of Philip II to viceroy of Peru, Don Francisco de Toledo, Bosque de Segovia, November 19, 1570, III, 3–4.

20. Autos de Cabildo, January 12, 1742, NA, pp. 90–91.

21. Auto de Elecciones by Almazán, August 2, 1731, AGN-UT.

22. In large municipalities there was a premium placed on informing the court of an infraction of an ordinance. In a case in Mexico City informers were given half of a ten-peso fine for disclosing the illegal sale of wine and oil (*Actas de Cabildo, de la Ciudad de México*, May 9, 1525, I, 38, Latin American Special Collection, University of Texas, Austin).

23. Ibid., January 1, 1591, X, 46.

24. Ibid., July 4, 1567, VII, 358.

25. Simmons, *Spanish Government*, p. 162.

26. Power of attorney from Joseph de la Garza y Arrellano and Juan Resio de León, Villa de San Fernando, June 25, 1736, BA, vol. IX (June 25, 1736–January 24, 1738), p. 1, Hunnicutt translations.

27. Power of attorney from Joseph de Urrutia, Villa de San Fernando, August 23, 1737, BA, vol. IX, p. 10.

28. Power of attorney from the officers and soldiers of the presidio de Nuestra Señora del Pilar de las Adaes for collection of annual salaries and allotment of gunpowder, Presidio of San Antonio de Béxar, January 24, 1758, BA, vol. IX, p. 46.

29. Power of attorney from Juan Resio de León for collection of salary from 1737 and 1738, Villa de San Fernando, March 22, 1738, BA, vol. X, p. 1, Hunnicutt translations.

30. Power of attorney from Ygnacio de la Garza Falcón for representation in pending and future suits, Villa de San Fernando, May 4, 1743, BA, vol. X, p. 84, Hunnicutt translations.

31. Power of attorney from Rosa Flores de Valdez . . . for representation in all pending and future claims, Villa de San Fernando, June 26, 1743, BA, vol. X, p. 95.

32. Moore, *The Cabildo in Peru under the Bourbons,* p. 102.

33. Fisher, *The Intendant System,* p. 14.

34. Ibid., p. 28.

35. In contrast, the *alcaldes mayores* who governed territorial divisions in the province of New Mexico not only assumed judicial roles but also, in the absence of *cabildos,* assumed most functions normally reserved to municipal councils. Unlike the San Antonio *cabildo,* this was true of the Santa Fe *cabildo* from at least the 1740s until the close of the eighteenth century, when the local government was nearly the property of *alcaldes mayores* (Simmons, *Spanish Government,* pp. 166–69).

36. The town *fueros,* moreover, were supplemented by the promulgation of the *Lex Romana Visigothorum* and the *Fuero Juzgo,* both of which strengthened respect between king and citizenry. The *Fuero Real,* a compilation of laws, rights, and customs introduced by Alfonso X in 1264, and the celebrated *Siete partidas,* published in 1348, confirmed the fact that subjects' rights were vested in the laws of the municipalities. (*Las siete partidas,* partida 2, título 10, ley 1; partida 2, título 10, ley 2; partida 2, título 10, ley 3, pp. 332–34; Hume, *Spain, p.* 18; Mariejol, *The Spain of Ferdinand and Isabella,* p. 281; Mayer, *Historia de la instituciones,* II, 126; Chapman, *A History of Spain,* p. 162; Altamira, *History of Spain,* pp. 146–81; Valdeavellano, *Historia de España,* p. 487).

37. *Recopilación de leyes,* libro 1, título 14, ley 39.

38. Moore, *Cabildo in Peru under the Hapsburgs,* p. 13; Valdeavellano, *Historia de España,* p. 585; *Recopilación de leyes,* libro 5, título 3, ley 1.

39. *Recopilación de leyes,* libro 5, título 2, ley 14; libro 5, título 3, ley 1; Encinas, *Cedulario indiano,* II, 104, III, 31.

40. Decree of Góraz, Villa de San Fernando, April 14, 1735, BA, vol. VI, p. 83; Decree of Montes de Oça, Villa de San Fernando, February 6, 1745, BA, vol. XVII, p. 7; Austin, "Municipal Government," p. 314.

41. Manuel de Sandoval's statement on debts and credits, Villa de San Fernando, October 4, 1733, BA, vol. IV, Miller translations, p. 28.

42. Manuel de Sandoval, Presidio de San Antonio, April 19, 1736, BA, vol. IV, p. 47.

43. Vicente Albarez [*sic*] Travieso, Presidio de San Antonio, April 19, 1736, BA, vol. IV, p. 52.

44. Ibid., p. 54.

45. *Fundación española del Cuzco y ordenansas para su gobierno. Restauraciones mandadas ejecutar del primer Libro de Cabildos de la Ciudad por el viceroy del Perú, Don Francisco de Toledo,* p. 83.

46. Ibid.

47. *Recopilación de leyes,* libro 5, título 8, leyes 20, 6.

48. A paradox in Spanish legal absolutism was seen in the axiom, "Obedezco pero no cumplo." It might be construed "as a device that imparted flexibility to the Laws of the Indies, as elasticity proven necessary to adjust the Castilian code to another social environment, thousands of miles from the capital of the empire. . . . From the viceroy down to the local cabildos the infrequent, acknowledged non-

observance of a cédula was a step toward the easing of tension [between] the governed and the government" (Moore, *Cabildo in Peru under the Bourbons,* p. 31.)

49. Statement of Juan Leal Góraz regarding allegations, Presidio de San Antonio, August 29, 1734, BA, vol. V (October 5, 1733–December 31, 1734), p. 98, McLean translations.

50. Statement of Manuel de Sandoval, in ibid., p. 102.

51. Statement of María Pérez de Cabrera, Presidio de San Antonio, September 6, 1734, vol. V (October 5, 1733–December 31, 1734), p. 103, McLean translations.

52. Statement of Manuel de Sandoval, in ibid., pp. 107, 108.

53. Statement of Juan de Barro, Presidio de San Antonio, April 11, 1736, BA, vol. IV (October 4, 1733), pp. 2, 3, Miller translations.

54. Ibid., p. 4.

55. Ibid.

56. Statement of Manuel de Sandoval, Presidio de San Antonio, in ibid., p. 6.

57. Statement of Juan Curbelo, in ibid., p. 11; statement of Marthin Lorenzo de Armas, in ibid., p. 9.

58. Statement of Rodríguez, in ibid., April 12, 1736, p. 12.

59. Statement of debenture, Villa de San Fernando, October 4, 1733, BA, vol. IV, p. 12; memorandum, Villa de San Fernando, March 17, 1735, BA, vol. IV, p. 22; statement, Carta quenta, Villa de San Fernando, October 4, 1733, BA, vol. IV, pp. 24–26; statement, Carta quenta, Villa de San Fernando, March 17, 1735, BA, vol. IV, pp. 24–26.

60. Statement of Manuel de Sandoval, Presidio de San Antonio, April 19, 1736, BA, vol. IV (October 4, 1733), Miller translations, p. 46.

61. Statement of Vicente Alvarez Travieso, Villa de San Fernando, April 19, 1736, BA, vol. IV, p. 48.

62. Ibid., pp. 48, 49.

63. List of Armas' possessions, in ibid., pp. 51–53.

64. Ibid.

65. List of Rodríguez's possessions, in ibid., pp. 56–58.

66. Statement by Vicente Alvarez de Travieso, in ibid., April 20, 1736, p. 61.

67. Statement by Marthin Lorenzo de Armas, Presidio de San Antonio, April 20, 1736, BA, vol. IV, p. 62.

68. List of Rodríguez's possessions, April 20, 1736, BA, vol. IV, pp. 58–59.

69. Statement by Juan de Barro, Presidio de San Antonio, April 21, 1736, BA, vol. IV, p. 67.

70. Statement by Vicente Alvarez Travieso, in ibid., p. 60.

71. Statement by Manuel de Sandoval, in ibid., April 23, 1736, p. 70.

72. The Ordenamiento de Alcalá de Henares was a collection of laws promulgated by the Cortes of 1348. It contains thirty-two titles, each containing various laws relating to the mode of conducting suits, contracts, last wills, crimes and punishments, and so on. Glossary, Vol. IV, p. 129, BA.

73. Statement by Manuel de Sandoval, Presidio de San Antonio, April 23, 1736, BA, vol. IV, p. 70. *Si combenarit de yurisdicione omnium yudicum* (correctly written, *si convenerit de jurisdicione omnium judicum*) is translated: "If an agreement shall have

been reached which proceeds from the legal authority of all the judges"; that is, it is seemingly a reference to the decision given by arbitrators, which was not necessarily unanimous, but according to law had to be rendered at least by a majority, with all the arbitrators present (*Las siete partidas,* partida 3, título 22, ley 17; Glossary, vol. IV, p. 130, BA). *Sumiciones (sumisiones)* translates as subjection to a special court or jurisdiction, waiving the right to be tried in one's own. The law here renounced is evidently one giving the litigant the right to choose the judge by whom his case is to be tried (*derecho de sumisión*) (Glossary in vol. IV, p. 130, BA).

74. Statement of Manuel de Sandoval, Presidio de San Antonio, April 30, 1736, BA, vol. IV, p. 81.

75. Ibid., May 8, 1736.

76. Ibid., pp. 103–107; April 30, 1736, Vol. I, pp. 83–87.

77. Ibid., May 9, 1733, vol. IV, pp. 89, III.

78. Moore, *The Cabildo in Peru under the Bourbons,* p. 107.

79. Ibid., p. 108.

80. *Actas de Cabildo, Mexico,* March 28, 1590, vol. X, p. 87, Latin America Special Collection, University of Texas, Austin.

81. Ibid.

82. Fisher, *The Intendant System,* p. 67.

83. Hatcher, "The Municipal Government," p. 321.

84. Affidavit by Cabildo concerning disorderly conduct of priest of San Fernando, July 22, 1745, BA, vol. IV, p. 25.

85. Decree for inspection by Cabildo of San Fernando of all weights and measures, Villa de San Fernando, April 29, 1752, BA, vol. 25 (April 7–September 25, 1752), p. 7, Hunnicutt translations.

86. Ibid.

87. Wilcox, "Archives of Laredo," p. 354.

88. Santiago de Jesús Sánchez, Justicia, Autto. Laredo, May 3, 1784, LA 1-39-193.

89. Góraz to Sandoval, Presidio de San Antonio, May 18, 1735, BA, vol. VI (January–April, 1735), pp. 123–27, McLean translations.

90. Reply to Captain Thoribio de Urrutia's injunction, Villa de San Fernando, September 15, 1750, BA, vol. XX (July 19, 1749–July 28, 1750), p. 314, Hunnicutt translations.

CHAPTER 9

1. "The Anglo-Americans who came into Texas with Stephen F. Austin were not in the true sense pioneers; they found not a wilderness, but a society already in existence, and a foreign power in possession. Neither were the traders who came across the Great Plains to traffic at Santa Fe and Southward into Chihuahua. Folk of European origin were already well established and had a society ready to do business. The forefathers of not a few had been established there some years before there was a Jamestown, quite a few more than that 1620 date which saw the Pilgrims arrive, and so, too, of other proud Anglo-American centers. The few hardy souls,

trappers generally, who slipped beyond the Divide and wandered southward, to Arizona, also found European men before them—not many, perhaps, save those around Tucson and Tubac. . . . Nowhere in the Borderlands was the Anglo-American a pioneer. His frontier in these parts ran head-on into another and older one. . . . That is part of the post-Spanish Borderlands story" (Bannon, *Spanish Borderlands*, p. 230).

Bibliography

Manuscript Materials

Eugene C. Barker Texas History Center, University of Texas, Austin. Archivo de San Francisco el Grande. Archivo General de la Nación. Archivo General de las Indias. Bexar County Archives. Historia (Compilation of Cédulas Relating to Texas and the Northern Provinces of New Spain, 1631–1719). Laredo Archives. Nacogdoches Archives. Saltillo Archives. W. B. Stephens Collection.

Coronado Special Collection Center, University of New Mexico, Albuquerque. Spanish Archives of New Mexico.

Bancroft Library, University of California, Berkeley. Archives of California. Archivo General de la Nación. Archivo General de las Indias.

Books

Actas de cabildo de la ciudad de México. 27 vols. Mexico City: Imprenta y Librería de Aguilar e Hijos, 1899–1911.

Adams, Eleanor B., and Fray Angélico Chávez, trans. *The Missions of New Mexico, 1776: A Description by Fray Francisco Atanasia Domínguez with Other Contemporary Documents.* Albuquerque: University of New Mexico Press, 1956.

Aiton, Arthur Scott. *Antonio de Mendoza: The First Viceroy of New Spain.* New York: Russell & Russell, 1967.

Almaráz, Félix Díaz, Jr. *Tragic Cavalier: Governor Manuel Salcedo of Texas, 1808–1813.* Austin: University of Texas Press, 1971.

Alegre, Francisco Javier. *Historia de la Compañía de Jesús en Nueva España.* 3 vols. Mexico City: J. M. Lara, 1842.

Altamira y Crevea, Rafael. *A History of Spain.* Patterson, N.J.: D. Van Nostrand Company, 1966.

Amador, Elias. *Bosquejo histórico de Zacatecas*. Zacatecas. Tip. de la Escuela de Artes y Oficios en Guadalupe, 1892.

Arleguí, M. R. P. José. *Crónica de la provincia de N. S. P. S. Francisco de Zacatecas*. Mexico City: Calle de los Rebeldes, 1851.

Bakewell, P. J. *Silver Mining and Society in Colonial Mexico: Zacatecas, 1546–1700*. Cambridge: At the University Press, 1971.

Bancroft, Hubert Howe. *History of California*. 7 vols. San Francisco: History Company, 1890.

——. *History of Mexico*. 7 vols. San Francisco: History Company, 1886.

Bannon, John Francis, ed. *Indian Labor in the Spanish Indies: Was There Another Solution?* Boston: D. C. Heath & Company, 1966.

——. *The Spanish Borderlands Frontier, 1513–1821*. New York: Holt, Rinehart & Winston, 1970.

——. *The Spanish Conquistadores, Men or Devils?* New York: Holt, Rinehart & Winston, 1960.

Benavides' Memorial of 1630. Translated by Peter P. Forrestal. Washington, D.C.: Academy of American Franciscan History, 1954.

Bielharz, Edwin A. *Felipe de Neve, First Governor of California*. San Francisco: California Historical Society, 1971.

Blackmar, Frank W. *Spanish Institutions of the Southwest*. Baltimore: The Johns Hopkins University Press, 1891.

Bolton, Herbert E. *Fray Juan Crespi, Missionary Explorer on the Pacific Coast, 1769–1774*. Berkeley & Los Angeles: University of California Press, 1927.

——. *The Mission as a Frontier Institution*. El Paso: Texas Western College Press, 1960.

——. *Rim of Christendom: A Biography of Eusebio Francisco Kino, Pacific Coast Pioneer*. New York: Macmillan, 1936.

——. *The Spanish Borderlands: A Chronicle of Old Florida and the Southwest*. New Haven: Yale University Press, 1921.

——. *Spanish Explorations in the Southwest, 1542–1706*. New York: Barnes & Noble, 1908.

——. *Texas in the Middle Eighteenth Century: Studies in Spanish Colonial History and Administration*. 1915. Reprint. Austin: University of Texas Press, 1970.

Borah, Woodrow. *New Spain's Century of Depression*. Ibero-Americana, 35. Berkeley & Los Angeles: University of California Press, 1951.

Brading, D. A. *Miners and Merchants in Bourbon Mexico, 1763–1810*. Cambridge: At the University Press, 1971.

Brinckerhoff, Sidney B., and Odie B. Faulk. *Lancers for the King: A Study of the Frontier Military System of Northern New Spain, with a Translation of the Royal Regulations of 1772*. Phoenix: Arizona Historical Foundation, 1965.

Buck, Samuel M. *Yanaquana's Successors*. San Antonio: Naylor, 1949.

Caruso, John Anthony. *The Mississippi Valley Frontier: The Age of French Exploration and Settlement*. Indianapolis: Bobbs-Merrill, 1966.

Castañeda, Carlos E. *Our Catholic Heritage in Texas, 1519–1936*. 7 vols. Austin: Von Boeckman-Jones, 1936–58.

Céliz, Francisco. *Diary of the Alarcón Expedition into Texas, 1718–1719*. Translated by Fritz Lee Hoffman. Los Angeles: Quivira Society, 1935.

Chabot, Frederick Charles. *With the Makers of San Antonio*. San Antonio: Artes Gráficas, 1937.

Chapman, Charles. *A History of Spain*. New York: Macmillan, 1925.

Chávez, Angélico. *La Conquistadora, the Autobiography of an Ancient Statue*. Patterson, N.J.: St. Anthony Guild Press, 1954.

———. *Origins of New Mexico Families*. Santa Fe: Historical Society of New Mexico, 1954.

Clarke, John G. *New Orleans 1718–1812: An Economic History*. Baton Rouge: Louisiana State University Press, 1970.

Cook, Sherburne F. and Woodrow Borah. *The Indian Population of Central Mexico, 1531–1610*. Ibero-Americana, 44. Berkeley & Los Angeles: University of California Press, 1960.

Cortés, Hernán. *Conquest: Dispatches of Cortés from the New World*. Edited by Irwin R. Blacker. New York: Grosset & Dunlap, 1962.

Coues, Elliot, ed. *The Expeditions of Zebulon Montgomery Pike to the Headwaters of the Mississippi River, through Louisiana Territory, and in New Spain, during the Years 1805-6-7*. 3 vols. New York: Francis P. Harper, 1895.

Crouch, Dora P.; Daniel J. Carr; and Azel I. Mundigo. *Spanish City Planning in North America*. Cambridge: MIT Press, 1982.

Crouse, Nellis M. *Lemoyne Iberville: Soldier of New France*. Ithaca: Cornell University Press, 1954.

Cumberland, Charles. *Mexico: The Struggle for Modernity*. London: Oxford University Press, 1968.

Cunningham, Charles Henry. *The Audiencia in the Spanish Colonies*. Berkeley & Los Angeles: University of California Press, 1919.

Da Cámara, Kathleen. *Laredo on the Rio Grande*. San Antonio: Naylor, 1949.

Davies, R. Trevor. *Spain in Decline, 1621–1700*. London: Macmillan, 1957.

Díaz del Castillo, Bernal. *The Discovery and Conquest of Mexico, 1517–1521*. Edited by Genaro García, translated by A. P. Maudslay. New York: Farrar, Straus & Cudahy, 1965.

———. *The True History of the Conquest of Mexico*. Translated by Maurice Keating. London: John Dean, 1800.

Domínguez, Herón E. *Zacatecas: Una recopilación sintetizada de datos históricos, geográficos, económicos . . . del Estado de Zacatecas en ocasión del IV centenario de la fundación de su capital*. Zacatecas, 1946.

Dunne, Peter Masten. *Pioneer Jesuits in Northern Mexico*. Berkeley & Los Angeles: University of California Press, 1944.

Elliot, John Huxtable. *Imperial Spain, 1469–1716*. New York: St. Martin's Press, 1964.

Encinas, Diego de, ed. *Cedulario de indiano recopilado por Diego de Encinas reproducción facsímil de la edición única de 1596 con estudios e índices de Alfonso García Gallo*. 4 vols. Madrid: Ediciones Cultura Hispánica, 1945.

Espinosa, Isidro de. *Espinosa's Diary of 1709*. Translated by Gabriel Tous. Preliminary Studies of the Texas Catholic Historical Society. Austin, 1930.

Espinosa, J. Manuel, trans. *First Expedition of Vargas in New Mexico, 1692*. Coronado Historical Series, 10. Albuquerque: University of New Mexico Press, 1940.

Fisher, Lillian Estelle. *The Intendant System in Spanish America*. Berkeley & Los Angeles: University of California Press, 1929.

Forbes, Jack D. *Apache, Navajo and Spaniard*. Norman: University of Oklahoma Press, 1964.

Forrestal, Peter P., trans. *Benavides' Memorial of 1630*. Introduction and notes by Cyprian J. Lynch. Washington, D.C.: Academy of American Franciscan History, 1954.

Fuentes, Patricia de. *The Conquistadores*. New York: Orion Press, 1963.

Fundación española del Cuzco y ordenansas para su govierno. Restauraciones mandadas ejecutar del primer libro de cabildos de la Ciudad por el virrey del Perú. Don Francisco de Toledo. Gráficos Samartí, 1926.

García, Rogelia O. *Dolores, Revilla and Laredo: Three Sister Settlements*. Waco: Texian Press, 1970.

Gibson, Charles. *The Aztecs under Spanish Rule: A History of Indians of the Valley of Mexico, 1519–1810*. Stanford: University of California Press, 1964.

Habig, Marion A. *San Antonio's Mission San José: State and National Historic Site, 1720–1968*. San Antonio: Naylor, 1968.

Hackett, Charles Wilson, ed. *Historical Documents Relating to New Mexico, Nueva Viscaya and Approaches Thereto, to 1773*. Collected by Adolph and Fanny R. Bandelier. 3 vols. Washington, D.C.: Carnegie Institution of Washington, 1923.

————, and Charmion Clair Shelby, eds. and trans. *Revolt of the Pueblo Indians of New Mexico and Otermin's Attempted Reconquest 1680–1682*. 2 vols. Albuquerque: University of New Mexico Press, 1942.

Hall, Frederick. *The History of San José*. San Francisco: A. L. Bancroft, 1871.

Hallenbeck, Cleve. *Alvar Nuñez Cabeza de Vaca: The Journey and Route of the First European to Cross the Continent of North America, 1534–1536*. Glendale, Cal.: Arthur H. Clark Company, 1940.

Hammond, George P. *Don Juan de Oñate and the Founding of New Mexico*. Santa Fe: El Palacio Press, 1927.

————. *New Spain and the Anglo-American West: Historical Contributions Presented to Herbert Eugene Bolton.* Lancaster, Penn.: Lancaster Press, 1932.

————. *The Rediscovery of New Mexico, 1580–1594: The Explorations of Chamuscado, Espejo, Castaño de Sosa, Morlete, and Leyva de Bonilla and Humana.* Albuquerque: University of New Mexico Press, 1966.

Hammond, George P. and Agapito Rey, eds. and trans. *Don Juan de Oñate, Colonizer of New Mexico, 1595–1628,* vol. I. Pages 309–28: "Record of the March of the Army, New Spain to New Mexico, 1596–98." Coronado Historical Series. Albuquerque: University of New Mexico Press, 1953.

————. *Expedition into New Mexico Made by Antonio de Espejo, 1528–83, As Revealed in the Journal of Diego Pérez de Luxan.* Los Angeles: Quivira Society, 1929.

Hanke, Lewis. *Aristotle and the American Indians.* London: Hollis & Carter, 1957.

————. *Spanish Struggle for Justice in the Conquest of America.* Philadelphia: University of Pennsylvania Press, 1949.

Haring, C. H. *The Spanish Empire in America.* New York: Harcourt, Brace & World, 1963.

Hill, Lawrence Francis. *José de Escandón and the Founding of Nuevo Santander.* Columbus: Ohio State University Press, 1926.

Historic Santa Fe Foundation. *Old Santa Fe Today.* Albuquerque: University of New Mexico Press, 1972.

Hughes, Anne. *The Beginnings of the Spanish Settlement in the El Paso District. University of California Publications in History.* Berkeley: University of California Press, 1914.

Humboldt, Alexander von. *Political Essay on the Kingdom of New Spain.* 4 vols. 1811. Reprint. New York: AMS Press, 1966.

Hume, Martin A. S. *Spain: Its Greatness and Its Decay.* London: C. J. Clay and Sons, 1899.

Irving, A. Leonard. *Baroque Times in Old Mexico.* Ann Arbor: University of Michigan Press, 1959.

Iturribarria, Jorge Fernando. *Oaxaca en la conquista.* Oaxaca: Universidad Benito Juárez de Oaxaca, 1965.

Jacobsen, Jerome V. *Educational Foundations of the Jesuits in Sixteenth Century New Spain.* Berkeley & Los Angeles: University of California Press, 1938.

James, William F., and George H. McMurray. *History of San José California.* San Jose: Smith Printing Co., 1933.

Janer, Florencio. *Condición social de moriscos de España: Causas de su expulsión y consequencias que éste produjo en el orden económico y político.* Madrid: Imprenta de la Real Academia de la Historia, 1857.

Jiménez Moreno, Wigberto. *Estudio de historia colonial.* Mexico City: Instituto Nacional de Antropología e Historia, 1958.

Jones, Oakah L. *Los Paisanos: Spanish Settlers on the Northern Frontier of New Spain*. Norman: University of Oklahoma Press, 1979.

———. *Pueblo Warriors and the Spanish Conquest*. Norman: University of Oklahoma Press, 1966.

Kessel, John L. *Kiva, Cross and Crown: The Pecos Indians and New Mexico, 1540–1840*. Washington, D.C.: National Park Service, 1979.

Kubler, George. *Mexican Architecture of the Sixteenth Century*. 2 vols. Westport, Conn.: Greenwood Press, 1948.

Le Fuente, Modesto. *Historia general de España*. 8 vols. Barcelona: Montaner y Simón, 1887.

Lane-Pool, Stanley. *The Moors in Spain*. London: T. Fisher Unwin, 1887.

Las Casas, Bartolomé de. *Brevísima relación de la destrucción de las Indias*. Mexico City: Secretaría de Educación Pública, 1945.

Laut, Agnes C. *Cadillac, Knight-Errant of the Wilderness*. New York: Bobbs-Merrill, 1931.

Leonard, Irving A. *Baroque Times in Old Mexico*. Ann Arbor: University of Michigan Press, 1959.

Livermore, Harold. *A History of Spain*. New York: Farrar, Straus & Cudahey, 1958.

Loomis, Noel, and Abraham P. Nagatir. *Pedro de Vial and the Roads to Santa Fe*. Norman: University of Oklahoma Press, 1967.

López de Gómara, Francisco. *Cortes: The Life of the Conqueror by His Secretary*. Translated by Lesley Byrd Simpson. Berkeley & Los Angeles: University of California Press, 1965.

López-Portillo y Weber, José. *La conquista de la Nueva Galicia*. Mexico City: Talleres Gráficos de la Nación, 1935.

Madariaga, Salvador de. *Hernán Cortés*. Buenos Aires: Editorial Sudamérica, 1941.

Maravall, José Antonio. *El concepto de España en la edad media*. Madrid: Instituto de Estudios Políticos, 1964.

Mariejol, Jean Hippolyte. *The Spain of Ferdinand and Isabella*. New Brunswick, N.J.: Rutgers University Press, 1961.

Mayer, Ernesto. *Historia de las instituciones sociales y políticas de España y Portugal*. 2 vols. Madrid: Anuario del Derecho Español, 1926.

Mecham, J. Lloyd. *Church and State in Latin America*. Chapel Hill: University of North Carolina Press, 1934.

———. *Francisco de Ibarra and Nueva Vizcaya*. Durham: Duke University Press, 1927.

Mendieta, Gerónimo de. *Historia ecclesiástica indiana*. Mexico City: Antigua Librería, 1870.

Menéndez Pidal, Ramon. *Historia de España*. 19 vols. Madrid: Espasa-Calpe, 1969.

Merriman, Roger Bigelow. *The Rise of the Sanish Empire in the Old World and in the New.* 4 vols. New York: Cooper Square Publishers, 1962.

The Missions of New Mexico, 1776: A Description by Fray Francisco Atanasio Domínguez with Other Contemporary Documents. Translated and annotated by Eleanor B. Adams and Fray Angélico Chávez. Albuquerque: University of New Mexico Press, 1956.

Moore, John Preston. *The Cabildo in Peru under the Bourbons, 1700–1824.* Durham: Duke University Press, 1954.

———. *The Cabildo in Peru under the Hapsburgs.* Durham: Duke University Press, 1954.

Moorhead, Max L. *New Mexico's Royal Road: Trade and Travel on the Chihuahua Trail.* Norman: University of Oklahoma Press, 1958.

———. *The Presidio: Bastion of the Spanish Borderlands.* Norman: University of Oklahoma Press, 1975.

Morfi, Juan Agustín. *History of Texas, 1673–1779.* Translated by Carlos Eduardo Castañeda. 2 vols. Albuquerque: Quivira Society, 1935.

Nixon, Pat Ireland. *The Medical Story of Early Texas, 1528–1853.* Lancaster, Penn.: Mollie Benett Lupe Memorial and the Lancaster Press, 1946.

Palou, Francisco. *Historical Memoirs of New California.* Edited by Herbert Eugene Bolton. 4 vols. Berkeley & Los Angeles: University of California Press, 1926.

Parry, John Horace. *The Audiencia of New Galicia in the Sixteenth Century: A Study in Colonial Government.* Cambridge: At the University Press, 1948.

———. *The Sale of Public Office in the Spanish Indies under the Hapsburgs.* Ibero-Americana, 37. Berkeley & Los Angeles: University of California Press, 1935.

———. *The Spanish Seaborne Empire.* New York: Alfred A. Knopf, 1967.

Peña, Francisco. *Estudio histórico sobre San Luis Potosí.* San Luis Potosí: Imprenta Editorial de "El Estandarto," 1849.

Pérez de Villagrá, Gaspar. *History of New Mexico.* Translated by Gilberto Espinosa. Los Angeles: Quivira Society, 1933.

Phares, Ross. *Cavalier in the Wilderness: The Story of the Explorer and Trader Louis Juchereau de St. Denis.* Baton Rouge: Louisiana State University, 1931.

Phelan, John Leddy. *The Millennial Kingdom of the Franciscans in the New World: A Study of the Writings of Gerónimo de Mendietta (1525–1604).* Berkeley & Los Angeles: University of California Press, 1956.

Portillo y Diez de Sollano, Alvaro del. *Descubrimientos y exploraciones en las costas de California.* Madrid: Escuela de Estudios Hispano-Americanos de Seville, 1947.

Pourade, Richard F. *Anza Conquers the Desert.* La Jolla: Copley Books, 1971.

Powell, Philip Wayne. *Soldiers, Indians, and Silver: The Northward Advance of New Spain, 1550–1600.* Berkeley & Los Angeles: University of California Press, 1952.

Priestly, Herbert Ingram. *José de Gálvez: Visitor-General of New Spain.* Berkeley & Los Angeles: University of California Press, 1916.

Prieto, Alejandro. *Historia geográfica y estadística del estado de Tamaulipas.* Mexico City: Tip. Escalerillas no. 13, 1873.

Recopilación de leyes de los reynos de las Indias mandadas imprimir y publicar por la magestad católica de Rey Don Carlos II. Madrid: Gráficas Ultra, 1943.

Revilla Gigedo, Conde de. *Instrucción que dio a su sucesor en el mando, Marqués de Branciforte sobre el gobierno de este continente en el tiempo que fué su virrey. México. June 30, 1794.* Mexico City: Imprenta de la Calle de las Escalerías, 1831.

Richard, Roberto. *La conquista espiritual de México.* Mexico City: Editorial Jus, 1947.

Robles, Vito Alessio. *Nicolás de la Fora, relación del viaje que hizo a los presidios internos situados en la frontera de la América septentrional pertenecientes al rey de España.* Mexico City: Editorial Pedro Robredo, 1939.

Rodríguez, María J. *Rodríguez Memoirs of Early Texas.* San Antonio: Passing Show, 1913.

Scholes, France V. *Troublesome Times in New Mexico, 1659–1670.* Albuquerque: University of New Mexico Press, for the Historical Society of New Mexico, 1942.

Scott, Florence Johnson. *Historical Heritage of the Lower Rio Grande.* Waco: Texian Press, 1966.

———. *Royal Land Grants North of the Rio Grande, 1777–1821.* Waco: Texian Press, 1969.

Scott, Samuel Parson, ed. and trans. *Las siete partidas.* Chicago: Commerce Clearing House, 1931.

Sepúlveda, Juan Ginés de. *Demócrates Segundo de la guerra contra los indios.* Edited by Angel Losada. Madrid: Instituto Francisco de Vitoria, 1951.

Shiels, W. Eugene. *King and Church: the Rise and Fall of the Patronato Real.* Chicago: Loyola University Press, 1961.

Simmons, Marc. *Albuquerque: A Narrative History.* Albuquerque: University of New Mexico Press, 1982.

———. *Spanish Government in New Mexico.* Albuquerque: University of New Mexico Press, 1968.

Simpson, Eyler N. *The Ejido: Mexico's Way Out.* Chapel Hill: University of North Carolina Press, 1937.

Simpson, Lesley Byrd. *Exploitation of the Land in Central Mexico in the Sixteenth Century.* Ibero-Americana, 36. Berkeley & Los Angeles: University of California Press, 1952.

Smith, Donald Eugene. *The Viceroy of New Spain*. University of California Publications in History. Berkeley & Los Angeles: University of California Press, 1913.

Sonnichsen, C. L. *Pass of the North: Four Centuries on the Rio Grande*. El Paso: Texas Western Press, 1968.

Sutherland, C. H. V. *The Romans in Spain*. London: Methuen & Company, 1939.

Tapia, Francisco Xavier. *El cabildo abierto colonial*. Madrid: Ediciones Cultura Hispánica, 1966.

Thomas, Alfred Barnaby. "Antonio de Bonilla and Spanish Plans for the Defense of New Mexico. 1772–1778." In *New Spain and the Anglo-American West: Historical Contributions Presented to Herbert Eugene Bolton*. Edited by George P. Hammond. Lancaster, Penn.: Lancaster Press, 1932.

Tibesar, Antoinine, ed. *The Writings of Junípero Serra*. 4 vols. Washington, D.C.: Academy of American Franciscan History, 1955–56.

Torquemada, Juan de. *Monarquía indiana*. 3 vols. 1723. Reprint. Mexico City: Salvador Chávez Hayhoe, 1944.

Torres Campos, Rafael. *Carácter de la conquista y colonización de las Islas Canarias*. Madrid: Imprenta y Litografía del Depósito de la Guerra, 1901.

Twitchell, Ralph Emerson. *Old Santa Fe: The Story of New Mexico's Ancient Capital*. Santa Fe: New Mexican Publishing Corporation, 1925.

Urteaga, Horacio H. *Fundación española de Cuzco y ordenansas para su gobierno, restauraciones mandadas ejecutar del primer libro de cabildos de la ciudad por el viceroy del Perú, Don Francisco de Toledo*. Lima: Talleres Gráficos Sanmartí, 1926.

Valdeavellano, Luis G. *Historia de España*. Madrid: Revista de Occidente, 1955.

Valle-Arizpe, Artemio de. *Historia, tradiciones y leyendas de calles de México*. Mexico City: Cía. General de Ediciones, 1957.

Velasco, A. Alcázar de, and Cleofas Calleros. *Historia del templo de Nuestra Señora de Guadalupe*. Juárez: Tipográfica Internacional, 1953.

Vetancurt, Agustín de. *Teatro mexicano: Descripción breve de los sucessos exemplares de la Nueva-España en el Nuevo Mundo Occidental de las Indias*. 4 vols. 1691. Reprint. Madrid: José Porrúa Turanzas, 1961.

Vicens Vives, Jaime. *Approaches to the History of Spain*. Translated and edited by Joan Connelly Ullman. Berkeley & Los Angeles: University of California Press, 1967.

Vidal, Salvador. *Ciudad de Zacatecas*. Zacatecas: Imprenta Flores, 1951.

Wagner, Henry R. *The Cartography of the Northwest Coast of America to the Year 1800*. 2 vols. Berkeley & Los Angeles: University of California Press, 1937.

———. *The Rise of Fernando Cortés*. Cortés Society. New York: Kraus Reprint Company, 1969.

Weber, David J. *The Taos Trappers: The Fur Trade in the Far Southwest, 1540–1846.* Norman: University of Oklahoma Press, 1971.

Weddle, Robert S. *Wilderness Manhunt: The Spanish Search for La Salle.* Austin: University of Texas Press, 1973.

West, Robert C. *The Mining Community in Northern New Spain: The Parral Mining District.* Ibero-Americana, 30. Berkeley & Los Angeles: University of California Press, 1949.

Woolford, Sam, ed. *San Antonio, a History for Tomorrow.* San Antonio: Naylor, 1963.

ARTICLES, MANUSCRIPTS, AND DISSERTATIONS

"Acta de la general visita al pueblo de San Agustín de Laredo, by Juan Fernando and Don José de Ossorio y Llamas, Laredo, June 1767." Copy and translation of the Charter Visita Document of 1767. Austin, Texas: General Land Office Building.

Adams, Eleanor B., ed. "Bishop Tamaron's Visitation of New Mexico, 1760." *New Mexico Historical Review (NMHR)* 28 (July, 1953): 192–221.

———, and John E. Longhurst. "New Mexico and the Sack of Rome: One Hundred Years Later." *NMHR* 28 (October, 1953): 243–50.

"An Anonymous Statistical Report on New Mexico in 1765." Translation and introduction by Donald C. Cutter. *NMHR* 50 (October, 1975): 347–52.

Austin (Hatcher), Mattie Alice, "The Municipal Government of San Fernando de Bexar, 1730–1800." *Quarterly (SWQ)* 8 (April, 1905); 277–352.

Beithe, Jean Pierre. "Las minas de oro del Marqués del Valle en Tehuantepec, 1540–1541." *Historia Mexicana* 8 (July–September, 1958): 122–29.

Bloom, Lansing B. "Early Weaving in New Mexico." *NMHR* 2 (July, 1927): 228–38.

———. "When Was Santa Fe Founded?" *NMHR* 4 (1927): 188–94.

———, and Chaves, Ireneo L., eds. and trans. "Instruction to Peralta by Vice-Roy." *NMHR* 4 (April, 1929): 178–87.

Bolton, Herbert E. "Defensive Spanish Expansion and the Significance of the Borderlands." In *The Trans-Mississippi West.* Edited by James Willard. Pages 1–42. Boulder: University of Colorado, 1930.

———. "The Jumano Indians in Texas, 1650–1771." *Texas State Historical Association Quarterly (TSHAQ)* 15 (July, 1911): 66–84.

———, trans. "Tienda de Cuervo's Ynspección of Laredo, 1757." *TSHAQ* 6 (January, 1903): 187–203.

Buckley, Eleanor Claire. "The Aguayo Expedition into Texas and Louisiana, 1719–1722." *TSHAQ* 15 (July, 1911): 1–65.

Cox, Isaac Joslin. "Early Settlers of San Fernando." *TSHAQ* 5 (January, 1899): 142–60.

———. "The Southwest Boundary of Texas." *TSHAQ* 6 (October, 1902): 81–102.

Cutter, Donald C., trans. "An Anonymous Statistical Report on New Mexico in 1765." *NMHR* 50 (October, 1975): 347–52.

"Descripción o mapa de las fundaciones hechas por el orden del excellentisimo Señor Conde de Revillagigedo, con sus nombres, misiones, distancias . . . consecuentes a la consulta de 1747 . . ." *Estado General de las Fundaciones Hechas por D. José de Escandon en la Colonia del Nuevo Santander Costa del Seno Mexicano.* 2 vols. Publicaciones del Archivo General de la Nación, XV. Mexico City: Talleres Gráficas de la Nación, 1929.

Dunn, William E. "Spanish Search for La Salle's Colony on the Bay of Espíritu Santo." *SHQ* 19 (April, 1916): 323–69.

Espinosa, Juan Manuel, ed. and trans. "Vargas' Campaign Journal and Correspondence, August 21 to October 16, 1692." In *First Expedition of Vargas in New Mexico, 1692.* Albuquerque: University of New Mexico Press, 1940.

Forbes, Jack D. "The Janos, Jocomes, Mansos and Sumas." *NMHR* 32 (October, 1957): 319–34.

———. "Unknown Athapaskans: The Identification of the Jano, Jocome, Jumano, Manso, Suma, and Other Indian Tribes of the Southwest." *Ethnohistory* 6 (Spring, 1959): 97–159.

Greenleaf, Richard E. "Land and Water Rights in Mexico and New Mexico, 1700–1821." *NMHR* 47 (April, 1972): 85–112.

Guest, Florian Francis. "The Establishment of the Villa de Branciforte." *California Historical Society Quarterly (CHSQ)* 41 (March, 1962): 29–50.

———. "The Indian Policy under Fermín Francisco de Lausén, California's Second Father President." *CHSQ* 45 (September, 1966): 195–224.

———. "Municipal Government in Spanish California." *CHSQ* 46 (December, 1967): 307–35.

Hackett, Charles Wilson. "The Retreat of the Spaniards from New Mexico in 1680, and the Beginnings of El Paso." *SHQ* 16 (January, 1913): 259–76.

Hammond, George P., and Agapito Rey. "The Rodríguez Expedition to New Mexico, 1581–82." *NMHR* 2 (July, 1927): 239–68.

Heizer, Robert F. "Archeological Evidence of Sebastián Rodríguez Cermenho's California Visit." *California Historical Quarterly (CHQ)* 20 (December, 1941): 315–38.

Houston, Virginia H. Taylor. "Surveying in Texas." *SHQ* 65 (October, 1961): 204–33.

"Instrucciones que han de observar Don José Tienda de Cuervo y Don Agustín López de la Cámara Alta, para el recognicimiento de la costa del Seno Mexicano, cuya conquista y reducción esta a cargo de Don José de Escandón." *Estado general de las fundaciones hechas por D. José de Escandón en la colonia del Nuevo Santander costa del seno mexicano,* vol. 1. Publicaciones del Archivo General del Archivo General de la Nación, XV. Mexico City: Talleres Gráficas de la Nación, 1929.

"Instructions to Peralta by Vice-Roy." Transcribed by Lansing B. Bloom; translated by Ireneo L. Chaves. *NMHR* 4 (April, 1929): 178–87.

Jenkins, Myra Ellen. "Spanish Land Grants in the Tewar Area." *NMHR* 47 (April, 1972): 113–34.

Jones, O. Garfield. "Local Government in the Spanish Colonies as Provided by the Recopilación de Leyes de los Reynos de las Indias." *SHQ* 19 (July 15, 1915): 65–90.

Kelsey, Harry. "A New Look at the Founding of Old Los Angeles." *CHQ* 55, no. 4 (Winter, 1976): 326–39.

Kress, Margaret Kenny. "Diary of a Visit of Inspection of the Texas Missions Made by Fray Gaspar José Solís in the Year 1767–68." *Southwestern Historical Quarterly* 35 (July, 1931): 28–76.

Marshall, C. E. "The Birth of the Mestizo in New Spain." *HAHR* 19 (1939): 161–84.

Mecham, J. Lloyd. "The Real de Minas as a Political Institution." *HAHR* 7 (1927): 45–83.

Miller, Robert Ryal, trans. & ed. "New Mexico in the Mid-Eighteenth Century: A Report Based on Governor Vélez Cachupín's Inspection." *SHQ* 79, no. 2 (October, 1975): 166–83.

Neasham, V. Audrey. "Spain's Emigration to the New World, 1492–1592." *HAHR* 19 (1939): 147–60.

Nuttall, Zelia. "Royal Ordinances Concerning the Laying Out of New Towns." *HAHR* 4, no. 4, (November, 1921): 743–53.

Pourade, Richard F. "Juan Rodríguez Cabrillo: Discoverer of California." *Journal of the West* 1 (July, 1962): 11–23.

"Relación de los méritos de Don José de Escandón." *Estado general de las fundaciones hechas por D. José de Escandón en la colonia del Nuevo Santander costa del seno mexicano.* 2 vols. Publicaciones del Archivo General de la Nación, XV. Mexico City: Talleres Gráficas de la Nación, 1929.

Salmerón, Zárate. "Relaciones de Nuevo México." In *Spanish Explorations in the Southwest, 1542–1706.* Edited by Herbert Eugene Bolton. New York: Barnes & Noble, 1908.

Scholes, Frances V. "Civil Government and Society in New Mexico in the Seventeenth Century." *NMHR* 10 (April, 1935): 71–111.

———. "Problems in the Early Ecclesiastical History of New Mexico." *NMHR* 7 (January, 1932): 32–74.

———. "The Supply Service of the New Mexican Missions in the Seventeenth Century." *NMHR* 5 (January, 1930): 93–115.

————, trans. "Documents for the History of the New Mexican Missions in the Seventeenth Century." *NMHR* 4 (April, 1929): 195–201.

————, and Eleanor B. Adams, eds. "Copia de los advertimientos generales tocante al gobierno de la nueva españa que el virrey conde de Monterrey dejó al marquis de Montescarlos." *Advertimientos generales que los virreyes dejaron a sus sucessores para el gobierno de Nueva España, 1590–1604.* In *Documentos para el gobierno para la historia del México colonial.* Mexico City: José Porrúa e Hijos, 1956.

————, and ————, eds. "Copia de los advertimientos que el virrey Don Luis de Velasco dejó al Conde de Monterrey para el gobierno de la Nueva España." *Advertimientos generales que los virreyes dejaron a sus sucessores para el gobierno de Nueva España, 1590–1604.* In *Documentos para el gobierno para la historia del México colonial.* Mexico City: José Porrúa e Hijos, 1956.

Simmons, Marc. "Spanish Irrigation Practice in New Mexico." *NMHR* 47 (April, 1972): 135–50.

Tapia, Andrés de. "Chronicle of Andrés de Tapia." In *The Conquistadores.* Edited by Patricia de Fuentes. New York: Orion Press, 1963.

Thomas, Alfred Barnaby. "Antonio de Bonilla and Spanish Plans for the Defense of New Mexico, 1772–1778." In *New Spain and the Anglo-American West: Historical Contributions Presented to Herbert Eugene Bolton,* edited by George P. Hammond, pp. 183–209. Lancaster, Penn.: Lancaster Press, 1932.

Tjarks, Alicia V., "Comparative Demographic Analysis of Texas, 1777–1793," *SHQ* 77 (January, 1974): 291–338.

Von Wuthenau, A. "The Spanish Military Chapels in Santa Fe and the Reredos of Our Lady of Light." *NMHR* 10 (July, 1935): 175–94.

Wagner, Henry R. "The Voyage to California." *CHQ* 3 (April, 1924): 3–24.

Wilcox, Seb S. "Laredo during the Texas Republic." *SHQ* 42 (October, 1938): 83–102.

————. "The Spanish Archives of Laredo." *SHQ* 49 (January, 1946): 341–60.

Theses and Dissertations

Boylan, Leona Davis. "A Study of Spanish Colonial Silver in New Mexico." Ph.D. dissertation, University of New Mexico, Albuquerque, 1970.

Butler, Robert. "The Cabildo and the Intendant." M.A. thesis, University of Texas at Austin, 1967.

Cutter, Donald C. "Moraga of the Military: His California Service, 1784–1810," M.A. thesis, University of California, Berkeley, 1954.

Daniel, James M. "The Advance of the Spanish Frontier and the Despoblado." Ph.D. dissertation, University of Texas at Austin, 1955.

Garner, Van Hasting. "Cultural Contact and Conflict in Late Seventeenth-Century New Mexico." Ph.D. dissertation, University of California, Santa Barbara, 1972.

Guest, Florian Francis, "Municipal Institutions in Spanish California, 1769–1821." Ph.D. dissertation, University of California, Los Angeles, 1961.

Hackett, Charles Wilson. "The Uprising of the Pueblo Indians of New Mexico, 1630–1682." Ph.D. dissertation, University of California, Berkeley, 1917.

Walz, Vina. "History of the El Paso Area, 1680–1692." Ph.D. dissertation, University of New Mexico, Albuquerque, 1951.

Index

Index

Index

Let There Be Towns was composed into type on a Compugraphic digital phototypesetter in ten and one-half point Galliard with two and one-half points of spacing between the lines. Galliard was also selected for display. The book was designed by Jim Billingsley, typeset by Metricomp, Inc., printed offset by Thomson-Shore, Inc., and bound by John H. Dekker & Sons. The paper on which this book is printed carries acid-free characteristics for an effective life of at least three hundred years.

Texas A&M University Press : *College Station*